POVERTY AND LIFE EXPECTANCY

Poverty and Life Expectancy is a multidisciplinary study that reconstructs Jamaica's rise from low to high life expectancy and explains how that was achieved. Jamaica is one of the small number of countries that have attained a life expectancy nearly matching the rich lands, such as the United States, despite having a much lower level of per capita income. Why this is so is the Jamaica paradox. This book provides an answer, surveying possible explanations, at the outset, of Jamaica's rapid gains in life expectancy in the 1920s and thereafter. The rich countries could invest large sums in reducing mortality, but Jamaica and other low-income countries had to find inexpensive means of doing so. Jamaica's approach especially emphasized that schoolchildren and their parents master lessons about how to manage disease hazards, and this led to a successful collaboration between public health authorities and the people. This book also argues that low-income countries with high life expectancy, such as Jamaica, provide more realistic models as to how other poor countries where life expectancy remains low can improve survival.

James C. Riley is a distinguished professor of history at Indiana University in Bloomington. He is the author of several books, including *Rising Life Expectancy: A Global History* (Cambridge, 2001) and *Sick Not Dead: The Health of British Workingmen During the Mortality Decline* (1997). He is a contributor to journals such as *Population Studies,* the *American Historical Review,* and the *Journal of Interdisciplinary History,* and recipient of research awards from the National Endowment for the Humanities and the National Institutes of Health.

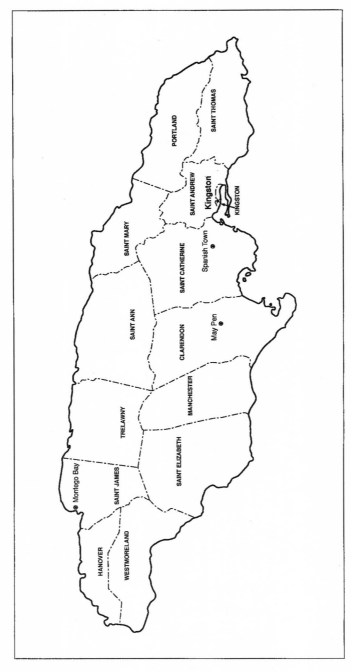

Frontpiece map: Jamaica's Parishes and Cities

POVERTY AND LIFE EXPECTANCY

THE JAMAICA PARADOX

James C. Riley
Indiana University, Bloomington

CAMBRIDGE
UNIVERSITY PRESS

CAMBRIDGE UNIVERSITY PRESS
Cambridge, New York, Melbourne, Madrid, Cape Town, Singapore, São Paulo

Cambridge University Press
40 West 20th Street, New York, NY 10011-4211, USA

www.cambridge.org
Information on this title: www.cambridge.org/9780521850476

First published 2005

Printed in the United States of America

A catalog record for this publication is available from the British Library.

Library of Congress Cataloging in Publication Data
Riley, James C.
Poverty and life expectancy : the Jamaica paradox / James C. Riley.
p.   cm.
Includes bibliographical references.
ISBN 0-521-85047-9
1. Life expectancy – Jamaica – History.   2. Jamaica – Population – History.
3. Poor – Jamaica – History.   4. Poverty – Jamaica – History. I. Title.
HB1322.35.J25R55   2005
304.6′457292–dc22   2005011524

ISBN-13   978-0-521-85047-6 hardback
ISBN-10   0-521-85047-9 hardback

The Rockefeller Archive Center allowed reproduction of photographs taken
by agents of the Rockefeller Foundation working in Jamaica. The National Library
of Jamaica provided images of latrines from A. Bruce McFarlane, *Hints on Hygiene
for Elementary Schools with Special Reference to the Tropics.*

To all librarians, who make scholarship possible,
and especially to the librarians at Indiana University

CONTENTS

LIST OF TABLES, FIGURES, AND ILLUSTRATIONS

TABLES

viii

PREFACE AND ACKNOWLEDGMENTS

Like many other people interested in population and health, I was struck by Jack Caldwell's 1986 article "Routes to Low Mortality in Poor Countries."[1] I worked on this topic for a time by studying the Indian state of Kerala and Costa Rica, the most widely known examples of low- or middle-income regions with high life expectancy. Initially my plan was to make Kerala, Costa Rica, and Sri Lanka the starting point for a general study. At a certain early stage, however, I decided to collect the information needed to build a chronology of life expectancy and infant mortality among countries with a population of at least 400,000 in the year 2000, going back in time in each case as far as permitted by the data and estimates I could find. That seemed necessary because existing studies of poor countries with low mortality rarely discuss the pattern of mortality decline across time, which, as a historian, I needed to understand. This chronology immediately revealed a larger number of what might qualify as good-health-at-low-income countries. Many scholars associate the period after World War II, and specifically the introduction of antibiotics in the 1940s and of new vaccines in the 1950s, with the inauguration of health transitions in poor countries. In fact, sustained reductions in mortality in low-income countries often began one, two, or even five decades earlier. This chronology also pointed up Jamaica as a case of high life expectancy and low income, even though it had not been one of the countries mentioned in studies of "good health at low cost," the term widely used to describe Costa Rica, Sri Lanka,

---

[1] John C. Caldwell, "Routes to Low Mortality in Poor Countries," *Population and Development Review*, 12 (1986): 171–220.

and Kerala.[2] A search for sources showed that Jamaica's experience could be studied in considerable detail with the aid of vital statistics of good quality. I changed my plan. In place of the general study of the good-health-at-low-income countries, I decided to concentrate on Jamaica.

Many institutions and people have contributed to this work, and I want to thank them without holding them responsible for parts of this study to which they may object. Fellowships from the Council for International Exchange of Scholars under its New Century Scholars program and, jointly, from the National Endowment for the Humanities and the Agency for Healthcare Research and Quality freed me from ordinary academic duties. Indiana University added a Research Leave Supplement, a travel fellowship from the Arts and Humanities Institute, additional travel funds from the President's Council on International Programs, and a grant-in-aid of research from the Vice President for Research. I am deeply grateful for this assistance.

I am grateful also to the people who helped me at one stage or another in research and writing. Dr. Peter Figueroa, then Chief Medical Officer in the Jamaican Ministry of Health, extended an invitation to visit Jamaica and do research there, gave me a cordial reception in Kingston, and made many helpful suggestions about people to meet, places to go, and things to read. He also provided a valuable critique of an early draft. Many scholars let me discuss issues and then asked questions or challenged interpretations; among them I wish to thank especially Vicki Lukere and Bruce Caldwell. Jack Caldwell, Pat Caldwell, Dennis Conway, Peter Figueroa, Allan G. Hill, Walter T. K. Nugent, and two anonymous readers for Cambridge University Press gave me a critique of earlier drafts. So did Ramsey Fischer, an undergraduate taking my course in global health history. William Bicknell of the Boston University School of Public Health provided information about recent assessments of health services in Jamaica.

In Jamaica I worked chiefly at the Sir Arthur Lewis Institute of Social and Economic Studies (SALISES) at the University of the West Indies (UWI), Mona; the University Library; and the National Library of Jamaica. Audrey Chambers, Norma Davis, and Kristin Fox at SALISES and Eppie D. Edwards of the National Library of Jamaica

---

[2] Scott B. Halstead, Julia A. Walsh, and Kenneth S. Warren, eds., *Good Health at Low Cost* (New York, 1985), which is the proceedings of a conference with sets of essays on Costa Rica, Kerala, and Sri Lanka, and also China.

provided cordial and efficient help. I also want to thank Sophia Jarrett and the staff at the Planning Institute of Jamaica, the staff at the Jamaica Archives in Spanish Town, and the reference librarians at UWI, Mona. At Mona, Affette McCaw-Binns, Aldrie Henry-Lee, and Michael Witter took time from their busy schedules to provide advice and leads. Elsie Le Franc at the Bridgetown, Barbados, campus of UWI provided advice and help by e-mail, as did Derwin Munroe of the University of Michigan at Flint. Marvin D. Sterling advised me about how Jamaicans talk about color and race. Also, I want to thank Frank Smith and Eric Crahan at the Press for the help they provided.

At the Rockefeller Archive Center the archivist Thomas Rosenbaum suggested research leads and Robert Battaly, assistant photograph archivist, helped me locate photographs.

The reference librarians at Indiana University and the National Library of Jamaica located information about some of the individuals who appear in this history. Bloomington interlibrary loan librarians secured many items from distant locations. And the librarians who, in the past, assembled the rich collections at UWI, the National Library of Jamaica, and Indiana University made this book possible.

INTRODUCTION

POVERTY AND LIFE EXPECTANCY

In most poor countries people live shorter lives than do their counterparts in rich countries. In Japan life expectancy at birth in 2000 for males and females together was 81 years; in Botswana and Sierra Leone it was less than 40 years.[1] But there are some countries where low income has not prevented the attainment of high life expectancy. As of 2000, some 30 low- and middle-income countries defied the logic that seems to tie life expectancy to a country's level of income. This is an account of one of those countries.

Students of life expectancy and income working in the 1960s believed that they had found that rising income allows rising survivorship. They surmised that life expectancy increases along with income, or that life expectancy gains follow income gains. Without any careful investigation of the matter, that was taken to be what had happened in the countries that had so far become rich, all of which also enjoyed high life expectancies. These included most of the countries of western and central Europe, in addition to the United States and Canada, Australia, New Zealand, and Japan. Perhaps that had happened in the Soviet Union also, where rapid economic growth had been accompanied by a rapid improvement in survival in some periods. But should people have to wait to gain long lives until their countries have begun a course of economic development that leads to being rich?

A critical look at the idea that life expectancy gains are made possible by prior or simultaneous gains in economic development and national

---

[1] United Nations Development Program, *Human Development Report 2002* (New York, 2002), pp. 149–52. Unless otherwise indicated, life expectancy will always refer to life expectancy at birth.

income first appeared in the book *Poverty and Health*, published in 1969 and written by John Kosa, Aaron Antonovsky, and Irving Zola. Later studies by Morris David Morris and Jack Caldwell pursued this question further.[2] Caldwell found a small group of countries that had defied the economic logic and an explanation for their success at evading the high income–high life expectancy association. In his reasoning, Costa Rica, Sri Lanka, and the Indian state of Kerala – the three cases he discussed at length – managed to gain high life expectancies by beginning with a different logic, one in which the emphasis fell not on economic growth but on social justice, meaning the equitable distribution of goods and services – especially equitable access to medical services, food, and education – and greater autonomy for women. The paradox of good health in low-income countries could be explained.

Costa Rica, Sri Lanka, and the Indian state of Kerala were not communist countries and areas, in the sense of having close ties to the Soviet Union or China, but they adhered to socialist ideals, so that in these and some other respects they resembled the social democracies of Western Europe. They were free and open societies committed to the lively discussion of ideas and policy that had, for reasons arising from local circumstances, elected social justice as a dominant value, favored schooling, and provided women with greater opportunities in schooling and decision making within households than most countries had done. The good news in Caldwell's essay was that people in poor countries could also find ways to live long lives. But there was some bad news, albeit implied. To gain the benefits Costa Ricans, Sri Lankans, and Keralans enjoyed in survivorship, other people would first have to adopt the values and modes of political and social behavior found in those three places. That is, they would have to embrace fundamental changes in their attitudes and habits of behavior.

Since Caldwell's essay was published, in 1986, life expectancy has risen in most countries, and more countries have joined the good-health-at-low-income group. But most of the movement into that group has not occurred among countries committed to social justice. Oman,

---

[2] John Kosa, Aaron Antonovsky, and Irving Kenneth Zola, *Poverty and Health: A Sociological Analysis* (Cambridge, MA, 1969); Morris David Morris, *Measuring the Condition of the World's Poor: The Physical Quality of Life Index* (New York, 1979); and John C. Caldwell, "Routes to Low Mortality in Poor Countries," *Population and Development Review*, 12 (1986): 171–220. Other scholars tackled the poverty–health relationship at the individual level. See Harold S. Luft, *Poverty and Health: Economic Causes and Consequences of Health Problems* (Cambridge, MA, 1978).

for most of its modern history an autocracy giving little evidence of sharing the values Caldwell found in Costa Rica, Kerala, and Sri Lanka, made exceptionally rapid gains in survivorship,[3] and a number of countries that Caldwell scorned for lacking female autonomy or openness, such as Jordan and Syria, joined the good-health-at-low-income group. Many countries that were then part of the Soviet Union have in the meantime lost life expectancy, particularly for males.

Furthermore, it must be said, the idea of achieving high life expectancy by adopting the values of social justice did not appeal to policymakers in poor countries with low survivorship. Leaders in poor countries had for a long time sought the advice of outside experts about how to stimulate economic growth and had often adopted unfamiliar, even quite drastic, economic policies. But they did not warm so readily to the idea of elevating life expectancy on the model of Costa Rica, Kerala, or Sri Lanka.

Although some authorities had written about this earlier,[4] it was not until the 1970s and later that many students of mortality and survivorship noticed how quickly the countries that had adopted Lenin's ideas about economic and social policy had added years of survivorship for their populations. The Soviet Union, China, and other countries associated with them, including such seemingly unlikely places as Albania,[5] had added rapidly to life expectancy at birth. Before their revolutions they had all, except East Germany, Czechoslovakia, and Hungary, lagged far behind global leaders in life expectancy. By the 1960s they had closed most of that gap. Indeed the Soviet Union, China, and their satellite states had added years of survivorship at a faster pace than they had added income or even industrial capacity.

In such systems, planning and control take the place of competition and free markets. But that was not the central feature of socialism as

[3] Allan G. Hill and Lincoln C. Chen, *Oman's Leap to Good Health: A Summary of Rapid Health Transition in the Sultanate of Oman* (Muscat, 1996).

[4] For example, Frank Lorimer, *The Population of the Soviet Union: History and Prospects* (Geneva, 1946) and Henry E. Sigerist, *Medicine and Health in the Soviet Union* (New York, 1947), found much to compliment in the Soviet health system and its hopes.

[5] Arjan Gjonça, *Communism, Health and Lifestyle: The Paradox of Mortality Transition in Albania, 1950–1990* (Westport, CT, 2001); Arjan Gjonça, Chris Wilson, and Jane Falkingham, "Paradoxes of Health Transition in Europe's Poorest Country: Albania 1950–90," *Population and Development Review*, 23 (1997): 585–609; and Ermelinda Meksi and Gianpiero Dalla Zuanna, "La mortalité générale en Albanie (1950–1990)," *Population*, 49 (1994): 607–35.

practiced in the Soviet Union, China, and their allies, nor was that central feature the equitable distribution of resources, which in those countries was more often a promise than a practice. What made it possible for people in those countries to add years of life expectation so rapidly was instead the democratization of access to things that individuals cannot command for themselves, especially education, public health amenities, and health care. Individuals can sometimes pay school fees and buy public health or medical services, but they cannot command the system that makes schools, doctors, clinics, vaccinations, safe water, and other public health resources available.

For some time before the 1970s, leaders of the Soviet Union and countries close to it had argued that they elevated life expectancy and provided universal education matching the capitalist countries well before their per capita income levels matched those in capitalist countries. The data behind those claims were suspect enough to leave most scholars uncertain about the veracity of the argument, at least until the 1980s. Then articles began to appear in which scholars wrote favorably about achievements in health and education in countries where socialism had been imposed and where the political systems had been, and remained, authoritarian. Other observers noticed the particularly sharp contrast between income and life expectancy in Cuba and the gains in life expectancy that had followed the 1959 revolution led by Fidel Castro.[6]

Thus far, research on the question of how some poor countries achieve high life expectancy has emphasized socialist examples. None of the socialist countries became rich lands, although most of them had, by the 1980s, attained life expectancies of 69 years or more. But no one came forward with a direct argument that Soviet or Chinese socialism should be adopted in poor countries in order to improve health. If Kerala, Sri Lanka, and Costa Rica had managed to match the rich

---

[6] In fact gains after 1959 continued earlier progress. S. Díaz-Briquets, "Determinants of Mortality Transition in Developing Countries before and after the Second World War: Some Evidence from Cuba," *Population Studies*, 35 (1981): 399–411; Sergio Díaz-Briquets, "Mortality in Cuba," in Ira Rosenwaike, ed., *Mortality of Hispanic Populations: Mexicans, Puerto Ricans, and Cubans in the United States and in the Home Countries* (New York, 1991) pp. 55–77; Rolando Garcia Quiñones, *La transition de la mortalidad en Cuba: Un estudio sociodemografico* (Havana, 1996); Hector Gutiérrez, "La mortalité par cause à Cuba avant et après la Revolution," *Population*, 39 (1984): 383–88; and Mervyn Susser, "Health as a Human Right: An Epidemiologist's Perspective on the Public Health," *American Journal of Public Health*, 83 (1993): 418–26, with 423–5 on Cuba.

countries in survivorship, which was an effect of policies adopted out of the community's desire for social justice rather than because people expected socialism to lead them to longevity. Moreover, in those three cases, socialist policies had been building for a long time. It was easy enough to conclude that their people had made choices that promoted better survival but quite another matter to conclude that the much larger group of poor countries with low life expectancy that had not made such choices could suddenly reverse course. Social justice laid the foundations of good survivorship, but what ideas and experiences laid the foundations of a preference for social justice? And is it necessary to take such exceptional steps in order to turn a poor country with low survivorship around?

The attempt to understand how some poor countries managed to achieve high life expectancy has typically eschewed a historical perspective. For the most part, scholars who asked this question in the 1970s and 1980s investigated the policies then being followed by Kerala, Sri Lanka, Costa Rica, and a few other countries outside the Soviet bloc, and implicitly assumed that explanations would be found in the present. As a historian I begin with another assumption, which is that explanations for present circumstances lie mostly in the past. When did the poor countries where people live long lives begin to stand out among their peers, and why? When did the most robust gains in life expectancy occur, and which programs, policies, and actions accompanied those gains and may explain them?

Jamaica provides the example of a poor country with high life expectancy that did not follow a socialist path. Under the British, up to independence in 1962, and under most of Jamaica's leaders since then, Jamaica has pursued openly capitalist economic policies, albeit in the incomplete manner and with the partial success that has characterized most low-income countries in the years since World War II. Thus Jamaica is an atypical case in the sense that it has been more unusual for poor capitalist countries to achieve high life expectancy than for poor socialist countries to do so. That makes this case more interesting. Jamaica's success in elevating life expectancy is to be explained, this book will argue, not by an attachment to singular and exceptional attitudes, such as a preference for social justice, but by more commonplace things that are, in principle, available to any country.

Investments in schooling, health, nutrition, and other human resources have come in recent years to be seen as important elements in strategies of economic development. Examining countries in Latin

America and the Caribbean, Jere Behrman carries the argument a step further, suggesting that human resources are as important for economic development as are free markets, economic stability, and infrastructure investments.[7] Since the 1960s, in that region, higher rates of growth have occurred most readily in the countries where people completed more years of school and life expectancy was higher. Hence "economies with greater human resources for a given level of initial per capita real income are more likely to be able to adapt to changing markets and technologies and to grow and prosper."[8] The main issues of this study of Jamaican experience deal with life expectancy as a payoff. But there is something to be gained from keeping Behrman's model in mind along with another question: How far did Jamaica's achievements in human resources pay off in economic development?

PREVIOUS EXPLANATIONS FOR JAMAICA'S HEALTH TRANSITION

Scholars seeking to understand how countries moved from a life expectancy at birth of below 40, or even below 30, years to levels above 70 years have concentrated on a few countries, writing most often about England and Wales, France, and Sweden. Most of the middle- and low-income countries, those with high and low life expectancies, have attracted much less scholarly attention. Jamaica is no exception. George W. Roberts wrote an extended study of Jamaica's population history, published in 1957, in which he mapped changes in survivorship to the 1950s. But Roberts treated factors behind the gains in life expectancy between the 1920s and the 1950s in just a few words, attributing them to expanding medical and sanitary services.[9] Gisela Eisner, working from data about innovations in those services, surmised that the chief life expectancy gains came from the control of epidemics in

---

[7] Jere R. Behrman, *Human Resources in Latin America and the Caribbean* (Washington, 1996).

[8] Ibid., p. 1.

[9] George W. Roberts, *The Population of Jamaica* (Cambridge, 1957), p. 309. The treatment is enlarged in George W. Roberts and Dorian L. Powell, *Recent Population Movements in Jamaica* (Paris, 1974), pp. 94–123, especially on the period 1946–1970. See also the author's introduction to the reprint of *The Population of Jamaica* (Cambridge, 1979). Dinesh P. Sinha, *Children of the Caribbean, 1945–1984: Progress in Child Survival, Its Determinants and Implications* (Kingston, 1988), places life expectancy in the English-speaking Caribbean in a global frame and details infant and child survival in the region from 1945 to the 1980s.

the latter decades of the nineteenth century, and from expanding medical and public health services in the early twentieth century.[10] Owen Jefferson, too, emphasized medicine, explaining Jamaica's good life expectancy as an effect of the introduction of western medicine to less developed areas, with the World Health Organization and other international agencies having played the leading role.[11]

The theme of expanding health services and western medicine has been followed by other authors and developed in most detail by George Cumper. Impressed by Jamaica's gains, particularly in infant mortality, Cumper examined the path the country had followed as a source of potential insight into how other countries, especially in Africa, might draw on the Jamaican experience. He argued that the principal factor behind Jamaica's improvement in the 1920s and 1930s consisted of wider medical services in the form of doctors and hospitals, in addition to "a vigorous promotion of public health measures," more sophisticated attitudes toward health, better information about health, and social and economic improvements. Those gains, he argued, came chiefly from the outside: from the Rockefeller Foundation's interest in hookworm eradication, from dedicated British doctors practicing in Jamaica, and from an enlightened colonial administration. Influenced by the idea that western medicine played a substantial role in controlling bacterial diseases, Cumper located most life expectancy gains in the period 1945–70.[12]

These scholars, especially Cumper, have contributed a great deal to this book, as also has Kalman Tekse, who took the trouble to compile a detailed record of Jamaican demographic data for the period up to the early 1960s.[13] But they left enough questions unanswered, and enough parts of the history not yet told, to make it worthwhile to visit this case again and in greater detail.

---

[10] Gisela Eisner, *Jamaica, 1830–1930: A Study in Economic Growth* (Manchester, 1961), pp. 337–44.

[11] Owen Jefferson, *The Post-war Economic Development of Jamaica* (Kingston, 1972), pp. 19–20, citing Kingsley Davis, "The Amazing Decline of Mortality in Underdeveloped Areas," *American Economic Review*, 46 (1956): 305–18, who mentions also the introduction of DDT and the subsequent control of malarial mosquitoes.

[12] George E. Cumper, "Jamaica: A Case Study in Health Development," *Social Science and Medicine*, 17 (1983): 1983–93, quote from p. 1989. See also J. Mayone Stycos and Judith Blake, "The Jamaican Family Life Project: Some Objectives and Methods," *Social and Economic Studies*, 3 (1954): 342–49, who cite public health, modern drugs, and modern medical techniques.

[13] Kalman Tekse, *Population and Vital Statistics: Jamaica, 1832–1964: A Historical Perspective* (Kingston, 1974).

The initial three chapters of this book will address Jamaica's status as a low-income country with high life expectancy, lay out the specific questions that need to be answered if explanations are to be found, and set the scene for gains in survivorship by discussing conditions in Jamaica around 1920, on the eve of the beginning of its health transition. Another three chapters follow, each taking a chunk of time in the period of gains. Chapter 4, much the longest, treats the period 1920–50, during which Jamaica added years of life expectancy at one of the fastest paces ever achieved. Chapter 5 considers the good years, the period 1950–72, when it seemed that Jamaica might become a rich land, or at least a middle-income country. And Chapter 6 discusses the long period of economic disappointment since 1972, in which life expectancy has continued to rise nevertheless.

HOW DO POPULATIONS BECOME LONG-LIVED?

In seeking to explain sustained gains in life expectancy, scholars have sometimes tried to identify a key or leading factor. This approach has produced debates about the relative importance of better nutrition, sanitary improvements, and medicine in the modern rise of life expectancy. But it is a flawed approach. It relies altogether too heavily on the experience of single countries, most often Britain, in periods that comprise only part of the overall health transition, most often the nineteenth century. A broader view, one that examines the experience of many countries across the longer era of life expectancy gains, from the 1770s to the present, leads to another approach. Many factors account for gains in survival, some operating in all countries in one period or another, and others only in certain countries and periods. One factor may lead in some countries in some periods, but none has been dominant or even singularly important, across the entire span of time and experience.

Rather than searching for a single or a leading factor, the research goal can be to identify, and where possible weigh the importance of, all the significant policies and programs that a country followed in making survival gains, looking also for the sequences and combinations of tactics deployed when specific diseases were managed or controlled and when mortality in particular age groups retreated. This approach operates within a theory of life expectancy gains that identifies the sizable number of factors ever usefully applied to mortality reduction and the idea of combinations of policies and programs. My version of this multifactor theory and approach is explained in *Rising Life Expectancy: A Global History*,[14] where the factors behind gains in survival are discussed under six tactical headings: public health, medicine, economic development, nutrition, individual and household behavior, and literacy and education.

Each of these six tactical areas in fact covers many different activities, all with their own histories of making contributions to gains in survival. Thus, for example, public health encompasses vaccinations against disease, beginning with smallpox; the preparation of vaccines and the training of people to deliver vaccines; the system of surveillance developed to monitor communicable diseases of leading importance; the development of water filtration and chlorination, waterborne sewage collection, treatment, and disposal, and of alternative modes for providing households with safe water and means for safe disposal of human waste; maternal and child health programs that attempt to disseminate services and information to the population at large; and many more specific programs. Each tactical area encompasses tens or scores of elements.

Most of the countries that began health transitions between the 1770s and 1900 were more or less simultaneously undergoing economic development. In many cases they were already, in the decade of initiation, richer in per capita income expressed in constant value than the low-income countries of the early twentieth century would be, and in some cases they were already richer than the lowest-income countries of the world would be in 2000. Thus the countries that pioneered health transitions could afford to invest in costlier things, of which many paid health dividends. They could, for example, build costly systems for piping filtered and chlorinated water into households and for removing wastewater and human waste to sewage treatment plants. They could build elaborate systems for medical research and for training nurses and doctors. They could send scientists out to the tropics to study disease vectors, such as mosquitoes, and tropical diseases. Before 1900 these countries already possessed prosperous middle classes whose members could individually invest in things that enhanced health, such as more spacious housing, equipment to clean their houses, education, and many other things. In the rest of the world, neither countries and colonies nor household members could make the same choices because the costs were too high. If these countries and

[14] (Cambridge, 2001).

9

people were to enhance health and life expectancy, they had to find less expensive ways of doing so.

That was certainly true of Jamaica. The descriptive material in this book deals with the discovery and application of less costly ways of raising life expectancy and with how one low-income country found a way to match the rich lands in life expectancy. Whereas the paths to low mortality followed by the rich lands emphasized capital-intensive improvements, poor countries had to find other resources to substitute for capital.

Low-income models of the successful attainment of good health are likelier to serve the needs of today's low-income countries that have not yet matched the rich countries in survival or that have fallen back in life expectancy in recent years. The resources these countries can bring to bear more closely resemble those available to Jamaica through the history of its attainment of high life expectancy than they do the resources of the rich lands.

"A SINGULARLY BLESSED ISLAND"

In 2000 life expectancy at birth and per capita income were distributed among 167 countries across the globe with populations of at least 400,000 in the manner shown in Figure 1.1. (In this figure, Jamaica appears as a solid circle with a life expectancy at birth of 75.3 years and a GDPpc of $3,639 expressed in 2000 U.S. dollars.) Higher income often coincided with higher life expectancy, and lower income with lower survivorship. But there were many exceptions, all being poorer countries with comparatively high life expectancy. A total of 65 of these countries had life expectancies of at least 65 years and incomes below $10,000. Containing some 48 percent of the world's population, they are an interesting group because their populations extract so much potential for survival from such meager resources.

More interesting still are the 15 countries with life expectancies of 70 years or more and per capita incomes under $5,000 (Table 1.1).[1] The people in these countries have used scarce resources still more effectively. They also represent a varied group of peoples and countries distributed widely across the world, on four continents.

Most of the attention given the phenomenon of good health at low income has concentrated on the cases of Costa Rica, Kerala,

The title of this chapter is a quote from Herbert T. Thomas, *The Story of a West Indian Policeman or Forty-Seven Years in the Jamaica Constabulary* (Kingston, 1927), p. 18. Lord Olivier, antagonism toward whom prompted Thomas to write his story of disenchantment, ironically used "the blessed island" as the subtitle of his 1936 book.

[1] Estimates of life expectancy and income have been taken from United Nations Development Program, *Human Development Report 2002* (New York, 2002), pp. 149–52, except for Cuba's income, which comes from United States Central Intelligence Agency, *World Factbook*, at www.cia.gov/cia/publications/factbook. The latter source supplies estimates for some other countries not reported in the *Human Development Report* or supplies variant estimates of life expectancy or income, which would add Bosnia and Herzegovina, Honduras, North Korea, Peru, Serbia and Montenegro, and the Solomon Islands.

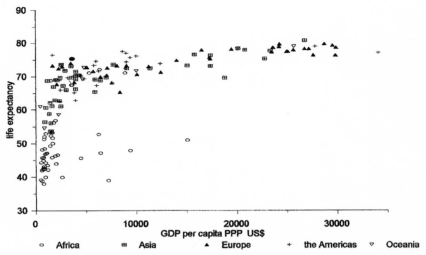

FIGURE 1.1. Life expectancy and per capita income in 2000 in 167 countries. *Sources:* World Bank, *World Development Indicators 2002*, CD-ROM (Washington, 2003); and, where estimates lack, United States Central Intelligence Agency, *World Factbook*, at www.cia.gov/cia/publications/factbook/geos/jm.html.

and Sri Lanka. These three deserve close scrutiny because they have been comparatively extreme cases, with lower incomes and higher life expectancies in the 1960s and 1970s than most other good-health-with-low-income countries. They have also been social democracies through most of the period since 1960, and their political systems have been marked by openness, popular participation, and the rule of law. They are cases that can be idealized. Each of the three has its own problems: in Kerala the chief problem has been persistent poverty; in Costa Rica with, by 2000, a higher income than others in the group, the leading problem has been a failure to meet popular expectations about economic growth; and in Sri Lanka it has been disappointed economic expectations and the long-standing conflict with Tamils who demand autonomy. These are significant problems, even if they are less imposing than the problems that most poor countries have faced in recent decades: desperate poverty, low survivorship, political disorganization and instability, corruption, and war.

Concentrating on these cases implies that the path to high life expectancy in poor countries lies with the characteristics of these three, either those that Caldwell emphasized – social justice, schooling, and female autonomy – or such others as open political systems and the policies of social democracy. The larger number of poor countries with

TABLE I.I. *Fifteen countries with low incomes and high life expectancies in 2000*

Country	Life expectancy	Per capita income in PPP* (2000 U.S.$)
Albania	73.2	3,506
Armenia	72.9	2,559
Azerbaijan	71.6	2,936
China	70.5	3,976
Cuba	76	1,700
Ecuador	70	3,203
El Salvador	69.7	4,497
Georgia	73.2	2,664
Jamaica	75.3	3,639
Jordan	70.3	3,966
Lebanon	73.1	4,308
Paraguay	70.1	4,426
Sri Lanka	72.1	3,530
Suriname	70.6	3,799
Syria	71.2	3,556

*Purchasing power parity.
Sources: United Nations Development Program, *Human Development Report 2002* (New York, 2002), pp. 149–52; United States Central Intelligence Agency, *World Factbook*, at www.cia.gov/cia/publications/factbook/geos/jm.html.

high life expectancy belies these generalizations, for that number includes countries where more aggressively capitalist economic systems prevail; political systems are marred by violence, corruption, and authoritarianism; and public policy does not seek to achieve social justice.

All cases deserve close study to discover what local circumstances made the attainment of high life expectancy possible. If the experience of these countries is to prove useful to other poor countries that have not yet met their potential in life expectancy, the most useful knowledge to acquire from that experience will come from tracking the variety of paths they have followed and finding which adaptations to local circumstances had the greatest benefit in added years of survival. A country need not first adopt a new politico-economic system, capitalism and democracy or social democracy, or a new culture and a new set of values in order to elevate life expectancy beyond what is possible from importing medical and public health technology, such as antibiotics, vaccines, and water purification systems, which all poor countries have tried to do.

Even populations and countries that have, quite serious problems on the scale of things in the last decades of the twentieth century, may nevertheless be able to achieve high life expectancy. Jamaica is an example of such a country, not in the sense that its problems have been as grave as those of the poorest countries with the lowest survivorship, but in the sense it has confronted and failed to resolve a serious array of problems. Listening to Jamaicans talk about their country and reading the pages of the widest circulation newspaper, the *Daily Gleaner*, including its often anguished letters to the editor, one learns how so many Jamaicans see their country's problems. Jamaicans will be the first to tell you that theirs is a troubled country, so troubled that it is easier to notice the bad than the good news.

Every country brings some advantages and some disadvantages to the circumstances that influence risks to survival. Jamaica is a new land in the sense that, the original settlers having been wiped out, immigrant populations created their own settlement patterns, made their own villages, and began anew. Since 1655, when the British took Jamaica from Spain, the island has enjoyed political stability and orderly political transitions, the brutal use of military and police power against slave and working-class rebellions notwithstanding. Jamaica's climate is in many ways an ally of good health. Year round warmth, except in the highlands, means that comparatively rudimentary housing can be satisfactory and that fuel is needed for cooking but not for heating homes. The same ally provides sunshine, a powerful disinfectant at least for tuberculosis bacilli. Jamaica has many rivers and, outside of the dry season, an abundant supply of fresh water in most areas. The growing season is year round, and the soil allows Jamaicans to cultivate a wide variety of fruits, vegetables, and nuts. But the warm climate also welcomes insect vectors of disease, especially mosquitoes, allowing them to reproduce through much of the year, and it exposes people to diseases rare in cooler climates, including hookworm and yaws.

Further problems arise in the human presence. The written demographic record of Jamaica begins with the depopulation of the Tainos who lived there when the Spaniards arrived in 1494 and who died out within a few decades, victims of diseases brought by the Spanish, violent attempts to press them into labor service, systematic murder, and cruelty. The extermination of the Tainos and the desire of Spanish and, from 1655, British colonial masters to cultivate sugarcane led to the introduction of slaves from Africa beginning in the early sixteenth century and, in the nineteenth century, indentured laborers from China, India, and Africa. The result was a population of immigrants from three continents, although mostly from Africa, who had to find ways to live together.

The motto that Jamaica adopted at independence in 1962, "Out of Many, One People," expressed an ambition more than a reality. Commentators on Jamaican history and culture emphasize the legacy of strife among racial and ethnic groups, most typically the aggression of Jamaicans from Africa toward fellow Jamaicans of Chinese, Indian, or mixed race background, but more rarely against people of European background, whether Jamaicans or not. Jamaica had a heterogeneous population in 1655 when the British arrived, which became more heterogeneous in the nineteenth century with the introduction of immigrants from China and India and from parts of Africa not previously represented. But Jamaicans from areas in Africa where people were forced into slavery always outnumbered all the other groups.[2] Antagonism toward other groups arose not from a minority position in numbers but from problems associated with the skewed distribution of income, wealth, education, political power, and opportunities for economic advancement. Jamaica's first long-standing problem therefore is not just suppressed opportunity, but frustration vented periodically in aggression and violence.[3] At the beginning and the end of the twentieth century the main groups, in descending order of their typical economic and social status, were as follows: whites, including Jews and "Syrians," a word used to describe people from the eastern Mediterranean;[4] light-skinned Afro-Jamaicans or, in the term formerly used by scholars and in general conversation to describe people of mixed African and European parentage, colored people;[5] Asian Indians called East Indians, originally indentured laborers working on sugar estates but, increasingly across the twentieth century, living in towns and

---

[2] See the proportions in Table 2.2.

[3] On social discord, see esp. Erna Brodber, "Socio-cultural Change in Jamaica," in Rex Nettleford, ed., *Jamaica in Independence: Essays on the Early Years* (Kingston, 1989) pp. 55–74. Fernando Henriques, who studied class and color around 1950, found that "social frustration is the hallmark of [Jamaican] poverty." See his *Family and Colour in Jamaica*, 2nd ed. (London, 1968), p. 161.

[4] On the post-1960s elite, see Lisa Douglass, *The Power of Sentiment: Love, Hierarchy, and the Jamaican Family Elite* (Boulder, 1994).

[5] Brian L. Moore and Michele A. Johnson, eds., *Squalid Kingston, 1890–1920: How the Poor Lived, Moved and Had Their Being* (Mona, 2000), p. 5 from the "Introduction."

operating businesses or filling professional jobs; Chinese, also usually urban and small shopkeepers; and people of more or less full African parentage.[6] Up to the 1960s most whites came from Britain, but after the British exodus many were Syrians. To a greater degree than in most multiracial or multiethnic populations, Jamaicans intermarried, so that each of these groups, while still recognizable by itself, also blends into all the others, and has done so since the nineteenth century.

The second long-standing problem is that although the land is rich, the people are not. Despite some periods of rapid economic growth, especially from 1950 to 1972, Jamaica is and has been a poor country. Too many of its inhabitants have not been able to find regular work or, lacking jobs, to earn enough by working small plots of land to rise above poverty. They have looked abroad for jobs, emigrating temporarily for work to Panama, Cuba, Britain, the United States, and Canada. Since the 1980s, many have made their residence abroad permanent. At any given time in the late nineteenth and throughout the twentieth century, tens of thousands of Jamaicans worked abroad. Thus migration has been the principal outlet, from the countryside to Kingston, and from all parts of the island to foreign labor markets.[7]

In the days of slavery, which ended with emancipation in 1834 and a four-year-long period called "apprenticeship" or preparation for freedom, a few families controlled the land and commerce of the island, and most people earned nothing, as slaves, and in material goods accumulated only a few personal possessions. That was a classically inequitable distribution of income and wealth. Even after 1838 the former slaves could accumulate few possessions and secure no more than meager incomes. Over time, the number of large landed estates declined, while

---

[6] On the questions of Jamaican identity, race, color, and class at and after independence, see Henriques, *Family and Colour in Jamaica*; Rex M. Nettleford, *Identity, Race and Protest in Jamaica* (New York, 1972), esp. pp. 19–37; and, by the same author, *Caribbean Cultural Identity: The Case of Jamaica: An Essay in Cultural Dynamics* (Kingston, 2003). Adam Kuper, *Changing Jamaica* (London, 1976); and Diane J. Austin, *Urban Life in Kingston, Jamaica: The Culture and Class Ideology of Two Neighborhoods* (New York, 1984), argue that distinctions in education, as well as those in wealth and color, shape Jamaica's class structure. Colin G. Clarke, *Kingston, Jamaica: Urban Development and Social Change, 1692–1962* (Berkeley, 1975), follows each group's changing size, residential areas, and occupations in Kingston. Jack Alexander, "The Culture of Race in Middle-Class Kingston, Jamaica," *American Ethnologist*, 4 (1977), 413–35, explores some of the many terms that Jamaicans use to discuss race and physical appearance.

[7] Dennis Conway, "The Importance of Migration for Caribbean Development," *Global Development Studies*, 2 (1999–2000): 73–105.

the average size of the remaining estates grew. Many Jamaicans acquired smallholdings.[8] The small freehold, often 5 acres or less, came to be established as a national ideal that would, for more than a century, be cited as the solution to economic distress, overpopulation, political discord, and other problems. But these freeholders were an agrarian proletariat who, until the 1920s, lacked organization or cohesion.[9] European missionaries tried to draw people to their churches, but most Jamaicans preferred Creole, or locally formed, blends of Christianity and African beliefs and practices. Revivalism emerged in the 1860s, Pentecostalism in the 1910s, and Rastafarianism in the 1950s, all representing variations on established religion that appealed especially to poor people.[10] These religious movements constitute one of the pillars of national life for the general population, but more often as outlets for venting frustration than as agencies pursuing concrete social aims.

During the second half of the nineteenth century, a middle class emerged. It was made up of mixed-race and black Jamaicans who were prosperous farmers and tradesmen and skilled artisans, school teachers, preachers, police constables, and clerks, these last mostly women.[11] It was a sizable group but not as prosperous as the middle classes of northwestern Europe and North America. Thus by about 1900 the population was distributed into three groups: a small and rich elite that was almost entirely of European background and two classes of Jamaicans: a middle class larger than the elite and growing in number and a general population of poor people, some living in Kingston and the towns of the island but most living in rural areas. For most of Jamaica's history, people had little opportunity to improve their economic position no matter how much entrepreneurial vigor they brought to the task or how long and hard they were willing to work. And for most of the country's history, the population remained predominantly

---

[8] See esp. Thomas C. Holt, *The Problem of Freedom: Race, Labor, and Politics in Jamaica and Britain, 1832–1938* (Baltimore, 1992), pp. 143–76.

[9] Sidney W. Mintz, *Caribbean Transformations* (Chicago, 1974), discusses characteristics in Jamaica and across the Caribbean.

[10] Barry Chevannes, *Rastafari: Roots and Ideology* (Syracuse, NY, 1994), pp. 20–21 and passim; and Diane J. Austin-Broos, *Jamaica Genesis: Religion and the Politics of Moral Orders* (Chicago, 1997), which deals with Jamaican Pentecostalism and its origins.

[11] Patrick Bryan, "The Black Middle Class in Nineteenth Century Jamaica," in Hilary Beckles and Verene Shepherd, eds., *Caribbean Freedom: Society and Economy from Emancipation to the Present* (Kingston, 1993), pp. 284–95.

rural. In 1960 nearly two-thirds of people lived in rural areas; in 2000 that proportion was still about 44 percent.[12]

The middle class grew in number and influence in the late nineteenth century by exploiting the opportunities for economic and social mobility presented by education, even if no more than a few years of primary schooling. But access to the schools and to jobs favored people of mixed African-European background with lighter skin color and European facial traits. By the 1930s and 1940s a middle class oligarchy had developed with its power concentrated in two political parties, the People's National Party and the Jamaica Labour Party. Both parties promised opportunities for the many, but the leaders of both were members of the mixed-race elite.

Jamaica's soil and climate are particularly well suited for the cultivation of sugar, bananas, and, at higher elevations in the Blue Mountains, coffee. Bauxite was discovered in 1946 and was soon mined for the aluminum industries of Britain, Canada, and the United States. All of these primary goods are produced in competition with other lands in the region or elsewhere in the world, making Jamaica a rival with other low-income countries in international markets. Export prices rise and fall for reasons outside Jamaican control, and so do the fortunes of Jamaica's economy, which has long relied heavily on export earnings. Tourism, an area where there was a little activity by the 1920s,[13] began to flourish in the 1950s and has proved to be the most important supplementary source of foreign exchange. There, too, Jamaica competes with its neighbors, which offer the same advantages of winter sun and fine beaches. None of these sectors of economic activity has provided a way out of poverty for the masses.

Jamaicans have governed themselves in local affairs since 1944, and in matters in general since 1962. The People's National Party (PNP) and the Jamaica Labour Party (JLP), which formed in the 1940s, have alternated in power. In rhetoric the PNP has in recent decades been the more leftist of the two, but in the policies followed the two parties have generally been difficult to distinguish. Both rely more on clientelism than on ideology to gain supporters, though for the most part middle-class Jamaicans have supported the PNP, and working people the JLP.

---

[12] See the proportions in World Bank, *World Development Indicators 2002*, CD-ROM (Washington, 2003).

[13] Frank F. Taylor, "From Hellshire to Healthshire: The Genesis of the Tourist Industry in Jamaica," in B. W. Higman, ed., *Trade, Government and Society in Caribbean History 1700–1920* (Mona, 1983), pp. 139–54.

Jamaica's long-standing problems are many. It is a land where most people usually have had enough to eat but where diets have often been unbalanced, favoring starchy foods. Unemployment and under-employment, persistent and unsolved matters, push Jamaicans not only to seek work abroad but also onto two parallel paths, one of intense entrepreneurship and the other of inactivity. Some Jamaicans do anything they can think of to scrape together a living, the most typical outlet being small-scale trading in fruits and vegetables. Others do as little as they can, preferring to avoid the frantic search for a slightly better standard of living, and the frustration associated with that search, by adapting to poverty or finding solace in spiritualism as the Rastafarians have done. Up to the 1950s, growing food on small plots was the most typical way of earning a living. People farmed small parcels of land and traded some of what they grew at markets in the towns and cities of the island. Since the 1970s, criminal activity, based partly on trade in ganja grown on the island and partly on drugs imported into Jamaica, often to be transshipped to the United States, Canada, and Britain, has provided another outlet.

Especially since the 1970s, Jamaicans have complained about corruption. Public servants are underpaid, but they nevertheless expect to live on their salaries. The police often demand bribes and are widely perceived to be corrupt. The political parties use bribes to influence voters and are also widely seen to be corrupt, even by their own partisans. Jamaica rates somewhere in the middle on Transparency International's index of corruption. The 2002 Corruption Perceptions Index rated Finland as least corrupt among the 102 countries ranked, and Bangladesh as most corrupt. Jamaica, which was first ranked in 2002, appeared in the 45th place, just below the middle and in a group with Brazil, Bulgaria, Peru, and Poland.[14]

CONCLUSION

Poverty and frustration with the difficulties of surmounting it mean that the phrase "a singularly blessed island" should be understood in an ironic way. The outstanding characteristic of Jamaica, at the beginning of the twenty-first century and across the past, back to the earliest European settlements, has been the poverty of the many. A

[14] See the Web page at www.transparency.org/pressreleases_archive/2002/2002.08.28. cpi.en.html.

people with expectations about themselves, Jamaicans have endlessly butted up against the problem of poverty without finding a solution other than escape. In the latter years of the twentieth century, many countries in Latin America and the Caribbean moved from low- to middle-income status, replacing GDPpc expressed in 2000 US dollars below $5,000 with levels between $5,000 and $10,000, and even above $10,000. But Jamaica has not.

What is exceptional is that Jamaicans have achieved so much in life expectancy with so little. Poverty has not prevented them from moving into the circle of the rich lands of the globe in survivorship.

2

WHAT NEEDS TO BE EXPLAINED?

This chapter addresses questions about the timing and pace of mortality decline and about the pattern of decline at specific ages. Jamaica's health transition will be compared with those in some other countries, with specific questions in mind. And causes of death in successive periods will be explored. With answers to these questions it will be possible to decide where explanations for mortality decline should be sought in time, in particular age groups, and in the control of specific diseases.

Overall mortality can be measured by life expectancy at birth, which is a helpful summary of the hazards to survival operating at all ages in a given year. There were no wars in Jamaica in this period, and civil unrest when it did occur did not produce enough deaths to stand out. Thus atypically low levels of life expectancy always indicate that an epidemic occurred that year, rather than a crisis in another form.

LIFE EXPECTANCY

Jamaica's Place among Other Countries. There is no evidence of any country making sustained gains in survivorship before the 1770s, when Denmark began the first health transition. Denmark and six other countries initiated health transitions between 1770 and 1850. All of them made slow progress in reaching a life expectancy of 70 years (Table 2.1). Jamaica, in contrast, began its health transition in the 1920s, when life expectancy at birth was about 36 years, the average of 1920–24, and reached a life expectancy of 70 years in 1977, about 50 years later, in one of the most rapid health transitions on record.[1]

---

[1] Oman, which began a health transition in the 1950s and reached a life expectancy of 70 years in 1993, moved slightly faster.

TABLE 2.1. *The pace of the early health transitions*

Country	Health transition began	Year in which life expectancy of 70 was reached	Time required to reach life expectancy of 70 years
Denmark	1770s or 1780s	1959	179 years
France	1790s	1960	165
Sweden	1790s	1948	153
England*	1800s	1956	151
Norway	1810s	1946	131
Belgium	1840s	1959	114
Canada	1840s	1956	111

*England alone for the initiation of a health transition, and England and Wales for reaching a life expectancy of 70 years.

Sources: DENMARK: Otto Andersen, "The Development of Danish Mortality 1735–1850," *Scandinavian Population Studies*, 5 (1979): 9–21; Hans Chr. Johansen, *Danish Population History 1600–1939* (Odense, 2002); Kirill F. Andreev, *Evolution of the Danish Population from 1835 to 2000* (Odense, 2002). FRANCE: Yves Blayo, "La mortalité en France de 1740 à 1829," *Population*, Special Number, 30 (Nov. 1975): 123–42; France Meslé and Jacques Vallin, "Reconstitution de tables annuelles de mortalité pour la France au XIXe siècle," *Population*, 44 (1989): 1121–58; and Human Mortality Database, www.mortality.org. SWEDEN: Gustav Sundbärg, *Bevölkerungsstatistik Schwedens 1750–1900* (Stockholm, 1970 reprint); *Historisk statistik för Sverige*, 3 vols. (Stockholm, 1969); and Human Mortality Database, www.mortality.org. ENGLAND: E. A. Wrigley and R. S. Schofield, *The Population History of England, 1541–1871: A Reconstruction* (Cambridge, 1989); and Human Mortality Database, www.mortality.org. NORWAY: Human Mortality Database, www.mortality.org. BELGIUM: Robert André and José Pereira-Roque, *La démographie de la Belgique au XIXe siècle* (Brussels, 1974); D. Veys, *Cohort Survival in Belgium in the Past 150 Years: Data and Life Table Results, Shortly Commented* (Leuven, 1983); Isabelle Devos, Allemaal Beestjes: Mortaliteit en morbiditeit in Vlaanderen, 18de-20ste eeuw, unpublished Ph.D. dissertation, Universiteit Gent, 2003; and World Bank, *World Development Indicators 2002*, CD-ROM (Washington, 2002). CANADA: Robert Bourbeau and Jacques Légaré, *Evolution de la mortalité au Canada et au Québec, 1831–1931: Essai de mesure par generation* (Montreal, 1982); and Human Mortality Database, www.mortality.org.

Denmark added years of survivorship from 1782, the midpoint year of the earliest estimate, to 2000 at a pace of just under 0.2 years addition for each year of calendar time.[2] Jamaica moved at a pace of nearly 0.5 years gain for each year of calendar time.[3]

[2] The 1780–84 estimate is from Otto Andersen, "The Decline in Danish Mortality before 1850 and its Economic and Social Background," in Tommy Bengtsson, Gunnar Fridlizius, and Rolf Ohlsson, eds., *Pre-Industrial Population Change: The Mortality Decline and Short-Term Population Movements* (Stockholm, 1984), 115–26; and that for 2000 is from the Human Mortality Database at www.mortality.org.

[3] From 1925 to 2000. See Appendix 1 for the sources.

All the countries that pioneered health transitions between 1770 and 1850 also became rich lands, although not in similar ways or with similar timing. That was not true of the larger group of countries that initiated health transitions between 1870 and 1913, which included several lands in Jamaica's region (Costa Rica, Cuba, Mexico, the United States, and probably Panama) in addition to Japan, Australia, and many countries in Europe.[4] And it certainly was not true of countries that initiated health transitions between 1913 and 1940, which (besides Jamaica) included Trinidad and Tobago, Sri Lanka, India and the state of Kerala, all of present-day Bangladesh and Pakistan, the Koreas, China, Turkey, and Vietnam. All the countries that began health transitions between 1913 and 1940 have remained poor, and some of them have also failed to attain life expectancies at birth of 70 years.

Life Expectancy in Jamaica. Life expectancy fluctuated around a low level in all countries in the long period before health transitions began, rather than remaining stable. It could be exceptionally low, even 10 years during periods of serious epidemics, but more typically the lowest level was 20–25 years. And it could be as high as 40 years, even a bit more. In their pre-transition eras, countries usually fall into one of two groups. In one group, survivorship was rather high, with life expectancy usually ranging between 30 and 40 years. In the other, survivorship was lower, life expectancy usually ranging between 20 and 30 years. The evidence about Jamaica is sparse and open to dispute, but what is known indicates that life expectancy in the slave population, which made up most of the population, fluctuated between 20 and 30 years. But in the era of freedom, Jamaica's people were favored with a life expectancy usually between 30 and 40 years.

Spaniards introduced African slaves to Jamaica in the early sixteenth century as the indigenous population of Tainos was being killed off, and from that time onward the population of Jamaica was made up mostly of people from Africa. Table 2.2 shows proportions recorded in censuses for the period 1844–1960 using census terms.[5] Thus the

---

[4] Some authorities find that Costa Rica's health transition began later, i.e., in the 1920s. Australia enters the picture – the earliest estimates for life expectancy are for New South Wales around 1860 – with already quite high levels of survival in the European population. John C. Caldwell, "Population," in Wray Vamplew, ed., *Australians: Historical Statistics* (Cambridge, 1987), pp. 23–41. There, life expectancy rose from the 1870s, if not earlier.

[5] In 1960 the terms were replaced, respectively, by African, Afro-European, European, Chinese or Afro-Chinese, and East Indian or Afro-East Indian.

TABLE 2.2. *Distribution of the population by racial and ethnic groups,*
1844–1960

Year	Blacks	Coloreds	Whites	Chinese and Afro-Chinese	Asian Indians and Afro-Indians	Others	Total
1844	293,128	68,529	15,776	0	0	0	377,433
1861	346,374	81,065	13,816	0	0	9	441,264
1871	392,707	100,346	13,101	0	0	0	506,154
1881	444,186	109,946	14,432	99	11,016	1,125	580,804
1891	488,624	121,955	14,692	481	10,116	3,623	639,491
1911	630,181	163,201	15,605	2,111	17,380	2,905	831,383
1921	660,420	157,223	14,476	3,696	18,610	3,693	858,118
1943	965,960	216,250	13,377	12,394	26,507	2,573	1,237,063
1960	1,236,706	235,494	12,428	19,939	54,266	50,981	1,609,814

Sources: George W. Roberts, *The Population of Jamaica* (Cambridge, 1957), p. 65; and Kalman Tekse, *Population and Vital Statistics Statistics: Jamaica, 1832–1964: A Historical Perspective* (Kingston, 1974), p. 78.

history of health deals mostly, but never entirely, with the health of Jamaicans initially from Africa. Survivorship began to improve earlier among whites than blacks, but the number of whites was never great enough to show up in an elevated life expectancy in the overall population. In the slave era and, for Europeans, some decades thereafter, the principal difference in survivorship arose within population groups. People who had been born in Jamaica, called Creoles, and those who had lived there for some years, had much better chances of survival at all ages than did new arrivals from Africa and Europe, who were especially likely to die within the first three years after arrival.

Using estate records for the period 1820–32 that included people from both groups, Roberts estimated life expectancy at birth for the West Indian slave population at 22.8 years.[6] His evidence showed

[6] George W. Roberts, "A Life Table for a West Indian Slave Population," *Population Studies*, 5 (1951–52): 238–43. Michael Craton, "Jamaican Slave Mortality: Fresh Light from Worthy Park, Longville and the Tharp Estates," *Journal of Caribbean History*, 3 (1971): 1–27, prefers a much higher life expectancy figure, perhaps 30 years in the 1730s and 40 years in the 1830s. But Craton subtracts deaths during the first three years after arrival, when mortality was quite high, and does not show how he arrived at his estimates. See also B. W. Higman, *Slave Population and Economy in Jamaica, 1807–1834* (Cambridge, 1976), p. 106, for crude death rates for the period 1817–32.

heavy mortality at ages above 30, compared to other age groups, which is unusual, and he estimated the probability of dying at ages 0–6 to total 40 percent. An expectation of 22.8 years is low, but not exceptionally so: life expectancy in France in the 1740s totaled about 24.8 years, and the official estimate for India in the 1890s is 22.4 years. Fertility among Jamaican slaves was also low, so that a life expectancy of 22.8 years was closer than would otherwise be the case to a level that ensures population decline.

Crude death rates declined from 40 per 1,000 people or more in the latter part of the slave era to an average of 32 in the period 1844–61, and 27 in the period 1861–71, all levels well below those among British troops serving in Jamaica, even though the troops were mostly young adults who would, back home in Britain, have had much better survival prospects.[7] But, as Tobias Smollett remarked, Jamaica was "the grave of Europeans."[8] Jamaicans did not die at the extraordinary rates of recently arrived British soldiers, but they did die at rates at the higher end of experience elsewhere. Mortality declined from the 1820s or 1830s until the 1860s, which was a decade of hard times.[9] Part of that improvement can be attributed to the gradually declining share of people born in Africa after the abolition of the slave trade in British possessions, in 1807, death rates being higher in that group, and, among Europeans, to the declining share of people born in Europe. But the more important factor was probably emancipation and the release of Jamaicans from slave labor and from fieldwork often done under brutal conditions in planting, cultivating, and harvesting sugarcane. In the years following the apprenticeship period, 1834–38, many former slaves were forced to leave their homes and provision plots by planters who refused to pay adequate wages for labor. These people dispersed into the countryside, which presumably lowered hazards

---

[7] Until they were moved to higher ground, away from malarial lowlands, British troops suffered heavier mortality than did slaves. Philip D. Curtin, *Death by Migration: Europe's Encounter with the Tropical World in the Nineteenth Century* (Cambridge, 1989), p. 27.

[8] Quoted by G. T. Lescene, "Brief Historical Retrospect of the Medical Profession in Jamaica," *West Indian Medical Journal*, 4 (1955): 217–42. See also Trevor Burnard, "'The Countrie Continues Sicklie': White Mortality in Jamaica, 1655–1780," *Social History of Medicine*, 12 (1999): 45–72.

[9] George W. Roberts, *The Population of Jamaica* (Cambridge, 1957), p. 176. For economic conditions in the 1860s see Douglas Hall, *Free Jamaica 1838–1865: An Economic History* (New Haven, 1959).

from the transmission of communicable diseases. Among the British, Afro-Jamaicans acquired the reputation of being a willful and disobedient people.[10]

The registration of births and deaths began in Jamaica in 1879,[11] and those data, along with results from periodic censuses, make it possible to construct statistical series and to estimate annual values of life expectancy. The estimates appear in Figure 2.1, which is given in arithmetic and log scale, the first to show the scale of change and the second to give a clearer picture of the pace of gains.[12] Estimates for the period up to 1964 have been made from annual records of deaths, which have not been published since 1964. Those overlap for a few years with estimates made by the World Bank for 1960–2000 in a series called *World Development Indicators*, which are smoothed by the method of estimation used. During the period of overlap, the estimates calculated here are about 2 years lower than those made by the World Bank.

Jamaica's most rapid gains occurred in the period 1925–40. Gains from 1945 to 1965 were nearly as rapid, but the pace slowed thereafter. Although one authority has argued that gains accelerated in the immediate postwar period,[13] the pace was in fact beginning to slow in the latter 1940s.

[10] E.g., *Handbook of Jamaica for 1882* (Kingston, 1882), p. 235, referring to the 1830s. Rex Nettleford explores a modern form of this trait, which he terms "chronic individualism."

So strong is this characteristic in the Jamaican psyche that what is socialized assertiveness is not infrequently mistaken for genetic aggression or insolent assertion, unavoidably violence-prone, particularly in response to any assault (real or imagined) on one's dignity and "personhood."

Rex M. Nettleford, *Caribbean Cultural Identity: The Case of Jamaica: An Essay in Cultural Dynamics* (Kingston, 2003), p. xxi. Lisa Douglass, *The Power of Sentiment: Love, Hierarchy, and the Jamaican Family Elite* (Boulder, 1994), p. 261, explores Jamaicans' belief "in the values of individualism and achievement."

[11] I found no evidence that registration, which amounted to a kind of official surveillance, led to any changes in infant or child mortality or in parental attentiveness to children.

[12] The annual values are given in Appendix 1, together with an explanation of how the estimates were made. For the period 1881–1964, annual estimates have been made from births, registered deaths, and estimates of the population at risk at each age. For 1960–2000 the figure also reports estimates from World Bank, *World Development Indicators 2002*, CD-ROM (Washington, 2003), which are available for most years. The World Bank estimates are derived indirectly, using other indicators as well as mortality data, and they are smoothed.

[13] Roberts, *Population of Jamaica*, p. 199, located the faster decline in the period 1946–51.

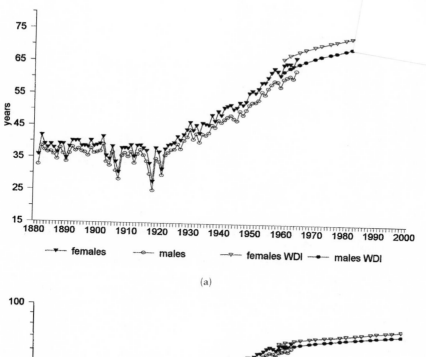

(a)

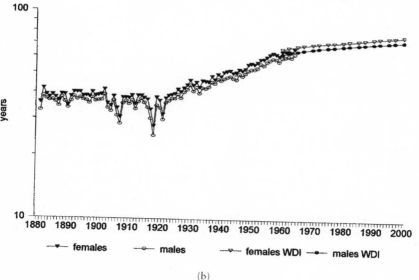

(b)

FIGURE 2.1. Life expectancy in Jamaica, 1881–2000. *Sources:* See Appendix A.

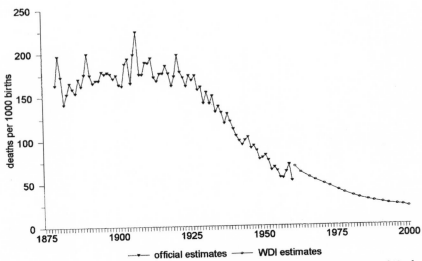

FIGURE 2.2. Infant mortality, 1879–2000. *Sources:* Kalman Tekse, *Population and Vital Statistics: Jamaica, 1832–1964: A Historical Perspective* (Kingston, 1974), pp. 168–73, for 1879–1964; and World Bank, *World Development Indicators 2002*, CD-ROM (Washington, 2003), for 1960–2000.

Infant mortality rates also began to decline in the 1920s, as appears in Figure 2.2, with the level varying sharply from year to year.[14] Infant mortality increased in the last two decades of the nineteenth century and into the early twentieth century, which may be partly a result of improving completeness in the registration of infant deaths and partly a real effect.[15] For the country as a whole, it began to decline in 1928. Annual birth and infant death data are available for Jamaica's 14 parishes, and a separate investigation of those records indicates that the 1928 turning point is an effect created by combining the data rather than a simultaneous turning point in the individual parishes.[16] Infant mortality was generally lower in the early 1930s than the early 1920s,

[14] Through 1959 the rates reported are official values. In more recent years the official estimates of infant mortality are known to be too low. Thus for 1960–2000 the figure reports estimates from the World Bank.

[15] More complete registration of infant deaths may contribute to the appearance of rising infant mortality in the 1880s, but that is unlikely to explain the longer trend rise if only because such an effect requires an improving registration of deaths without change in the completeness of birth registration.

[16] Kalman Tekse, *Population and Vital Statistics: Jamaica, 1832–1964: A Historical Perspective* (Kingston, 1974), pp. 196–202.

so that the second half of the 1920s, rather than specifically 1928, saw the initiation of Jamaica's infant health transition.

Figure 2.3 shows curves of the probability of dying by age for four periods from 1879–82 to 2000 for males and females separately.[17] There was little change before the 1920s, but afterward mortality declined at all the ages considered, from infancy up to 70–74.

Kingston remained the only Jamaican city with as many as 20,000 people until the late 1950s, when Montego Bay passed that threshold. Infant mortality in Kingston was initially higher than in the island as a whole, but in the late 1920s the capital became a less hazardous place to be born and a less hazardous place also for young children to live.

A closer look at specific age groups indicates that Jamaica's health transition began in the early 1920s when mortality among males and females aged 15–34 years first declined. In those ages, death rates fell in the early 1920s and the mid- and late 1930s, but not in between. Thus two dynamics emerge. Mortality in infancy and at ages 1–14 began to drop in the second half of the 1920s and continued to fall thereafter, while the decline began a few years earlier at ages 15–34. Once Jamaica's health transition was under way, mortality moved downward at a persistent and vigorous pace. Although maternal mortality remained high, deaths associated with childbirth continued to account for a small share of the total, so that male and female mortality declined at much the same pace until the 1980s. Then female gains slightly outpaced male gains.

Jamaican gains in life expectancy roughly paralleled those in Trinidad (Figure 2.4). Both colonies began health transitions in the 1920s. Trinidad had slightly higher levels of life expectancy into the 1950s. From the early 1960s, however, World Bank estimates suggest that Jamaica gained and preserved the advantage. By 2000 the World Bank estimated that Trinidadians had a life expectancy at birth of 72.6 years, against 75.3 years for Jamaicans.

Life Expectancy in Jamaica, the United States, and the Soviet Union.
Three issues prompt the comparisons made in Figures 2.5, 2.6, and 2.7,

---

[17] This figure reproduces World Health Organization estimates for 2000, which, for infant mortality, are too low. Compare with the adjusted estimate used in Figure 2.2.
 Figure 2.3 uses a logarithmic scale in order to show all ages on the same diagram. That scale gives a misleading picture about when the main changes occurred, making them appear to have come later than they did. This misimpression will be corrected in the introductory pages of chapters on 1920–1950, 1950–1972, and 1972–2000.

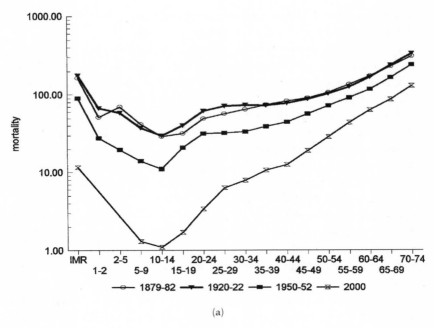

(a)

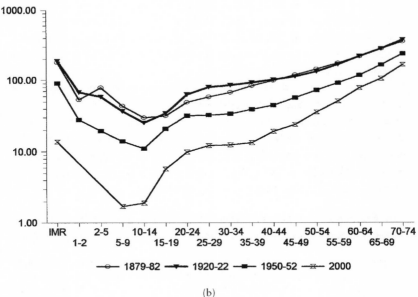

(b)

FIGURE 2.3. Mortality curves in four periods, 1879–2000. (a) Females, and (b) males. *Sources:* Kalman Tekse, *Population and Vital Statistics: Jamaica, 1832–1964: A Historical Perspective* (Kingston, 1974), pp. 238–39; and A. D. Lopez et al., *World Mortality in 2000: Life Tables for 191 Countries* (Geneva, 2002), pp. 294–95.

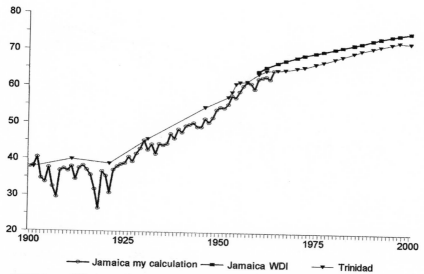

FIGURE 2.4. Life expectancy in Jamaica and Trinidad, 1900–2000. *Sources:* For Jamaica, see Appendix A; for Trinidad: Jack Harewood, *The Population of Trinidad and Tobago* (Paris, 1975), p. 34; Norma Abdulah, ed., *Trinidad and Tobago 1985: A Demographic Analysis* (n.p., n.d.), p. 164; and World Bank, *World Development Indicators 2002*, CD-ROM (Washington, 2003).

which show life expectancy in Jamaica, the United States, and Russia/ the Soviet Union across the period 1880–2000.[18] First, how did Jamaican experience compare with the other two countries in the pace and timing of gains? Second, how did Jamaicans fare in comparison with whites and blacks in the United States?[19] Third, how did Jamaican males fare in comparison with Russian males, among whom life expectancy trended down as the Russian economic system weakened in the 1970s and 1980s? (Jamaica, too, suffered a lengthy period of economic stagnation, which will be discussed in Chapter 6.)

Among these three countries, the United States has maintained a persistent lead in life expectancy (Figure 2.5). Russia/the Soviet Union nearly caught up with the United States in the 1960s, but then fell back because female survivorship stopped rising and male survivorship

[18] The worldwide influenza epidemic of 1918–19 caused a sharp spike in mortality. Life expectancy in the Soviet Union fell to an exceptionally low level during the 1933 famine and again during World War II.

[19] The comparison is with U.S. nonwhites for 1880–1970, the only form for which data were collected, but in that period the nonwhite population was mostly made up of blacks.

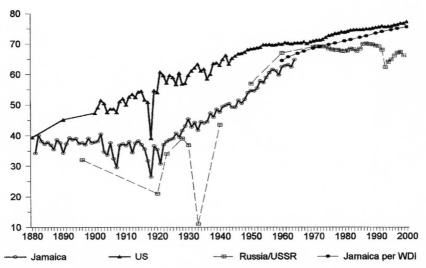

FIGURE 2.5. Life expectancy in three countries. *Sources:* For Jamaica the sources given for Figure 2.1 in Appendix A; for the United States before 1900, Michael R. Haines, "Estimated Life Tables for the United States, 1850–1910," *Historical Methods*, 4 (1998), 149–69, and for 1900–2000 official estimates from United States National Center for Health Statistics, *National Vital Statistics Reports*, 51, No. 3 (Washington, 2002), available at www.cdc.gov/nchs/about/major/dvs/mortdata.htm; and for Russia/the Soviet Union, Alain Blum, *Naître, vivre et mourir en URSS, 1917–1991* (Paris, 1994); and, for 1975–99, the Human Mortality Database, at www.mortality.org.

dropped. For most of the period in this comparison, Jamaica had an advantage over Russia, partly owing to dramatically low levels of life expectancy in Russia in crisis periods. But even in ordinary years, Jamaica had the advantage. Russia's gains in the period 1920–60 were even more rapid than Jamaica's, but Jamaican life expectancy continued to improve after 1972, amidst economic stagnation, and Jamaica nearly closed the gap with the United States in the 1990s.

Figure 2.6 shows life expectancy for U.S. whites and nonwhites and for Jamaicans across the period 1880–2000. (The nonwhite group whose life expectancy is estimated in the United States is composed of all nonwhites up to 1970, then exclusively of blacks.) The health transition of U.S. nonwhites, most of them blacks descended from slaves brought to America from Africa, began earlier than Jamaica's, and in the 1910s and 1920s U.S. nonwhites moved ahead of their Jamaican counterparts. Jamaicans closed the gap with U.S. nonwhites by about 1960 and thereafter made faster gains, so that by 2000 Jamaican life expectancy was closer to that of U.S. whites than of U.S. blacks.

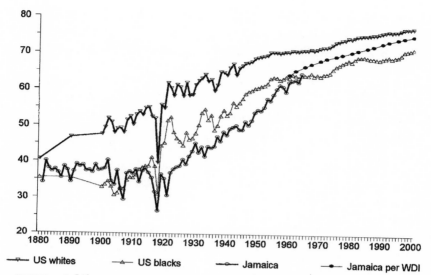

FIGURE 2.6. Life expectancy in Jamaica and the United States. *Sources:* See Figures 2.4 and 2.5 and the estimates for 1880 and 1890 for nonwhites from Douglas C. Ewbank, "History of Black Mortality and Health before 1940," *Milbank Quarterly*, 65, Suppl. 1 (1987), 100–28.

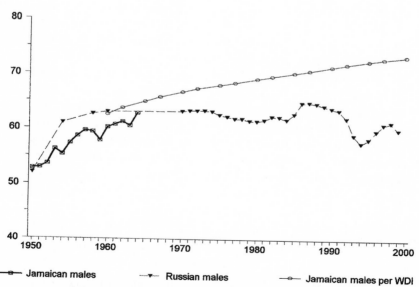

FIGURE 2.7. Life expectancy for males in Jamaica and Russia. *Sources:* See Figure 2.4.

Russian males had the advantage over Jamaican males in the 1950s, as Figure 2.7 shows. Thereafter, however, Russian males fell behind, so that by the end of the 1990s their life expectancy was about 13 years less than that of Jamaican males.

Life Expectancy in Jamaica, Costa Rica, India, Nigeria, the United States, and England/the United Kingdom. These six countries were sharply differentiated in income around 1870, but less so in life expectancy (Table 2.3). In the decades that followed, the United States and England/the United Kingdom moved ahead earlier in survivorship. Jamaica and Costa Rica caught up between 1913 and 1975, but India and Nigeria did not. For Jamaica the explanation of its position as a poor country with high survivorship is to be found in the period beginning around 1925, when death rates began to decline in a persistent way, up to about 1975, and in the circumstances that existed in 1925 and thereafter, which made a health transition possible.

IF THE DATA ARE LESS THAN PERFECT

Colonial authorities in Jamaica expressed confidence in the quality of most of the population and health data they reported, and later scholars have accepted that judgment.[20] It may seem unlikely that authorities were able to collect reasonably comprehensive information about births and deaths in a country where most people lived in rural areas and where colonial authorities regarded the local population as willful and disobedient. But internal tests of the data do not suggest that the errors were large.

By the 1870s, Jamaicans were moving about the Caribbean as employment possibilities presented, going to Costa Rica to build a railroad to the Atlantic coast and to cultivate bananas, to Panama in the 1880s to work on the French canal project and from 1904 to work on the U.S. canal, and to Guatemala, Cuba, and elsewhere, mostly to clear land for or to work on sugar and banana plantations.[21] Those opportunities

---

[20] Roberts, *Population of Jamaica*, pp. 23–27; and Tekse, *Population and Vital Statistics*, pp. 1 and 3.

[21] Aviva Chomsky, *West Indian Workers and the United Fruit Company in Costa Rica, 1870–1940* (Baton Rouge, 1996), pp. 35–44; Elizabeth McLean Petras, *Jamaican Labor Migration: White Capital and Black Labor, 1850–1930* (Boulder, 1988); Velma Newton, *The Silver Men: West Indian Labour Migration to Panama, 1850–1914* (Kingston, 1984); and Michael L. Conniff, *Black Labor on a White Canal: Panama, 1904–1981* (Pittsburgh, 1985).

TABLE 2.3. Income and life expectancy in six countries, 1870–1998 (GDPpc in 1990 U.S.$ PPP)

	Costa Rica		England and Wales/U.K.		India		Jamaica		Nigeria		United States	
	GDPpc	Life exp.	GDPpc	Life exp.	GDPpc	Life exp.	GDPpc	Life exp.	GDPpc	Life exp.	GDPpc	Life exp.
1870	553*	28.6 to 37.7	3,191	40.8†	533	24.6	553*	38.4‡			2,445	44.0
1913	1184*	34.6	4,921	53.7†	673	21.5	1184*	37.5			5,301	52.5
1950	1,963	55.6	6,907	69.0†	619	31.0	1,314	54.6	753	31.3	9,561	68.2
1973	4,319	68.7	12,022	72.1	853	50.8	1,642	69.2	1,442	43.8	16,689	71.4
1990	4,755	75.4	16,411	75.6	1,309	59.1	1,877	73.2	1,242	49.1	23,214	75.2
1998	5,346	76.9	18,714	77.2	1,746	62.4	2,035	75.0	1,232	48.8	27,311	76.6

* In the group of countries with this GDPpc level.
† England and Wales only.
‡ 1881.

Sources (for the income estimates): Angus Maddison, The World Economy: A Millennial Perspective (Paris, 2001), pp. 185, 195, 215, 224. For the life expectancy estimates for various countries, refer to the following: ENGLAND and WALES: see Table 2.1. COSTA RICA: Leonardo Mata and Luis Rosero, National Health and Social Development in Costa Rica: A Case Study of Intersectoral Action (Washington, 1988), p. 56. INDIA: P. N. Mari Bhat, "Mortality and Fertility in India, 1881–1961: A Reassessment," in Tim Dyson, ed., India's Historical Demography: Studies in Famine, Disease and Society (London, 1989), p. 93; and World Bank, World Development Indicators 2002, CD-ROM (Washington, 2003). The estimate for the 1870s is probably too high. JAMAICA: See Figure 2.1. NIGERIA: United Nations Population Division, Selected World Demographic Indicators by Countries, 1950–2000, Working Paper No. 55 (n.p., 1975), p. 55; and World Bank, World Development Indicators 2002, CD-ROM (Washington, 2003). UNITED STATES: Michael R. Haines, "Estimated Life Tables for the United States, 1850–1910," Historical Methods, 4 (1998), 149–69; United States, Historical Statistics of the United States: Colonial Times to 1970, 2 vols. (Washington, 1975), Vol. I, p. 55; and World Bank, World Development Indicators 2002, CD-ROM (Washington, 2003).

were curtailed in the 1930s, but in the 1940s Jamaicans began to move to Britain (up to about 1962), the United States, and Canada.[22] Emigration relieved unemployment in Jamaica, initially among people who had only their labor to sell, but later, by the 1950s and 1960s, the emigrants were increasingly people, especially young adults, with more years of schooling than the national average. The emigrants often visited their families in Jamaica and sent remittances.[23]

For many years in the nineteenth century, those movements were not recorded and, afterward, when the authorities tried to monitor migration numbers, the reporting was incomplete. Sizable differences are evident when populations counted at censuses are compared to those estimated by adjusting the prior census for registered births, deaths, and net migration. Those differences are usually attributed to underreported emigration, a persistent problem.[24] It is possible, even likely, that emigration continued to be underreported in the 1940s, 1950s, and onward to the present. If so, then the population at risk to death in Jamaica may be overstated in official estimates at the ages most affected, usually 15 through about 40 years but, given the characteristics of postwar emigration, up to about 80 years.

Reporting of births and deaths began to show signs of strain in the 1960s and continued to do so to the end of the century, with particular problems in the registration of births, infant deaths, and adult deaths from violence. Adjusted figures for the censuses of 1943 and 1960 indicate that infants and young children were undercounted.[25] A number

---

[22] Owen Jefferson, *The Post-war Economic Development of Jamaica* (Kingston, 1972), p. 22; Shirley J. Smith, Industrial Growth, Economic Opportunities, and Migration within and from Jamaica, 1943 to 1970, unpublished Ph.D. dissertation, University of Pennsylvania, 1975, pp. 28–29, 179–96, and 360–72; Ceri Peach, *West Indian Migration to Britain: A Social Geography* (London, 1968); and Virginia R. Dominguez, *From Neighbor to Stranger: The Dilemma of Caribbean Peoples in the United States* (New Haven, 1975), esp. pp. 74, 79, and 85.

[23] Bonham C. Richardson, *Panama Money in Barbados, 1900–1920* (Knoxville, 1985), pp. 155–59, discusses remittances by Barbadians working in Panama in some detail; Newton, *The Silver Men*, p. 104, reports that Jamaicans sent money home via postal money orders and in cash.

[24] R. R. Kuczynski, *Demographic Survey of the British Colonial Empire*, 3 vols. (London, 1948–1953), Vol. III, p. 233, indicates that emigration was underrecorded in annual estimates before 1921 and between the 1921 and 1943 censuses. Richard A. Lobdell, *Economic Structure and Demographic Performance in Jamaica, 1891–1935* (New York, 1987), p. 216, concurs.

[25] Compare Census Research Programme, University of the West Indies, *Estimates of Intercensal Population by Age and Sex and Revised Vital Rates for British Caribbean*

of scholars suggest that official Jamaican estimates understate infant mortality in the period 1965–2000.

International agencies typically report official estimates. Thus the life expectancy estimates calculated by Jamaican authorities and many international agencies are overstated. Some scholars have tried to make adjustments by surveying the extent of underregistration. In a literature review, Affette McCaw-Binns et al. found a high rate of registration of births, 94 percent in a 1986 survey, but low and deteriorating rates for the registration of infant deaths, especially those in the first few days after birth, and of stillbirths.[26] The World Bank estimates of infant mortality, used here, are meant to take underregistration into account, but the estimates from surveys differ so much that it is difficult to have full confidence in the corrections.[27] For an entirely different reason – delays in the operations of the Coroners Court – there is also an unknown degree of underregistration or belated registration of deaths from violence and from motor vehicle accidents, which appears to have worsened in the 1990s.

For 1960 the official estimate of infant mortality, 48.8 deaths per 1,000 births, is well below the World Bank estimate, at 67.8 per 1,000. For 1970 the difference is even greater, 27.1 versus 47.8, although both estimates indicate about the same amount (although not rate) of decline. Since then, official estimates are more difficult to find, and some agencies have resorted to the tactic of repeating a 1993 estimate

---

Countries, 1946–1960 (n.p., 1964), pp. 14–15, with results from the censuses in Tekse, *Population and Vital Statistics*, pp. 30–36. The adjustments also correct for age misreporting at 10–19 years but do not correct census figures at higher ages. See also Jay H. Glasser, "Implications of Declining Mortality for the Organization of Health Care: The Case of Jamaica," in Harald Hansluwka et al., eds., *New Developments in the Analysis of Mortality and Causes of Death* (Bangkok, 1986), pp. 509–26.

[26] But the surveys are not exactly comparable since they deal with different regions. Affette M. McCaw-Binns et al., "Registration of Births, Stillbirths and Infant Deaths in Jamaica," *International Journal of Epidemiology*, 25 (1996): 807–13. See also P. Desai et al., "Infant Mortality Rates in Three Parishes of Western Jamaica, 1980," *West Indian Medical Journal*, 32 (1983): 83–87; Kristin Fox, Infant Mortality Rates in Jamaica, 1993, unpublished paper, 1994 (available at SALISES); and Ruth Rice Puffer and Carlos V. Serrano, *Patterns of Mortality in Childhood* (Washington, 1973), pp. 70–71.

[27] Moreover, the World Bank, like other international agencies reporting life expectancy and infant mortality estimates, provides little or no documentation about the corrections made, creating further uncertainty.

of 24.5 deaths per 1,000.[28] However, the World Health Organization (WHO) estimate for 2000 is 13.7 for males and 11.6 for females.[29]

In sum, the number of Jamaicans living in Jamaica may be over-stated in many population estimates, even those for recent years; since about 1960, infant mortality is likely to be understated, and deaths from violence, and to a lesser degree from vehicular accidents, are not reported or are reported too late to be used in mortality estimates. A. D. Lopez et al. at WHO estimated life expectancy at birth in 2000 at 72.8 years for males and 76.6 years for females. Taking all these adjustments into account, life expectancy for 2000 would be reestimated at 70.7 for males and 74.6 for females.[30] These adjustments reduce life expectancy by two years, to 72.5 years. They have a significant but not a large effect. Only far more dramatic adjustments would remove Jamaica from its position as a country with low income but good health. Moreover, these adjustments do not undermine general confidence in the picture of trends in age-specific mortality and life expectancy based on official data, even after 1960.

Nevertheless, these cautions are enough to suggest that life expectancy in Jamaica in 2000 was not as high as estimated in the *Human Development Report* or by Lopez et al. for WHO. Life expectancy then was probably between 72.5 and 75.3, or about 74, years.

CAUSES OF DEATH

Each disease has its own characteristic features, which we usually think about in terms of signs and symptoms, the things that physicians notice and patients complain about. For demographers studying mortality, however, it is more important to think about some of the other particularistic features of diseases, especially the proportion of people with the disease who die (lethality), the ages at which diseases most typically occur and end in death, differences in disease and age-specific mortality associated with sex, and other population characteristics,

---

[28] E.g., Planning Institute of Jamaica, *Economic and Social Survey Jamaica 2000* (Kingston, 2001), p. 20.5, citing a study done by the Jamaican Ministry of Health in association with the United Nations Children's Fund.

[29] A. D. Lopez et al., *World Mortality in 2000: Life Tables for 191 Countries* (Geneva, 2002), pp. 294–95.

[30] That is, infant mortality at 24.5 per 1,000 for males and females alike; a 10 percent reduction in the size of the population at risk at ages 15–79 for males and females; and, for males only, a 10 percent increase in mortality at ages 15–34 to account for deaths from violence.

such as urban or rural residence, that affect mortality and disease risk. Demographers must grapple with modes for controlling diseases, especially those likely to result in death or to increase the likelihood of death from another cause. What must people do to reduce the chances of getting a particular disease or, if they get it, to reduce the chances of dying from it? How may avoidance, prevention, treatment, or management control the effects of a disease?

Up to 1920. In the era of slavery and for the remainder of the nineteenth century, Jamaicans faced a broad spectrum of diseases, which are identified by references made by inhabitants of the island and visitors, and in the formal medical literature beginning with Thomas Dancer's medical guide for Jamaicans without access to doctors, first published in 1801.[31] Among British troops in the nineteenth century, the leading causes of death were yellow fever, malaria, typhoid fever and probably also typhus, and tuberculosis, and significant numbers of men also died from diseases of the digestive and circulatory systems.[32]

Jamaican authorities began to register deaths and certify causes in 1878. Registration was "reasonably complete" from the beginning, reporting 13,011 deaths in the initial year and 15,084 in the second year, for crude death rates of 23.3 and 27.0 per 1,000, respectively.[33] But for a long time, medical certification was incomplete: most deaths were recorded without a cause. The highest quality cause-of-death data refer to certified cases, which, for the period 1881–1900, comprise 21 percent of registered deaths. Deaths in Kingston were more often certified than those in rural parishes, and more adult than infant and child deaths, but few deaths among the oldest people, were certified. And of course, certified deaths were biased toward people who could afford to consult doctors and who lived closer to doctors.

---

[31] Thomas Dancer, *The Medical Assistant; or Jamaica Practice of Physic: Designed Chiefly for the Use of Families and Plantations* (Kingston, 1801). To preserve health, Dancer urged a mixture of practices associated with the nonnaturals and filth theory ideas: exercise; select food and drink carefully (e.g., avoid meat in hot climates); bathe, but not too often; ventilate homes; burn the clothing of the sick; and fumigate foul odors with tobacco, vapors of vinegar, or other substances.
See also Benjamin Moseley, *A Treatise on Tropical Diseases, and on the Climate of the West Indies* (London, 1787).

[32] Curtin, *Death by Migration*, p. 85; and Lescene, "Brief Historical Retrospect."

[33] The quote and the data come from the "Historical Supplement, 1878–9 to 1945," first published in Jamaica, *Annual Report of the Registrar General's Department* (Kingston, 1947), pp. 25 and 28, for 1945.

TABLE 2.4. *Ten leading causes of death in Jamaica, 1881–1920, among certified deaths*

Cause	Proportion of deaths, 1881–1900	Proportion of deaths, 1901–1920
Diarrhea, enteritis, and typhoid fever	9.8 percent	13.0 percent
Pulmonary tuberculosis	9.1	9.1
Accidents	7.2	5.4
Malaria	7.1	7.3
Heart disease	5.8	6.5
Nephritis	5.7	7.9
Cerebral hemorrhage	4.1	3.1
Pneumonia	3.3	4.3
Syphilis	2.1	3.2
Bronchitis	1.6	1.8
Puerperal causes	1.6	1.5

Source: Jamaica. *Annual Report of the Registrar General's Department* (Kingston, 1946), pp. 36–7.

The certified deaths give a picture of four leading causes of death in the period 1881–1900: diarrheal diseases, tuberculosis, malaria, and one external cause, accidents (Table 2.4). The same causes led among certified deaths in the period 1901–20.[34]

The registrar general also collected information about causes of death from relatives and neighbors who reported and registered deaths, so that causes are known also for many uncertified deaths, although these are likelier to be stated in terms of symptoms, such as fever or convulsions. These data modify the picture given in Table 2.4, because they show that some deaths, such as those from puerperal fever and syphilis, were much likelier to be certified than others, presumably because they occurred more often in hospitals or under the care of a doctor. The more comprehensive data also repair many of the omissions for infants and children. Table 2.5 shows the leading causes of death in an unexceptional year, 1896–97. Even though unexplained causes lead the list, it is apparent that a few diseases caused most deaths. Deaths attributed to convulsions, which occurred mostly among infants and young children, are likely to include many in which diarrhea was a

[34] The source for these data is given in the previous footnote. Typhoid fever deaths have been added to those for diarrhea and enteritis on grounds that the differentiation is suspect.

TABLE 2.5. *Leading causes of death in 1896–97*

	Number	Proportion of deaths
Ill-defined or not given	3,097	19.9 percent
Malarial diseases	2,807	18.1
Convulsions	1,381	8.9
Phthisis (pulmonary tuberculosis)	1,191	7.7
Old age	1,126	7.2
Dysentery, diarrhea, enteritis, and enteric fever	1,114	7.2
Whooping cough	495	3.2
Heart and circulatory system	376	2.4
Accidents and violence	253	1.6

Source: Annual Report of the Registrar General's Department for 1896–97 (Kingston, 1897), which appears in Jamaica, *The Annual General Report of Jamaica, together with the Departmental Reports* (Kingston, 1897), pp. 262–87.

leading symptom; if all deaths attributed to convulsions were assigned to the category of diarrheal diseases, that category would account for 16.1 percent of all deaths. Using that assignment, malarial diseases, diarrheal diseases, and phthisis (i.e., respiratory tuberculosis) accounted together for 41.9 percent of all deaths, in addition to deaths in the unexplained category that would, if the cause were known, add more cases from these causes.

Table 2.6 shows the age distribution in the main causes and all causes in 1896–97, emphasizing the leading importance of deaths in infancy and childhood. In the period 1881–1900, infant deaths accounted for 28.4 percent of all deaths, and during 1901–20, for 27.8 percent. Any substantial reduction in mortality in Jamaica would have to reduce infant and child mortality by controlling diarrheal diseases and malaria, and to curtail young adult mortality by controlling tuberculosis.

1920–2000. Table 2.7 shows the leading causes of death in the period 1920–22. Diarrheal diseases and convulsions, malaria, fevers, and respiratory tuberculosis accounted for 46 percent of all deaths. Convulsions can be associated with diarrheal disease and some other maladies, and fevers can be associated with infectious diseases in general but especially with malaria and tuberculosis. (The association of fever with malaria is a long-standing feature of cause-of-death reporting in

TABLE 2.6. *Age distribution of all deaths and deaths from leading causes, 1896–97*

	Ill-defined and not given	Malarial fevers	Convulsions	Pulmonary tuberculosis	Old age	Dysentery, etc.	Whooping cough	All deaths
0–1	1,367	871	1,083	4	0	320	227	4,760
1–4	409	828	178	21	0	216	233	2,506
5–14	166	277	66	47	0	58	34	883
15–24	173	234	20	316	0	79	0	1,189
25–44	337	262	22	526	0	159	0	2,179
45–64	437	209	9	227	2	159	1	1,834
65 and up	191	119	3	45	1,118	122	0	2,122
Age not given	17	7	0	5	6	1	0	62
TOTAL	3,097	2,807	1,381	1,191	1,126	1,114	495	15,535
Proportion certified	5.7	11.4	2.5	31.3	11.4	46.6	4.6	23.6

Source: See Table 2.5.

TABLE 2.7. *Leading causes of death in 1920–22*

Cause	Per 10,000	Recombined as		Recombined as	
Enteric fever	4.72	Diarrheal diseases	25.85	Diarrheal	52.71
Dysentery	3.65				
Diarrhea and enteritis	15.30				
Worms and parasites	2.18				
Convulsions	26.86				
Malaria	4.94	Malaria	47.39		
Fevers	42.45				
Pulmonary tuberculosis and phthisis	18.39				
Heart and circulatory diseases	7.24				
Chronic Brights disease	5.43				
Pneumonia	6.10				
TOTAL THESE CAUSES	137.26				
TOTAL ALL CAUSES	257.83				

Sources: Jamaica, *Annual Report of the Registrar General's Department* (Kingston, 1921–1923).

Jamaica; authorities in the medical department argued that tuberculosis deaths were also concealed among fevers and in 1938 suggested that about one-third of deaths from fevers should be attributed to tuberculosis.[35] The exclusion of convulsions and fevers from any estimate will necessarily understate the level of mortality from diarrheal diseases, malaria, and tuberculosis. But the addition of convulsions and fevers will make it difficult to pick out turning points because, first, those symptoms cannot unambiguously be associated with a named disease and, second, the proportion of deaths attributed to symptoms rather than named diseases was shrinking.

Table 2.8 shows the changing proportion of deaths attributed to convulsions, fevers, diarrheal diseases, malaria, and tuberculosis across the period from 1920–22 to 1990. Diarrheal disease mortality declined early and rapidly, falling to less than half its 1920–22 level by the late 1930s, with the fastest decline occurring before 1931. For several

[35] AGR 1938, Medical Department report. Earlier, in 1932, Hugo Muench tried, using regression, to allocate deaths attributed to fevers and convulsions to specific diseases. See RAC, RF, RG 1.1, 437, Box 1, folder 8.

TABLE 2.8. *Leading disease categories and the decline of mortality in Jamaica, 1920–90*

| | Crude death rate | Share of all deaths accounted for by | | | | | |
		Diarrheal diseases	Convulsions	Malaria	Fevers	Tuberculosis	Sum of these five*
1920–22	25.78	9.2	10.4	1.9	16.5	7.1	45.1
1931–35	18.20	4.8	9.0	2.8	13.2	6.3	36.1
1936–40	16.12	4.3	7.6	3.1	9.4	5.7	30.0
1941–45	14.47	4.6	6.7	3.3	5.4	5.3	25.5
1946–50	12.92	4.9	6.4	3.6	4.5	5.2	23.4
1951–55	11.20	4.1	5.0	3.5	2.0	3.7	18.3
1962	8.52	7.9	1.2	0.1	0.3	0.8	10.2
1968–70	7.80	6.3	0	0	0	0.4	6.7
1988–90	6.10	1.8	0	0	0	0.1	1.9

*Take note of rounding errors.

Sources: Jamaica, *Annual Report of the Registrar General's Department* (Kingston, various years) for the years indicated up to 1962; Statistical Institute of Jamaica, *Statistical Yearbook 1982* (Kingston), pp. 140–45, for 1968–70; and Statistical Institute of Jamaica, *Demographic Statistics 1993* (Kingston), pp. 78–89, for 1988–90.

decades thereafter, this category claimed a roughly stable share of deaths and remained a significant cause of death until after 1970. Health authorities of the day believed that the category "fevers" included mostly malaria and tuberculosis, but it may also have encompassed typhoid fever, an important diarrheal disease. It is less likely to have included diseases, such as measles, in which fever occurs with spots or lesions on the skin. Tuberculosis, taken separately or adding in a share of deaths from fevers, declined more sharply in the 1920s and 1930s than during the 1940s, and then, from the late 1940s, dropped to a much lower level. It is difficult to find a turning point in malaria mortality, perhaps because that point is concealed by fevers. Taking malaria and fevers together, the decline was most rapid between 1931–35 and 1941–45, and again from 1951–55 to 1962. Altogether the share of these three disease categories in overall mortality dropped by 43.2 points between 1920–22 and 1988–90.

These results depend, in part, on the ambiguities of diseases poorly described among uncertified causes of death, which accounted for 72.2 percent of all causes in 1920–22 and 14.9 percent in 1962. Since certification rates were much higher in Kingston, these approximate findings can be tested for reliability by examining the pattern in the leading city. Kingston received a disproportionate share of medical and public resources, including the earliest sanitary systems and the main hospital. The parishes of Kingston and St. Andrews touched a malarial area on the western side. As the site of the island's main tuberculosis clinic and, later, its tuberculosis hospital, Kingston drew patients from all parts of the island. Figure 2.8 shows trends in diarrheal diseases, pulmonary tuberculosis, and malaria in Kingston for some years between 1920 and 1940 and in Kingston/St. Andrews for 1945–1956.[36] Diarrheal disease mortality diminished between the early 1920s and the late 1930s, but then resisted further decline; tuberculosis mortality was trending down until the construction of a sanitarium in the city, which confused the picture by drawing people with tuberculosis to Kingston; malaria was never a major cause of death there. The Kingston data affirm the picture for diarrheal diseases.

The available data are imperfect, but they show several things. Communicable diseases led causes of death up to the beginning of Jamaica's

[36] Another advantage in looking just at data from Kingston is that convulsions and fevers were given as causes of death much less often there than in other parts of the island.

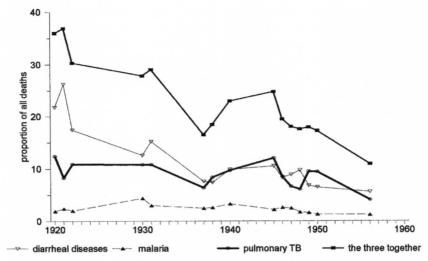

FIGURE 2.8. Mortality in Kingston from certain diseases, 1920–1956. *Sources:* Jamaica, *Annual Report of the Registrar General's Department* (Kingston), for the years indicated in the figure

health transition. Fewer deaths from diarrheal diseases, malaria, and tuberculosis accounted for most of the mortality decline up to the 1960s. The decline in deaths from diarrheal diseases, mostly water-borne, began about the same time in the rest of Jamaica as in Kingston; this fact is an important clue. But mortality from respiratory tuberculosis diminished earlier in Kingston in the 1920s and 1930s, whereas for the island, certified deaths attributed to this disease increased in the 1930s before declining.

CONCLUSION

Beginning in the 1920s, mortality declined at all ages from infancy through 70–74 years. Communicable diseases – especially diarrheal diseases, malaria, and tuberculosis – ranked as the leading causes of death in the years before Jamaica's health transition began. Mortality from those causes decreased sharply in the latter 1920s, 1930s, and 1940s, making 1925–1950 the period of most rapid gains in survivorship.

This study now turns to a series of four chapters. The first of these will examine Jamaica's situation on the eve of its health transition, around 1920, looking mainly at what are sometimes called the proximate determinants of mortality, meaning the background factors that influence the individual's susceptibility to disease. The three chapters after that will take up successive periods of life expectancy gains: 1920–50, 1950–72, and 1972–2000. The first breakpoint, 1950, corresponds closely with the introduction of antibiotics into Jamaica in the late 1940s, so that the year 1950 divides the discussion into pre- and postantibiotic eras. The year 1972 marks a sudden change in Jamaica's economic fortunes and in the trend of the standard of living. Among these three, the most important period is 1920–50, because the gains then were so substantial and so rapid. Hence the chapter on that period will be much the longest.

3

THE SITUATION AROUND 1920

With the advantage of hindsight we can see that Jamaica in 1920 stood on the eve of beginning its health transition. The purpose of this chapter is to survey factors that might have contributed to this transition, looking at medicine and public health; the economy, the standard of living, and the distribution of income; government activities; and the schools. In each area, much had been done in prior decades to duplicate British institutions, within the limits of Jamaican resources. For decades, colonial authorities had surveyed and resurveyed conditions in Jamaica and come up with progressive ideas about how to reform and improve conditions. But their actions had always been piecemeal and incomplete, limited by scarce resources. Their ideas for reforms and improvements came from Britain, which could afford them, whereas Jamaica could not.[1]

The most obvious feature of life and survivorship in Jamaica in the decades leading up to 1920 is the absence of any trend of improvement. Somewhat less obvious, but perhaps more important, is to see in the prior period of institution building the creation of an infrastructure and attitudes that could be mobilized to improve survivorship once ways were found to do that.

MEDICINE AND PUBLIC HEALTH

In comparison to many other colonies of the European powers and poor countries, Jamaica had extensive medical resources even in the

[1] A. S. Forrest and John Henderson, *Jamaica* (London, 1906). Henderson describes the manner of life and the attitudes of Jamaicans and British in the early 1900s, and Forrest adds remarkable watercolors, especially of market life.

era of slavery. An oversupply of doctors in Britain led medical men to settle in Jamaica in the late eighteenth and early nineteenth century, mainly to extend care to the European population. Some of the larger plantations retained British practitioners to treat the plantation owner's family and slaves. Thus emancipation posed something of a crisis for the medical community, throwing plantation doctors out of work. Many left Jamaica. From the mid-1830s into the 1860s, especially in rural areas, Jamaicans had less access to European-style medical care.[2]

In the latter part of the nineteenth century, British medical men took with them to the colonies the idea that medical treatment should be centered in hospitals. By the 1910s Jamaica had a large public hospital in Kingston, a hospital for child deliveries, also in Kingston, a lunatic asylum and a lepers home, and 18 district hospitals, many of them heavily used by indentured laborers from India but less often by the local population.

In the 1860s a health care system led by district medical officers (DMOs) of health was introduced, just ahead of Britain's own creation of a system of local health officers. The Jamaican system bears some resemblance to the feldsher scheme in Russia, in which from the 1870s army medics who had learned on the job provided medical care in the countryside. (Similarly, slaves who worked as hospital attendants provided health services in Jamaica after emancipation, along with a few doctors, myal men, and women.) But the DMOs were licensed practitioners rather than briefly trained physicians' assistants. And the Jamaican system bears some resemblance to the British system, except that the DMOs had little or nothing to do with sanitation and sanitary inspection and much to do with the direct provision of health services.[3]

Beginning in 1867, colonial authorities appointed DMOs for 40 districts across the island, their functions including the provision of free medical care for indigents and supervision of the parish hospital, the constabulary, and the almshouse. The DMOs could practice privately

---

[2] On health care after emancipation, see Nadine Joy Wilkins, "Doctors and Ex-Slaves in Jamaica, 1834–1850," *Jamaican Historical Review*, 17 (1991): 19–30; and Patrick Bryan, *The Jamaican People 1880–1902: Race, Class and Social Control* (London, 1991), pp. 166–67.

[3] Samuel Ramer, "Who Was the Russian Feldsher?" *Bulletin of the History of Medicine*, 50 (1976): 213–25; and Jeanne L. Brand, *Doctors and the State: The British Medical Profession and Government Action in Public Health, 1870–1912* (Baltimore, 1965), pp. 108–12.

at set fees, which they had to reduce for most patients who did not qualify as paupers but could not afford full fees.[4] Although they could report sanitary problems to the superintending medical officer of the Island Medical Service, the DMOs had no authority to order such problems corrected. Thus, for practical purposes, Jamaica had almost nothing in the way of sanitary authorities as late as 1918. A law requiring each dwelling to have a sanitary closet went entirely unenforced.[5]

Most of the people who served as DMOs were men who had trained in Britain. They became eligible for a pension after 20 years of service, and most of them returned to Britain after 20 to 30 years in the colony.

The scale of DMO services slowly expanded. By the 1880s, when the number of districts had been increased to 45, the DMOs were expected to attend a central clinic each day as well as treat patients in the patients' homes. Thus Jamaica developed and maintained a scheme in which medical practitioners were scattered through the island rather than being concentrated in the towns and cities. In the reporting year 1884–85, DMOs treated 10,044 cases and performed 504 operations.[6]

In 1861 there were about 8,800 people for every licensed doctor in Jamaica. By 1900 that number had dropped to about 6,100, and by 1920 to 5,400, people per registered practitioner. At least as early as 1902, some medical doctors – by one account "several" – were Afro-Jamaicans who had trained abroad and returned to practice, but most physicians in Jamaica were still British born.[7]

One of the duties of DMOs was to vaccinate children against smallpox; this vaccination was declared to be compulsory in 1865. Although successful vaccinations, performed in the latter years of the century at a rate of 20,000–30,000 a year, rarely reached the level necessary to protect the entire population, health authorities reported few cases of smallpox and few deaths. Beginning in the early twentieth

---

[4] Thus a national system of DMOs was created in Jamaica some five years in advance of the national system created in England and Wales in 1872. Mary Manning Carley, *Medical Services in Jamaica* (Kingston, 1943), describes the Jamaican system.

[5] See the reports made by M. E. Connor after his survey for hookworm in mid-1918 in RAC, RF, RG5, Series 3, 437, Box 180, folder 2245. Connor reported that some parishes had sanitary inspectors but that they were untrained and ineffectual.

[6] AGR 1884–85, Island Medical Department report, pp. 40–50.

[7] W. P. Livingstone, *Black Jamaica: A Study in Evolution* (London, 1899), p. 206. Also Erna Brodber, The Second Generation of Freemen in Jamaica, 1907–1944, unpublished Ph.D. dissertation, University of the West Indies Mona, 1984, pp. 38 and 41.

century, each year DMOs also helped to distribute several hundred thousand 5-gram doses of quinine, the most widely deployed treatment for malaria.[8] Jamaicans also called on Island Medical Department dispensers for medications and medical treatment, and they used informal practitioners, including balmists, women knowledgeable about herbal treatments, and practitioners of folk medicine in the traditions of obeah, myal, and revivalism.[9]

In addition to the DMO system, the colonial administration counted it important to build hospitals, mostly small local facilities. The *Handbook of Jamaica for 1882* reports that the 18 government hospitals had 1,012 beds.[10] The Kingston city dispensary, formed in 1876, provided medical attendance and medicines to the working class and poor of the capital, but it required enrollment and, for people with jobs, the payment of an annual fee. Health authorities in Jamaica successfully controlled yellow fever by quarantine. A traveling dispensary and hospital, organized in 1915, treated yaws among people too poor to pay the 2s fee charged by DMOs, moving from district to district dispensing Salvarsan, and also treated hookworm. By plan, the medical officer accompanying the traveling dispensary would lecture on sanitation in the schools, using a magic lantern, although this was not immediately possible because the other work required too much time.[11] In 1912 authorities adopted a new law requiring the notification of cases of certain diseases; by 1920 there were 16 diseases on the

---

[8] The colonial government began to promote quinine use in 1910, selling doses at post offices. At that point quinine was erroneously thought to prevent malaria rather than merely to control some of its symptoms. Mark F. Boyd and F. W. Aris, "A Malaria Survey of the Island of Jamaica," *American Journal of Tropical Medicine*, 9 (1929): 309–99.

[9] Brodber, Second Generation of Freemen, pp. 34–36; Martha Warren Beckwith, *Black Roadways: A Study of Jamaican Folk Life* (Chapel Hill, 1929), pp. 131 and 144; Barry Chevannes, *Rastafari: Roots and Ideology* (Syracuse, NY, 1994), pp. 19 and 30–31; Diane J. Austin-Broos, *Jamaica Genesis: Religion and the Politics of Moral Orders* (Chicago, 1997), pp. 51–54 and 63; and William Wedenoja, "Mothering and the Practice of 'Balm' in Jamaica," in Carol Shepherd McClain, ed., *Women as Healers: Cross-Cultural Perspectives* (New Brunswick, 1989), pp. 76–97. Also W. F. Elkins, *Street Preachers, Faith Healers and Herb Doctors in Jamaica, 1890–1925* (New York, 1977).

Chevannes reports that in more recent times Jamaicans have typically resorted to western medicine to treat diseases but may turn to traditional healers to treat social ills.

[10] *Handbook of Jamaica for 1882* (Kingston, 1882), p. 218. This source reports annual changes in the number of hospitals and beds.

[11] AGR for 1914–1915, Island Medical Department report.

list including chicken pox, alastrim,[12] typhoid fever, and pulmonary tuberculosis.

Ideas current in Britain made their way to the colonies, appealing especially to British colonial servants, who cherished the thought of a British home, deemed themselves reluctant residents of the colonies, and usually resettled in Britain.[13] Thus the early twentieth-century mothercraft movement, under which bourgeois wives and mothers would teach working-class women how to be better mothers, soon appeared in commentaries on the West Indies. But in Jamaica it proved easier to form committees of well-intentioned women among British residents than to establish contact with working-class households. Rubert Boyce, pathologist and specialist in tropical medicine and the then head of the Liverpool University Yellow Fever Bureau, mentioned in 1910 the idea of a broad campaign of health propaganda among the people and the specific idea of using the schools to teach public health and mosquito control.[14] Those ideas became plans in the 1910s, although by 1920 little had yet been done to implement them.

Ideas also flowed from colony to colony, so that comments and proposals by officials in one colony on problems and their solutions often repeated those found in official reports from another colony. For example, education authorities in Jamaica made many of the same complaints that appear in Department of Education reports from Ghana, proposed many of the same solutions, and echoed laments about scarcity of the money needed to implement their solutions.[15]

In 1912, A. Bruce McFarlane, principal of Mico College, the oldest and largest teacher-training school, was asked by the Jamaica Board of Education to prepare a textbook on hygiene aimed at teachers in training and, through them, at schoolchildren. He put together a collection

---

[12] Alastrim is either a mild form of smallpox or a mild disease similar to smallpox. Modern authorities continue to describe it both ways. It has a case fatality rate of about 1 percent, and Jamaican authorities tried to prevent it with smallpox vaccinations.

[13] E.g., Frank Cundall, *Jamaica in 1928* (London, 1928), p. 90.

[14] Rubert W. Boyce, *Health Progress and Administration in the West Indies* (London, 1910), pp. 41–48. Boyce traveled to the West Indies in 1909 to report on yellow fever.

[15] Compare especially the Education Department reports from the two colonies in the period 1890–1920 in AGR; and *Annual Departmental Reports Relating to the Gold Coast and British Togoland*, microfilm (Wakefield, 1979–1980), which includes the annual *Reports on the Education Department* from 1895 onward. For specific complaints, compare programs introduced in Tanganyika in the 1920s with those introduced in Jamaica in the same period, using David F. Clyde, *History of the Medical Services of Tanganyika* (Dar es Salaam, 1962), esp. pp. 127–30, and the discussion below of maternity and child welfare programs.

TABLE 3.1. Selections from McFarlane's *Hints on Hygiene*

Housefly control	Set out soapy water, or a slice of bread with honey on it
Killing germs	Boil water or milk, clean up dirt, clean sores and wounds
Malaria	Recognize by its symptoms, treat with quinine
Mosquito control to prevent malaria and yellow fever	No stagnant water near houses, cut down hollow trees, kill larvae with kerosene and destroy breeding sites, introduce small fish to feed on larvae, use mosquito nets
Tuberculosis	If you have consumption, either do not spit or use a spitting cup or a rag, disinfect spit with carbolic lotion or burn the rag; fresh air and sunshine hurt this disease, while overcrowding helps it
Yaws	How to recognize the disease; bathe sores with boiled water, kill the germs in sores with a lotion, and tie the treated sores with clean cloth; isolate people with yaws

Source: A Bruce McFarlane, *Hints on Hygiene for Elementary Schools with Special Reference to the Tropics* (Kingston, 1912), pp. 10–12 and passim.

of *Hints on Hygiene for Elementary Schools with Special Reference to the Tropics* "giving information which everyone should intelligently possess" without technical language.[16] In a small-format booklet with 105 pages, McFarlane distilled central lessons from filth and germ theory, explaining how to kill germs by boiling water and milk, the role of mosquitoes and houseflies in disease transmission and how to control their numbers, the importance of cleaning wounds, why meat should be well cooked, how to prevent the transmission of tuberculosis, and many other lessons (Table 3.1).[17] McFarlane introduced readers to disinfectants, especially carbolic lotion; the recognition and treatment

---

[16] (Kingston, 1912), quote from introduction.

McFarlane had, in 1902, published *Outline of the Geography and History of Jamaica* (Toronto, 1902), a text for elementary school students that informed about Jamaican rather than British history.

[17] Filth theory describes the ideas about disease transmission, especially for epidemics, that were most widely held in the West in the mid–nineteenth century. It was this line of thought that led to the argument that population health would be improved by general and bodily cleanliness, refuse collection and disposal, some forms of insect control, and the ventilation of living quarters. Filth theory also promoted water filtration and the construction of waterborne waste disposal systems. For further information see James C. Riley, *Rising Life Expectancy: A Global History* (Cambridge, 2001), pp. 60–67.

XXXIII. SANITARY LATRINE.

(a)

ILLUSTRATION 3.1a. Images of "good and bad latrines" from McFarlane's *Hints on Hygiene,* pp. 95–96.

of yaws; and the diseases transmitted through human waste. Moreover, he made suggestions about how to teach these lessons to young children. *Hints on Hygiene* included illustrations of the favored sanitary latrine of the day, an outhouse with a pail underneath the seat and a back trap door for removal of the pail, which McFarlane called an "outoffice," and a picture of an insanitary latrine, an outhouse with a seat but with waste material spreading out on the surface of the soil (Illustration 3.1). McFarlane also composed a simple table of some important

(b)

ILLUSTRATION 3.1b. Images of "good and bad latrines" from McFarlane's *Hints on Hygiene,* pp. 95–96.

communicable diseases, their early signs and how to recognize them, and the necessary period of isolation for the sick, which are reproduced in Table 3.2 with some minor modifications.

Elsewhere, lengthy and dense books mentioning these lessons and aimed mostly at public health experts had been written since the 1870s. Only much more recently had writers prepared more concise collections that could be understood by the general reading public, primary school teachers, and more advanced primary school students.

TABLE 3.2. *Schedule of infectious diseases*

Diseases	Incubation period*	Early signs	Day of the definite illness on which the rash appears	Period of isolation required after accidental exposure to infection	Period of isolation required after suffering from the disease†
Diphtheria	Within a week	Gradual illness, soreness and stiffness of throat, running at the nose; maybe croupy breathing and hoarseness	No rash	2 weeks	Until the doctor pronounces the patient to be free
Measles	10 days to a fortnight	Sneezing, running at the eyes, coughing	4th but often the 3rd The patient is highly infectious for 3 or 4 days before the rash appears	3 weeks	Until 3 weeks after the rash has gone
Whooping cough	10 days to a fortnight	Fits of dry coughing and straining	No rash Highly infectious from the beginning of disease and long before the whooping stage	3 weeks	A child may go to school in 6 weeks from the commencement of the "whoop" provided the spasmodic cough has ceased
Smallpox	10 days to a fortnight	Chill or convulsion, headache, backache, vomiting	Early on 3rd day	3 weeks	Until the whole of the skin is free from crusts

Chicken pox	2 to 3 weeks	Scattered pimples about the body	Successive crops of the eruption appear from day to day on the 1st, 2nd, 3rd, 4th, 5th, and 6th days, sometimes even up to the 10th day	3 weeks	Until every crust has fallen. This is in 2, 3, or even 4 weeks.
German measles	Within 3 weeks	Headache, sore throat, and sometimes rash about the face	1st or 2nd Infectious 2 or 3 days before rash appears	3 weeks	Until 3 weeks have elapsed from the beginning of the illness
Mumps	Within 4 weeks	Chilliness, stiffness and swelling below the ears	No rash	4 weeks	Allow 1 week from the subsidence of all swelling
Typhoid fever	Within a month	Headache, chilliness, disturbed sleep, maybe diarrhea	From the 7th day until the decline of the fever	None	Until at least 3 weeks after the temperature has become normal. The evacuations from the bowels and bladder must be disinfected
Scarlet fever	Within a week	Sudden vomiting, sore throat, headache, shivering; rash usually appears first about neck and upper chest	Early on 2nd day	2 weeks	6 weeks as a minimum after appearance of rash, and then after all "peeling" and discharges from eyes, nose, etc, have ceased

* *Incubation period* is the time that elapses between the exposure to infection and the appearance of the first sign of illness.
† The patient is unsafe even after the periods stated, unless the body and the clothes worn at the time of seizure are thoroughly disinfected.

Jamaica was one of the first countries outside Europe and the United States to acquire such a collection of direct lessons.[18]

For readers, much of what McFarlane wrote consisted of new information. That becomes evident in the series of articles on the living conditions of the poor that appeared in Jamaica's widest circulation newspaper, the *Daily Gleaner*, between 1896 and 1920, and that provide evidence about the reporters' ideas on public health and disease transmission.[19] The successive writers believed that filth – dirty yards and streets, stagnant water, foul odors, bad milk – contributed to disease and death, as also did poor quality housing, and poverty. They understood and agreed with basic filth theory and the arguments of social reformers who associated disease and premature death with poverty, especially in cities. The *Daily Gleaner*'s writers also knew that it was bad for houses and latrines to be "alive with insects," for houses to lack privies, and for city water authorities to allow water to become contaminated with cholera material. They knew that people suffering from infectious diseases should not sell milk. But they were uncertain about what it was that allowed cholera to be transmitted through water, and they did not explain why the sick shouldn't sell milk. In 1920 the *Daily Gleaner* reported on Dr. I. W. McLean, medical officer for the United Fruit Company, who had called for an expansion of Kingston's sewage system and a better organized sanitary department. But the *Daily Gleaner*'s own writer still emphasized the control of dust and filth and the removal of disgusting odors.[20] To judge from these writers, the community of people trying to form and inform public opinion in Jamaica had mastered many of the lessons of filth theory about the need for cleanliness in and around dwellings, but had only begun to understand germ theory and the specific steps individuals could take to protect themselves from disease. McFarlane provided direct and concise advice about disease prevention drawn from filth and germ theory.

Mortality in England and Wales had begun to decline around 1800. By the end of the nineteenth century, death rates were also falling for

---

[18] Compare Walter Moore Coleman, *The People's Health: A Textbook of Sanitation and Hygiene for the Use of Schools* (New York, 1914). Coleman intended to reach schoolchildren, but his book is much longer (307 pages) and is usually indirect in its advice and warnings.

[19] See Brian L. Moore and Michele A. Johnson, eds., *Squalid Kingston, 1890–1920: How the Poor Lived, Moved and Had Their Being* (Mona, 2000), where the articles are reprinted together with discussion about identifying the writers.

[20] Moore and Johnson, eds., *Squalid Kingston*, pp. 147–53, and, for the quote, p. 26.

Europeans living in the West Indies.[21] Those achievements and gains in scientific knowledge about the causes of disease and modes of disease transmission gave medical people and sanitarians, by 1920, much greater confidence in their capacity to prevent many diseases and reduce the lethality of others. Speaking to a 1924 conference of people working in tropical medicine and hygiene convened in Kingston by the United Fruit Co., John L. Todd claimed that medicine had, in the past quarter century, learned how to let Europeans and their animals live and prosper in the tropics, and mastered "malaria, yellow fever, trypanosomiasis, relapsing fevers, syphilis, yaws, dysentery, typhus" and other diseases. What Todd meant (as the context shows) was that tropical medicine and hygiene had learned the causes and modes of transmission of these diseases, as well as how to prevent some of them and to treat others successfully.[22] Among treatments counted as effective, he mentioned specifically the combination of emetine and bismuth subnitrate for amebic dysentery.

By 1920 the British had built a familiar medical and public health establishment in Jamaica, one outfitted with British doctors, hospitals and a dispensary on the British model, compulsory vaccination against smallpox, a system for registering births and deaths, notification of new cases of certain diseases, and the quarantine of incoming vessels carrying people with dread diseases. Most of this had been in place by 1880. The creation of this system of health care and disease prevention coincided with, and may have contributed to, a reduction in mortality for Europeans living in Jamaica. By comparing this institutional history to the annual course of Jamaican life expectancy in Figure 2.1, however, we can see that the construction of this health care system had not yet led to general gains in survivorship.

The 1918 influenza pandemic arrived in Jamaica in early October and by early December had mostly run its course, causing losses so heavy that 1918 is the worst year in the life expectancy record (Figure 2.1).[23] But the other bad years, 1890, 1903–04, 1906–07, which includes the earthquake of 1907, and 1917, indicate that the

---

[21] Philip D. Curtin, *Death by Migration: Europe's Encounter with the Tropical World in the Nineteenth Century* (Cambridge, 1989), p. 160.

[22] John L. Todd, *Proceedings of the International Conference on Health Problems in Tropical America* (Boston, 1924), pp. 17–27, quote from p. 18.

[23] David Killingray, "The Influenza Pandemic of 1918–1919 in the British Caribbean," *Social History of Medicine*, 7 (1994): 59–87. Killingray suggests that the official count understated mortality and that as many as 10,000 people may have died.

problem of epidemic disease had not yet been mastered. By 1920 Jamaica had a comparatively advanced health system, given what was available in most countries in the region. But it did not yet have a system capable of managing disease well enough to elevate life expectancy.

THE ECONOMY AND SOCIAL WELFARE

Agriculture remained the largest sector of the Jamaican economy in 1920, accounting for some 45 percent of the GDP and, according to the 1921 census, employing 55 percent of the labor force.[24] Sugar and, from the 1870s, bananas made up the main export crops. Until the 1960s, when new equipment was introduced, sugar was a labor-intensive crop, but prices fell sharply in the 1880s and 1890s and did not recover for a long time. Bananas compensated for the lost revenues from sugar exports in the period 1890–1930 but demanded much less in the way of labor resources and thus provided fewer jobs. From the 1830s onward the local production of varied crops for local consumption took the place of lost exports without, however, providing a path of economic growth.

Most Jamaicans made their living growing foodstuffs on small plots of land. About a third of the island's land is suitable for continuous crop cultivation, but many smallholders worked marginal land. Even though such activity left people poor – "the people are poor, just poor, beggarly poor"[25] – the Jamaican imagination was and continued to be captivated by the idea of smallholdings and independent livelihoods. The Land Settlement Program launched in 1929, one of the first steps taken by government authorities to try to stimulate economic opportunities for working-class Jamaicans, proposed to create more smallholdings by buying land to be resold in small units after roads, houses, water supplies, and village facilities had been provided. The program of land acquisition actually went forward, but the improvements scheme did not, so that most people who were newly settled on small farms went to unimproved sites.[26] Nevertheless the number of landholdings

---

[24] Gisela Eisner, *Jamaica 1830–1930: A Study in Economic Growth* (Manchester, 1961), pp. 120 and 163.

[25] J. C. Monaghan, U.S. consul in Kingston to E. C. Meyer, Feb. 19, 1915, in RAC, RF, RG5, Series 1.2, Box 12, folder 173.

[26] Shirley J. Smith, Industrial Growth, Economic Opportunities, and Migration within and from Jamaica, 1943 to 1970, unpublished Ph.D. dissertation, University of Pennsylvania, 1975, p. 39.

less than five acres jumped from 109,000 in 1902 to 153,000 in 1930.[27]
When the American physician M. E. Connor visited Jamaica in 1918
to survey for hookworm, he concluded, after discussions with British
authorities, that economic growth could occur only if the people could
produce more from their agricultural plots.[28]

Jamaica's main economic problem in the entire period from emancipation in 1834 to 1920, and thereafter, was the shortage of jobs.[29]
Where so many people earn their livings as farmers on smallholdings,
it is difficult to gauge levels of employment. But it can be said that the
labor force was underemployed, and that most people had too little
opportunity to engage in gainful tasks. Population growth averaged
1.2 percent a year in the period 1870–1920, a not particularly rapid
pace but one that outran growth in the supply of cultivable land. Thus
when jobs became available in Central America and Cuba, Jamaicans
seized the opportunity. They turned also to higglering (small-scale trade
mainly in fruit and vegetables) and to domestic service.[30] The result was
an oversupply of market stalls offering fruits, vegetables, and other inexpensive consumer items; an oversupply of servants; and meager earnings in both areas. Jamaica's economy was oriented toward the market,
but in ways that put poor people in competition with one another.

In the nineteenth century, the United Kingdom applied laissez-faire
policies at home and in the colonies, but in the colonies in an exagger-
ated form. Enterprises domiciled in Britain and the preferred colonies,
Canada and Australia, had no government subsidies or overt advantages over rivals, but they did have the advantage of exploiting the
colonies on favorable terms. Manufactured goods were bought from
abroad, chiefly from Britain, at much higher prices, judged in units of
labor expended on them, than the prices paid for sugar or bananas and
in a business organization in which British firms controlled shipping,

---

[27] Eisner, *Jamaica 1830–1930*, p. 220.
[28] See the conclusion to Connor's formal report in RAC, RF, RG5, Series 3, 437,
Box 180, folder 2245.
[29] Owen Jefferson, *The Post-war Economic Development of Jamaica* (Kingston, 1972),
p. 3 and passim.
[30] B. W. Higman, "Domestic Service in Jamaica, since 1750," in B. W. Higman, ed.,
Trade, Government and Society in Caribbean History 1700–1920 (Mona, 1983),
pp. 117–38, explains the rising demand for servants in the late nineteenth century
as an effect of the growth of the middle class. See also the novel by Herbert G. De
Lisser, *Jane's Career: A Story of Jamaica* (New York, 1971 reprint of the 1914 ed.),
which explores a servant's place in the Kingston social hierarchy and the deference
of the rural poor to the middle class.

insurance, finance, and distribution. Thus if laissez-faire capitalism prevailed in Britain, a perversion of it prevailed in Jamaica, where British firms could exclude rivals from countries outside the empire and also prevent the emergence of competition from within. It was much more difficult for a Jamaican to start an enterprise in Jamaica than for a British citizen to do so. That was the imperial system of capitalism.

In 1920 Jamaica was a poor country with a small, rich, elite and a growing middle class. Besides the persistent shortage of jobs, the problems of the day were, and had long been, housing of poor quality, petty crime, inadequate assistance from private or public sources, adulterated food, deficient sanitary services, and poorly balanced diets. The poor had rioted and rebelled often enough to make the rich fearful, but the rich cultivated detachment from and disdain toward the poor. The *Daily Gleaner*'s series of articles on the poor of Kingston and nearby areas, published between 1896 and 1920, called for more effective government action to clean up neighborhoods and improve housing. But repeated visits to the same neighborhoods over the years showed little change, although, by 1920, the reporter could write about some new voluntary organizations, including the Child Saving League created in 1916 to provide cheap infant care for working mothers and advice on child care, the Housing Commission recently appointed by the governor, and the Women's Social Services Club whose members interested themselves in sanitation, better housing, advising mothers about how to raise their children, and providing medical care for the sick poor.[31] That is, in these lengthy articles from the *Daily Gleaner*, there are some signs of engagement, but disengagement seems to have kept the upper hand. The journalists writing for the *Daily Gleaner* insisted, as do some modern observers, that well-off Jamaicans were largely unaware of and unconcerned about the circumstances of people in poverty.[32]

Benjamin E. Washburn arrived in Kingston in January 1920, having previously worked for the Rockefeller Foundation in eastern North Carolina, Trinidad, and British Guiana. Jamaica "is far behind Trinidad in every way and there are more conditions adverse to successful [public

[31] Moore and Johnson, eds., *Squalid Kingston*, pp. 142–54.
[32] This theme recurs in Anthony C. Winkler, *Going Home to Teach* (Kingston, 1995), e.g., p. 13: "Jamaicans, especially those who are well-off, are notorious for their callousness towards the poor." Winkler was writing in the early to mid-1990s about the situation in the mid-1970s, but most statements such as this one seem to be meant to be timeless. Also in the novel by Anthony Winkler, *The Painted Canoe* (Chicago, 1989), pp. 285–96, in a description of the attitude of a "brown" doctor toward his poor patients and their attitude toward him.

health] work than any place I have ever seen or heard of." Things he wanted to buy, which were mostly goods imported from Britain, and also lodging, were expensive compared even to New York City. There was little suitable housing to find outside Kingston, itself "a dirty, tumbled down heap." But the people offered more promise because they were, Washburn thought, more American in their ways than counterparts in other parts of the British West Indies.[33] Many years later, Washburn remembered a contrast between his experience in North Carolina and Jamaica. In North Carolina the whites were receptive to his public health work but the blacks were not, while in Jamaica the reverse was true.[34]

Another American doctor had visited in 1913 as a member of the Thompson-McFadden Pellagra Commission. J. F. Siler of the U.S. Army Medical Corps found pellagra only at the lunatic asylum, but he found many circumstances that favored other diseases. Up to 10 people crowded together in a single house. The people ate a diet low in protein and rich in carbohydrates and featuring especially bread, yams, plantains, potatoes, and some vegetables and fruits. He could not rank the many diseases that occurred in Jamaica, but he observed hookworm, malaria, tuberculosis, and many others.[35] In rural areas people lived in modest huts scattered about the countryside. In Kingston the poorer people lived in compounds or yards, with a half dozen or more huts facing an open space where people socialized and cooked out of doors, and the children played.

Jamaican housing had long been seriously deficient (Illustration 3.2). The 1911 census reported that 81 percent of dwellings contained only one or two rooms with an average of 4.5 people per dwelling, compared to 4.8 per dwelling in 1891. Between 1911 and 1921, more Jamaicans added flooring and replaced thatched roofs with shingle or metal roofs. But the typical house remained small, with a single windowed room. In 1921, 17 percent of the island's houses still lacked any flooring.[36] Observers remarked overcrowding, the poor quality of construction materials, flimsy building, and the absence of such amenities

[33] Quotes from BEW to J. A. Ferrell, Jan. 20, 1920, in RAC, RF, RG5, Series 1, Subseries 2, 437, Box 100, folder 1372; and BEW to H. H. Howard, Feb. 27, 1920, in ibid.

[34] Washburn was interviewed in September 1970. See RAC, RF, RG13, comments made on September 15, 1970.

[35] J. F. Siler, "Medical Notes on Jamaica," in RAC, RF, RG5, Series 2, 437, Box 43, folder 261.

[36] Jamaica, Colonial Reports, *Report for 1921* (London, n.d.), p. 5; and Eisner, *Jamaica 1830–1930*, p. 344.

(a)

ILLUSTRATION 3.2a. Four illustrations of housing in the 1920s: A typical village home. *Sources:* RAC, RF, RG Photographs, 437, Box 115, folder 7199, number 5027; RAC, IHB, RG 1.1, 437, Box 5, folder 51, in Edward W. Flahiff's 1932 report "Housing Conditions in the Parish of Trelawny."

as piped water, electricity, or sanitary facilities.[37] In the countryside, most people lived in wattle houses with walls often not sealed with mud and with thatched roofs. Siler found that the people, fearing the night air, tightly closed all doors and windows at dusk, so that the more solidly built houses were poorly ventilated at night.[38]

Gisela Eisner estimated gross domestic product for certain years in the period 1830–1930, and her estimates appear in Figure 3.1. After a lengthy period without growth, personal consumption in Jamaica began to expand in the 1910s, but slowly and from a low level. In 1920 Jamaicans had, on average, about £17 each to spend (in current values), against £120 for their counterparts in the United Kingdom.[39]

---

[37] Patrick Bryan, *The Jamaican People 1880–1902: Race, Class and Social Control* (London, 1991), pp. 172–4; and, for 1938, Claus F. Stolberg, ed., *Jamaica 1938: The Living Conditions of the Urban and Rural Poor: Two Social Surveys* (Kingston, 1990), esp. pp. 44–51.

[38] J. F. Siler, "Medical Notes on Jamaica," in RAC, RF, RG5, Series 2, 437, Box 43, folder 261.

[39] The U.K. per capita GDP in current values is calculated from data in C. H. Feinstein, *National Income, Expenditure and Output of the United Kingdom 1855–1965* (Cambridge, 1972), pp. T5 and T121.

(b)

ILLUSTRATION 3.2b. Four illustrations of housing in the 1920s: Home classed as "good."

About half of the consumer spending went in buying food, which is little different from the earlier pattern and a clear sign of a low standard of living.[40] Nevertheless, by 1920 Jamaicans were spending slightly more on items other than food and clothing, and slightly more on other consumer goods and services.

[40] Eisner, *Jamaica 1830–1930*, pp. 324–25.

(c)

ILLUSTRATION 3.2c. Four illustrations of housing in the 1920s: Home classed as "bad."

Details about the distribution of income and wealth are lacking, but no one doubts that a prosperous elite commanded a disproportionate share of income and property. Thus the average person had less than £17 to spend, though Eisner's estimate includes the value of food and housing that people provided for themselves, without going through the market.[41] The key question for present purposes is whether

[41] Eisner, *Jamaica, 1830–1930*, pp. 4–5, but not the value of domestic service or other nonwage jobs.

(d)

ILLUSTRATION 3.2d. Four illustrations of housing in the 1920s: Home classed as "bad."

Jamaicans in general shared in these slight gains in spending power, and a reliable answer is difficult to find. It is entirely possible that this slight increase in the per capita average went entirely to the elite, but it is also possible that the general populace was somewhat more prosperous in 1920 and had more discretionary income. In either case, the general public's income and spending capacity had not yet translated into lower death rates.

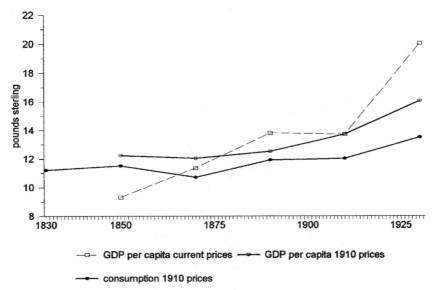

FIGURE 3.1. Per capita GDP and consumption, 1830–1930. *Sources:* Gisela Eisner, *Jamaica 1830–1930: A Study in Economic Growth* (Manchester, 1961), pp. 118–19; and Kalman Tekse, *Population and Vital Statistics: Jamaica, 1832–1964: A Historical Perspective* (Kingston, 1974), pp. 16, 168, and 170, with the estimates for 1850 and 1870 interpolated from census figures for 1844, 1861, and 1871.

GOVERNMENT

Since 1884 Jamaica had been governed by an elective Legislative Council and a governor appointed from London. Adult males qualified to vote on payment of at least 10 shillings a year in property tax to the parish, and to run as candidates by having an income of at least £150 a year. Since 1895 each parish had elected one member of the council along with members of the 14 parochial boards from the same pool of qualified voters, widened somewhat in 1909 and with women gaining the franchise in 1919. E. F. L. Wood, who visited the West Indies and British Guiana in 1921–1922, found that "the great majority of the electors are persons of coloured or African descent."[42] British authorities controlled the national government, the governor appointing 15 members of the Legislative Council and, moreover, having the right

---

[42] E. F. L. Wood, *Report by the Honourable E. F. L. Wood, M. P., on his Visit to the West Indies and British Guiana* (London, 1922), p. 12.

to overrule the Legislative Council. Typically, most or all of the elected members of the Legislative Council were Afro-Jamaicans, and most of the men appointed by the governor were whites. The Rockefeller agent working in Jamaica reported that Afro-Jamaicans on the council were usually willing to support proposals to create or expand medical and public health services but that the governor's people, who represented the planter class and the biggest taxpayers, usually resisted.[43]

Parochial boards, which administered the poor law and health services and built and maintained roads, likewise combined elected and appointed members. In numbers these boards were dominated by Afro-Jamaicans, light and dark-skinned, as appears from the photographs that Washburn and others made.[44] But the colonial government retained control of parish finances, underfunding local needs to the point that most boards were in deficit. Wood suggested reforms that would have strengthened the hand of the governor and the colonial government, but in 1922 and for years thereafter, in the Colonial Office in London, Wood opposed the centralization of sanitary authority in Jamaica, preferring to keep the boards in charge.[45] He also assessed Jamaica's health problems, finding excessive infant mortality and unnecessarily high mortality from malaria, dysentery, tuberculosis, and certain other diseases. For those problems he recommended less government involvement and greater "personal initiative and voluntary co-operation."[46] In sum, Wood favored closer government control over finances but more personal responsibility for health. This was not so much Wood's idea as it was a statement about the preferences of the day held by progressive British colonial authorities.

Government spending accounted for 4.5 percent of gross domestic product in Jamaica in 1910, and 6.9 percent in 1930.[47] Like consumers, by 1920 the government was able to spend somewhat more on programs and activities that might have improved survivorship, but it had not yet set the improvement of survival as a goal of public policy or public spending.

---

[43] Washburn interview, RAC, RF, RG 13, Sept. 17, 1970.

[44] E.g., RAC, RF, Photograph Collection, Box 115, folder 7199, photograph 13282 of the St. Mary board with Washburn on Feb. 10, 1925.

[45] BEW to H. H. Howard, July 2, 1925, in RAC, RF, RG5, Series 1, Subseries 2, Box 230, folder 2935.

[46] Ibid., p. 59, for the West Indies, not just Jamaica.

[47] Eisner, *Jamaica 1830–1930*, p. 122.

EDUCATION

With emancipation came an attempt to provide schools for the free population, mission societies building schools, the colonial government offering grants for teacher salaries, and the Mico Charity taking responsibility for training teachers.[48] School fees were discarded in 1892, which led to surging growth in the number of schools and students. By the end of 1920 there were 693 elementary schools (government and denominational together), 92,176 registered students, and four teacher-training colleges.[49] That year the colonial government spent £93,030 on the elementary schools, just over £1 per registered student. In theory the schools provided elementary education to students aged 5 to 15 years, but in practice there was never enough space to accommodate all children of those ages. Although the colonial government underfunded the school system, it did provide for annual visits by the school inspectors, who were typically graduates of British universities and who wrote revealing reports about the curriculum, learning, teacher quality, school sanitation, and many other matters. Year in and year out, the inspectors rated Jamaican schools in five categories from exceptional to failing, finding most to be second or third class. But colonial authorities never found the resources needed to build better schools, train more teachers, or outfit the schools with books and other materials.[50]

The schools faced many problems, including attendance rates around 60 percent, wastage (enrollment fell off sharply after the second and third years), inadequately trained teachers, deficiencies in equipment and materials, and poorly made buildings. The curriculum was modeled on that of Britain's with students learning British history, geography, and politics. Four colleges could not train enough teachers, and

---

[48] On education up to about 1920 see: Charles E. Asbury, "Public School System of Jamaica," *United States Bureau of Education Bulletin*, 49 (1919): 30–37; Mary Manning Carley, *Education in Jamaica* (London, 1942); Mllicent Whyte, *A Short History of Education in Jamaica* (London, 1977); Shirley C. Gordon, *Reports and Repercussions in West Indian Education, 1835–1933* (London, 1968); and Vincent Roy D'Oyley, *Jamaica: Development of Teacher Training through the Agency of the Lady Mico Charity from 1835 to 1914* (Toronto, 1964). See also Shirley C. Gordon, *A Century of West Indian Education: A Source Book* (London, 1963), where government-sponsored reports on schools in the West Indies are reprinted.

[49] AGR 1920–21, Education Department report, pp. 61–71.

[50] The inspectors' reports appear in Jamaica, *The Governor's Report on the Blue Book and Departmental Reports* (Kingston, various years); and in the AGR, Education Department reports.

most of the men and women working as teachers had had five or six years of primary education but no further training; they were called "pupil teachers." Inspectors regularly complained about the lack of enthusiasm among teachers and criticized them for relying heavily on drill and rote learning. Colonial authorities produced plans for technical and vocational schools, publicly funded secondary schools, and a university, but there was never enough money to pay for these things. Decade after decade the schools remained substandard in the eyes of British authorities.

Wood reported in 1922 that the school system, meaning the local system and further education in Britain, was producing a "black intelligentsia" ready to enter the liberal professions and to invest their skills in improving conditions in Jamaica. That was a group apart from the cadre of primary school teachers who were overwhelmingly Afro-Jamaicans, more often light-skinned and still mostly male, but with growing numbers of female and dark-skinned teachers. Wood described the teachers as politically active and contentious; they were organized in the Jamaica Union of Teachers, formed in 1894.[51] Gardening and hygiene had recently been added to the curriculum, and Wood commended the schools for using good local textbooks on those two subjects (i.e., for hygiene, McFarlane's *Hints on Hygiene*). Literacy was rising, even if the inspectors remained dissatisfied with the standard attained by most children. The proportion of people aged 5 years and above who were able to read and write, measured in each census by asking people whether they could read and write, had grown steadily from 13.3 percent in 1861 to 52.2 percent in 1921.[52] Ordinary Jamaicans prized education, seeing it as the leading means of social and economic mobility available to them.

British authorities remained in charge of education at the top, but the days when the schools relied on missionaries to teach and manage the schools were long past. The 1892 legislation eliminating school fees had made the schools into an egalitarian force in national life and had made them the most dynamic institution in the land and the institution that most broadly engaged Jamaicans.

---

[51] Wood, *Report by the Honourable E. F. L. Wood,* pp. 59, 65, and 68, discusses elementary school teachers, the need for public health improvements, and the place of hygiene in the curriculum. See also a history of elementary education by one of the school inspectors, George Hicks, who had served since 1876, in AGR 1913–14, Education Department report, pp. 22–28.

[52] George W. Roberts, *The Population of Jamaica* (Cambridge, 1957), p. 78.

CONCLUSION

By the early 1920s medical and government authorities in Jamaica were confident that much could be done to reduce the incidence of disease and premature death. But they had lived through many years of frustration at a shortage of money to pay for the reforms and improvements they could envision. Around 1920 the emphasis in government reports began to fall less on new initiatives to be taken by colonial authorities, less on more doctors or hospitals and hospital beds, and more on what Lewis A. Crooks, the medical officer of health in St. Andrew parish, which surrounds Kingston, called "the personal factor."[53] People needed to learn what to do to protect themselves against disease, they needed to be more attentive about protection, and they needed public authorities to encourage such attentiveness through inspections and health education. Jamaica's medical and public health establishment had come to the view that the people could safeguard themselves from disease despite the barriers posed by poverty, overcrowding, poor housing, and "ignorance as to the risks of insanitary conditions." In Crooks' words, "if properly constructed houses were placed at the disposal of the working classes and a campaign of education as to the insanitary conditions of the present shacks was instituted, both in the schools and for the general public, I am of opinion that very great improvement would take place in the conditions in which the working classes live."[54]

[53] See Crooks' report in AGR 1920–1921, Central Board of Health report, pp. 348–51, quotes here from pp. 348 and 350. By 1920 Kingston had spilled into adjacent St. Andrew parish, but this parish still contained rural areas too.
[54] Wood restated these arguments in his 1922 report to parliament.

4

RAPID GAINS IN LIFE EXPECTANCY:
1920–1950

Between 1920 and 1950, Jamaicans added life expectancy at one of the most rapid paces attained in any country. The expectation at birth rose from 35.9 years in 1920–24 to 54.6 years in 1950 along the chronological path sketched in Figure 2.1. In many countries, it has been argued,[1] life expectancy rose faster after World War II than in any earlier period. This was not true in Jamaica. There, the most rapid gains were made in the latter 1920s. The pace was still quite high between 1930 and 1960, but it was no higher in the postwar years than in the 1930s.

Table 4.1 contrasts age-specific mortality in 1920–22 and 1949–51. The proportion of people surviving increased at all ages, even 75 years and above, although it rose most dramatically in the age groups 1–14 and 20–34.[2] Whereas many countries that began health transitions earlier than Jamaica went through a long initial stage of declining childhood mortality that preceded a drop in infant mortality, in Jamaica infant mortality diminished simultaneously with mortality in the age group 1–14, although not quite as rapidly. The crude birth rate fell slightly, from 36.4 in the 1920s to 31.5 in the 1940s, beginning to decline about the same time as infant mortality.[3]

---

[1] See e.g. "The Situation and Recent Trends of Mortality in the World," *Population Bulletin of the United Nations*, 6, 1962 (New York, 1963), p. 9.

[2] Age reporting for people aged 85 years and above is certainly suspect, and it may be that the highest age groups did not yet experience gains.

[3] The departure of Britons during the 1920s and 1930s led the share of the European population in Jamaica to drop from 1.7 percent in the 1921 census to 1.1 percent in 1943. Between these two censuses the proportion of people counted as colored also declined, from 18.3 to 17.5 percent of the total, while that of people counted as black rose from 77 to 78.1 percent. Roberts, *Population of Jamaica*, p. 65. Since death rates were lower in the European and colored populations than among blacks, these changes worked against gains in survivorship, albeit in a small way.

TABLE 4.1. *Age-specific death rates, 1920–22 and 1949–51*

	Females			Males		
	1920–22	1949–51	Percent change	1920–22	1949–51	Percent change
IMR*	176.1	73.7	−58.2	187.3	86.2	−54.0
1–4	39.3	9.4	−76.1	41.2	10.9	−73.5
5–9	6.4	2.3	−64.1	7.9	2.6	−67.5
10–14	5.2	2.2	−56.7	4.4	1.4	−67.2
15–19	8.5	3.9	−54.6	6.8	2.3	−66.3
20–24	12.6	4.4	−64.7	13.7	5.6	−58.8
25–34	14.9	5.0	−66.6	16.7	5.2	−68.6
35–44	15.5	7.6	−51.3	19.9	8.3	−58.3
45–54	19.6	11.4	−42.0	25.4	14.8	−41.7
55–64	30.4	19.2	−36.8	41.4	25.2	−39.2
75 and above	146.8	114.3	−21.9	171.0	146.8	−14.2

* Infant mortality rate, i.e., infant deaths in the year divided by births in the year.
Source: Kalman Tekse, *Population and Vital Statistics: Jamaica, 1832–1964: A Historical Perspective* (Kingston, 1974), pp. 32–36, for the census data from which, for 1949–51, the population at risk was estimated by interpolation; also pp. 170–73 and 256–67.

Across the 30 years of the period 1920–50, certain changes in causes of death led the mortality decline:

1. Deaths attributed to infectious and parasitic diseases dropped from about 71 percent of total deaths in 1920 to about 30 percent in 1950.[4]
2. Deaths attributed to enteric fever, dysentery, and diarrhea and enteritis dropped from 23.7 to 4.8 per 10,000 persons.
3. Deaths from convulsions declined from 26.9 to 10.0 per 10,000.
4. Deaths from malaria dropped from 4.9 to 3.5 per 10,000; from undifferentiated fevers (including many cases of malaria and tuberculosis), from 42.5 to 3.0; and from pulmonary tuberculosis, from 18.4 to 6.1.
5. Deaths attributed to heart and circulatory diseases increased from 7.2 to 13.5 per 10,000.

[4] Jamaica, *Annual Report of the Registrar General's Department* (Kingston, 1921 and 1951). "About" because deaths that I attribute to infectious and parasitic diseases include medically certified cases that can unambiguously be associated with such causes and deaths attributed to convulsions, fevers, diarrhea, and other symptoms usually associated with such diseases.

Many more deaths were attributed to specific diseases rather than to symptoms, undifferentiated causes, or unreported causes in 1950 compared to 1920. This shows up clearly in the category of heart and circulatory disease, to which many deaths previously said to be due to old age, debility, or ill-defined causes were by 1950 assigned. Thus heart disease mortality appears to have increased, which is quite unlikely because mortality at the ages most closely associated with heart and circulatory disease, 45 years and above, declined. Mortality from specific diseases in the diarrheal cluster and from malaria and pulmonary tuberculosis dropped sharply, and the transfer of deaths from vague to specific causes almost certainly leads to an understatement of the actual decline for each of these diseases, because many deaths not given a cause in 1920 or attributed to symptoms were probably due to these diseases. In Jamaica most people who died from diarrheal diseases did so in infancy or early childhood, and those who died from tuberculosis did so mostly at 25–44 years. Malaria mortality was heaviest at 0–9 years and at 25 years and above.[5]

These ages and causes are the specific areas where gains in survivorship were most pronounced and that most need to be explained. Sections of this chapter will consider a series of possible explanations beginning with income and the standard of living; housing and nutrition; medical care and access to it; sanitary improvements; individual knowledge about disease risks and hygiene; schools, literacy and the child-to-parent campaign; campaigns against particular diseases; and the transition toward social autonomy that began in the 1930s. This is an exhaustive list of the factors that might have contributed to these gains in survival. The principal question is: Where are the strong signs that a particular factor contributed to these gains?

INCOME, STANDARD OF LIVING, AND THE PUBLIC SECTOR

International trade contracted at the beginning of World War I, in 1914, with particularly harsh effects for economies such as Jamaica's, which earned a sizable share of the domestic product through exports. In 1913 sugar output fell to the lowest level since 1710.[6] Economic conditions in the 1920s were mixed. Global export trade revived after

---

[5] AGR 1950, Registrar General's Department report, pp. 31–35.
[6] Michelle Harrison, *King Sugar: Jamaica, the Caribbean, and the World Sugar Industry* (New York, 2001), p. 121.

TABLE 4.2. *Per capita GDP, 1910–50*

	Per capita GDP in 1950 prices
1910	£45.2
1930	50.1
1938	52.3
1942	46.1
1950	50.6

Sources: Gisela Eisner, *Jamaica 1830–1930: A Study in Economic Growth* (Manchester, 1961), pp. 87 and 98; Alfred P. Thorne, "Size, Structure and Growth of the Economy of Jamaica," *Social and Economic Studies,* 4, supplement (1955): 19 and 81; Kalman Tekse, *Population and Vital Statistics: Jamaica, 1832–1964: A Historical Perspective* (Kingston, 1974), p. 25; and G. E. Cumper, "The Development of the West Indies," in G. E. Cumper, ed., *The Economy of the West Indies* (Kingston, 1960), p. 15.

the war, but demand for Jamaican products remained weak. The news turned bad in decisive ways in the 1930s, during the world depression, when export prices dropped and the opportunity to export labor to Cuba and Central America disappeared.[7] Certainly, by the standard of local perceptions, economic misery deepened. Table 4.2 shows incomes across the period 1910–50 in 1950 prices.[8] Per capita GDP fluctuated but failed to rise. Nor are there signs of redistribution toward poorer groups. This was not a period in which greater disposable income gave Jamaicans an opportunity to improve health by spending more for housing, health care, screens and mosquito nets, and other health amenities.

Distinguishing the condition of dwellings as good, fair, or bad, the next census, taken in 1943, reported 45.6 percent in the bad category. In 1950 much rural housing was still small, of poor quality, crowded, and unsupplied with piped water. Some households still lacked sanitary

[7] There was some growth in tourism and sugar exports in the 1930s, but not enough to compensate for contraction in other areas. On tourism see Frank Taylor, "The Tourist Industry in Jamaica, 1919–1939," *Social and Economic Studies,* 22 (1973): 205–28.

[8] See also Frederic Benham, *The National Income of Jamaica, 1942,* Bulletin No. 5, Development and Welfare in the West Indies (Bridgetown, 1942), for detail on 1942, including estimates of the domestic production of food and the rental value of houses, which were mostly constructed by owners.

latrines.[9] Many people refused to install screens, saying that they cut off air circulation but perhaps also swayed by their high price as imported goods.[10] Urban housing, of better quality, was often over-crowded, so that even middle-income households often shared small flats or dwellings.[11] But there was one area of improvement in hous-ing. From 1921 to 1943 the average number of people per house and per room declined, so that housing was slightly less crowded by the end of this period. Nevertheless in 1943 the typical household of five persons lived in a one-room dwelling of about 10 feet by 12.[12] Less crowding might mean that other household members were less often or less seriously exposed to anyone in the household with tuberculo-sis. In the 1940s most people were still being exposed to tuberculosis, as successive tuberculin testing and x-ray exams showed.[13] But fewer active cases were being reported, and mortality from tuberculosis was declining.

Public authorities began to notice nutritional problems among Ja-maicans in the 1910s. In 1918 education supervisors reported that some students exhibited signs of poor nutrition.[14] Attempts in the 1920s and 1930s to estimate the extent of poor nutrition among children produced widely varying results, partly because of the want of a consistent def-inition of malnutrition; partly because surveys were made at different times of the year, with nutrition being poorest in the spring, before crops matured in May and June; and partly because nutritional prob-lems varied from year to year and in different parts of the country. A survey in Kingston in 1935 estimated that 20 percent of school children were malnourished; another survey in 1939 of nearly 12,000 children concluded that 29.6 percent of Kingston children were malnourished, compared to 15.5 percent of the rural sample; yet another survey in

---

[9] The 1943 census reported that 10.9 percent of houses had toilets, 69.7 percent pit latrines, 0.8 percent buckets, and 18.5 percent no facilities for disposing of hu-man waste. See Colin G. Clarke, *Kingston, Jamaica: Urban Development and Social Change, 1692–1962* (Berkeley, 1975), p. 143.

[10] See the 1941 report for the U.S. Army Corps of Engineers in RAC, RF, RG 1.1, 437, Box 1, folder 31.

[11] International Bank for Reconstruction and Development, *The Economic Develop-ment of Jamaica* (Baltimore, 1952), esp. pp. 43–4, 125, and 265; and Clarke, *Kingston, Jamaica*, pp. 60–61, 94–98, 142–43, and 202.

[12] George Cumper, *The Social Structure of Jamaica* (Kingston, 1949), pp. 32–33.

[13] See below, this chapter

[14] AGR 1915, Education Department report, esp. pp. 8–9; and AGR 1918, Education Department report, p. 6.

1943 produced an estimate of 41 percent of Kingston children with poor nutrition.[15]

School authorities initiated a pilot program of lunches in 1936 in Kingston, and in 1938 they recommended that kitchens be added to every school and lunches be provided to all children who did not go home for lunch, without charge to the needy.[16] By 1949 schools with adequate facilities provided hot lunches and the others served either milk, bread, butter, and fruit, or lemonade and bread. Many schools grew some of what they served in their own gardens, which had been set up as part of an agricultural training program aimed at preparing children to operate small farms.[17]

B. S. Platt, head of the British Medical Research Council's Nutrition Unit, reported in 1946 that the meals served in the schools were neither of high enough quality nor supplied to enough children to solve the problem of poor nutrition among school-age children. Comparing height and weight between West Indian and London children, Platt found the West Indian girls and boys of 1944 to be typically taller than their London counterparts of either 1905–12 or 1938, but slighter. West Indian children aged 5 1/2 to 14 years closely matched London children of 1905–12 in weight, but did not weigh as much as London children of 1938.[18]

The evidence about nutrition is troubled by the changing level of urgency that British and local authorities brought to the issue. They found more poor nutrition in the 1930s because they looked harder for it. There is certainly no indication that child nutrition was improving before the 1940s. The highest proportions of Kingston school children reported as undernourished came in 1945 and 1946.[19]

The standard of living of individuals and households shows little improvement across 1920–50, and thus little change in the capacity

---

[15] Agricultural Policy Committee of Jamaica, *Nutrition in Jamaica* (Kingston, 1945). AGR 1930, Education Department, p. 233, reports that malnutrition was common among students in primary schools, even among students who were well dressed and seemed to be from more prosperous families.

[16] Jamaica, Colonial Reports, *Annual Report on the Social and Economic Progress of the People of Jamaica, 1938* (London, 1939).

[17] Jamaica, *Annual Report of the Ministry of Education 1949* (Kingston, n.d.); and Jamaica, *Annual Report of the Ministry of Education 1945–46* (Kingston, n.d.).

[18] B. S. Platt, *Nutrition in the British West Indies* (London, 1946), esp. pp. 32–33. See also C. A. Moser, *The Measurement of Levels of Living with Special Reference to Jamaica* (London, 1957), pp. 28–43.

[19] Moser, *Measurement of Levels of Living*, p. 40.

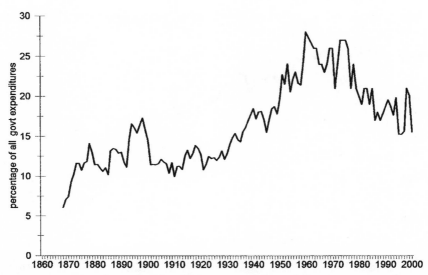

FIGURE 4.1. Spending on health and education as a share of all government spending, 1867–2000. *Sources:* Jamaica, *The Annual General Report of Jamaica, together with the Departmental Reports* (Kingston, various years); Jamaica, *The Governor's Report on the Blue Book and Departmental Reports* (Kingston, various years); *Handbook of Jamaica* (London and Kingston, various years); Jamaica, Ministry of Education, *Annual Report of the Ministry of Education* (Kingston, various years); Statistical Institute of Jamaica, *Statistical Yearbook of Jamaica* (Kingston, various years); and Planning Institute of Jamaica, *Economic and Social Survey* (Kingston, various years).

of individuals to spend money on things that may have meliorated health hazards. But the colonial government compensated for that to a significant degree by spending more on health and education, as Figure 4.1 shows. Between the mid-1920s and 1940 the portion of all spending devoted to health and education rose by half again, ironically to peak just after the 1938 labor revolt.[20] In constant values, public sector spending increased by about 20 percent from 1925 to 1940 and by 57 percent from 1925 to 1950.

MEDICINE AND PUBLIC HEALTH

The public health system led by district medical officers (DMOs) introduced in 1867 remained in operation throughout the period 1920–50. In the 1940s there were 42 districts with 45 doctors, all part time still except for the Kingston DMO. Treatment remained free to anyone

[20] On the labor revolt, see below this chapter.

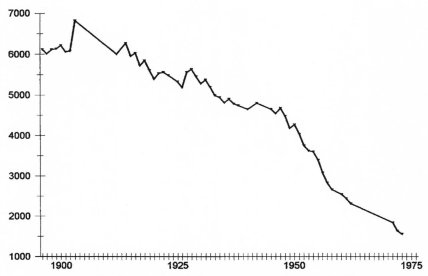

FIGURE 4.2. People per registered doctor, 1895–1972. *Sources:* See Figure 4.1.

earning less than 12s a week, and other people could obtain tickets for reduced fees of 1s to 1s 6d instead of the standard fee of 4s.[21] The DMOs also practiced privately, along with a growing number of physicians in private practice. Thus Jamaica developed and maintained a scheme in which medical practitioners were scattered through the island even though the largest number worked in Kingston and its vicinity. The number of people per registered medical practitioner hovered around 6,000 for a long time but began to decline somewhat in the 1910s and then more rapidly in the 1950s (Figure 4.2). The number of Jamaica-born doctors probably increased in the 1930s and 1940s, but most practitioners continued to arrive from Britain and, when they gave up their practices, to return there.

Surveys conducted in the aftermath of the 1938 labor revolt indicate, at least in the rural parish of St. Mary, that the system of district clinics remained in operation but that people did not have much confidence in them. For serious complaints people turned to what they could afford from private practitioners. The 1938 surveys also mention free clinics where children were treated and mothers given medicines and information about childcare and feeding. In the Pen, a poor neighborhood

[21] Mary Manning Carley, *Medical Services in Jamaica* (Kingston, 1943), describes the system.

in Kingston, a survey found that the only medical services available were from hospitals or missionaries.[22]

During the 1940s the government began building more maternal and child health clinics; by 1945 there were 85 clinics in operation across the island. It was in this period that maternal mortality declined, amid a temporary and slight fall in fertility.[23] By the late 1940s Jamaica had one of the most extensive networks of health clinics of any underdeveloped country, and medical care was more generally available than it had been in 1920. The new clinic system must have further reduced mortality in infancy and early childhood, but about the people who used these facilities or the services provided, not enough is yet known to assess their effect. It can be said with more assurance that Jamaica had begun to build a national system of primary health care that was easily accessible and provided services at no cost or minimal cost. The government also invested more in hospitals, expanding existing facilities, building new units, and, in 1940, opening a tuberculosis sanitarium. Even though the DMO system created in 1867 had not itself expanded much and had not kept up with population growth, Jamaicans nevertheless had better access to health services in the 1940s than they had in the 1910s. Pregnant women, infants, children, as well as people of all ages sick enough to require hospitalization, benefited the most from higher public sector spending on health care.

Health authorities in the 1910s singled out four diseases that were widespread and that could, in their judgment, be prevented, managed, or treated successfully. The smallpox vaccination program begun in the nineteenth century and aimed also at alastrim continued throughout this period, and four diseases, hookworm, yaws, malaria, and tuberculosis, were added as specific medical targets.[24] Among these diseases, hookworm, commonplace in the general population, caused few deaths but lowered resistance to other diseases. Yaws occurred mostly in children of school age, producing unsightly sores but rarely causing death. Malaria was both an important comorbidity, like hookworm, adding to the seriousness of other diseases and a significant cause of death in

---

[22] Claus F. Stolberg, ed., *Jamaica 1938: The Living Conditions of the Urban and Rural Poor: Two Social Surveys* (Kingston, 1990), pp. 13–14 and 61.

[23] Affete McCaw-Binns, "Jamaica, 1991–1995," in Marjorie A. Koblinsky, ed., *Reducing Maternal Mortality: Learning from Bolivia, China, Egypt, Honduras, Indonesia, Jamaica, and Zimbabwe* (Washington, 2003), pp. 123–30, on maternal mortality. Fertility rose sharply from the late 1940s to peak in 1960 (see Figure 5.5).

[24] Authorities also worried about ackee poisoning, syphilis and other venereal diseases, and, in 1921, an alastrim epidemic.

its own right. And tuberculosis was a – perhaps *the* – leading cause of death in Jamaica and an important cause of death across the globe in the early twentieth century.

Hookworm. Hookworm infection, infestation, or disease – all three terms are used – can be detected by the presence in human stools of eggs in significant numbers and in combination with certain symptoms.[25] Slow-healing sores, usually on the feet and legs, mark the early stages of the disease, while in the latter stages anemia and lassitude often occur.[26] Although hookworm caused few deaths, heavy worm burdens (i.e., worm loads that surpassed the nutrition available for the ordinary needs of the individual and the worms) diverted nutritional resources, leaving the victim with little energy, even unable to work, and lowering resistance to other diseases. Thus people anemic from hookworm were more susceptible to tuberculosis.[27] Some children with hookworm were stunted and underweight: Benjamin Washburn photographed a girl of 17 who was 4′ 3″ tall and weighed 84 lb before treatment, but who recovered strength rapidly after four treatments.[28] A diet rich in protein, iron, and vitamins resists serious damage from hookworm infection unless the initial load of worms is overwhelming, so that the prevalence of anemia and lassitude in Jamaicans by itself testifies to deficiencies in one or more of these things in ordinary diets.

[25] Asa C. Chandler, *Hookworm Disease: Its Distribution, Biology, Epidemiology, Pathology, Diagnosis, Treatment and Control* (New York, 1929); John Ettling, "Hookworm Disease," in Kenneth F. Kiple, ed., *The Cambridge World History of Human Disease* (Cambridge, 1993), pp. 784–88; Asa C. Chandler and Clark P. Read, *Introduction to Parasitology, with Special Reference to the Parasites of Man*, 10th ed. (New York, 1961), pp. 418–38, esp. 429; and Z. S. Pawlowski, G. A. Schad, and G. J. Stott, *Hookworm Infection and Anaemia: Approaches to Prevention and Control* (Geneva, 1991).

[26] Benjamin Earle Washburn, *A Country Doctor in the South Mountains* (Asheville, NC, 1955), p. 14, for the preliminary signs.

[27] B. E. Washburn, *As I Recall* (New York, 1960), p. 5, inferred this association from his experience in the 1910s and 1920s. Celia V. Holland and Malcolm W. Kennedy, eds., *The Geohelminths: Ascaris, Trichuris, and Hookworm* (Boston, 2001), p. 307, argue that helminthic infection causes immune changes that assist the development of tuberculosis. J. E. Fincham, M. B. Markus, and V. J. Adams, "Could Control of Soil-transmitted Helminthic Infection Influence the HIV/AIDS Pandemic?" *Acta Tropica*, 86 (2003), 315–33, suggest that hookworm infection may assist the development of HIV and AIDS.

[28] RAC, Special Collections, BEW Papers, Box 8, Folder 7. Washburn does not report whether the girl also grew taller and gained weight. In the same folder see a photograph of brother and sister, the brother, infected with hookworm, four years older but a foot shorter than his sister.

Jamaican health authorities most often mentioned tuberculosis, influenza, typhoid fever, and dysentery as diseases made more common or more serious by heavy levels of hookworm infestation in individuals. Surveys done in 1913 found that more than two-thirds of inmates at the General Penitentiary tested positive and that the disease was widespread in the general population.[29] British medical authorities were aware of the hookworm problem even earlier, but they had no plan for treatment or control.

H. H. Howard, an agent of the Rockefeller Foundation's International Health Board, arrived in Jamaica in early 1915 to investigate whether a program of hookworm eradication already tried out in the southern United States and elsewhere in the Caribbean might be useful in Jamaica.[30] Although British authorities were initially skeptical that outsiders, and more especially Americans, would be able to help, they decided to work with the International Health Board, invited a medical director, accepted the cost-sharing terms offered by the Rockefeller Foundation, and began a campaign against hookworm in 1919 at May Pen in Clarendon parish.[31] The Arkansan P. B. Gardner first directed the Jamaica Hookworm Commission, but Washburn, from Rutherfordton, North Carolina, led it from the beginning of 1920. In 1920 the campaign moved on to the southern parts of Clarendon parish and then to the adjacent St. Catherine parish, site of Spanish Town, at that time the second largest city in Jamaica. There, before

[29] RAC, RF, RG5, Series 2, 437, Box 43, folder 265.

[30] U.S. scholars have usually treated the Rockefeller Foundation and the International Health Board unsympathetically, as agents of imperialism and big business. There is some truth in that point of view, but it has obscured the role that Rockefeller agents played in reducing morbidity and mortality in at least some of the places where they conducted hookworm campaigns.

On the Foundation's history and its international activities in health, see esp. John Farley, *To Cast Out Disease: A History of the International Health Division of the Rockefeller Foundation (1913–1951)* (Oxford, 2004). However, Farley is wrong (pp. 61–87, esp. p. 84) in depicting the hookworm campaigns in British possessions as failures. On U.S. activism in the Caribbean in this period, see Dana Gardner Munro, *Intervention and Dollar Diplomacy in the Caribbean, 1900–1921* (Princeton, 1964).

[31] Connor's preliminary survey of hookworm infestation, done in June and July, 1918, took 11,887 specimens, of which two-thirds were positive. Connor offered astute advice about potential allies and problems, but his plan to begin in Clarendon parish turned out to be a mistake. Infection rates there were actually low, the people were scattered and difficult to reach, the May Pen district was remote from any town, and parochial authorities had hardly begun to build the latrines they had promised to complete ahead of time. RAC, RF, RG5, Series 3, 437, Box 180, folder 2245.

improvements began, 8 percent of the houses had satisfactory latrines, some street gutters swarmed with the larvae of anopheline and culex mosquitoes, and the town and parish were generally unsanitary. No schools in the survey area had satisfactory latrines, and so the Central Board of Health ordered the construction of pit latrines for the schools and for public buildings.[32]

The hookworm campaign had two immediate goals. It was meant to improve the health of the population, especially ordinary working people, so that they could work more of the time, work harder, earn more, and prosper. Rockefeller agents, like British colonial authorities, believed that Jamaicans could improve their standard of living only if working people could produce more from their land. And, because "the rural population as a whole goes to the bush and deposits excrement on the surface of the ground," the campaign was meant to control "soil pollution," the casual deposit of human waste that exposed people to hookworm and to diarrheal disease.[33] "The prevention of soil pollution . . . consists in stopping the scatter of human bowel material through the use of sanitary (fly-proof) latrines."[34] Local health authorities took the lead in pushing the idea of a sanitary latrine (i.e., not just a latrine but one of satisfactory design) for every house, and they invested more in public health, with spending rising sharply in the early 1920s as the parish boards began their part of the hookworm campaign, which was to "sanitate" the countryside and villages by persuading householders to build latrines. These latrines were to be simple structures that could be made with locally available materials by people with minimal skills at carpentry and construction and at as little cost as possible to householders or the parish (Illustrations 4.1 and 4.2).

Washburn and the International Health Board had bigger hopes, too: "The object is to take hookworm as an example of a preventable disease and, through the different phases of the campaign, to impress upon the people the desirability and necessity of practicing disease prevention in their homes and of teaching them, by demonstration, the benefits of keeping well." Once convinced of the utility of hookworm control for

---

[32] AGR 1920–1921, Central Board of Health, p. 334–35.

[33] Quote from Connor's 1918 report, in RAC, RF, RG5, Series 3, 437, Box 180, folder 2245, p. 5 of the formal report.

[34] See Washburn's annual report for 1921 in RAC, RF, RG5, Series 3, 437, Box 181, folder 2247, pp. 6–10, quote from p. 10.

ILLUSTRATION 4.1. An existing, and unsatisfactory, latrine. *Source:* RAC, RF, RG Photographs, 437, Box 115, folder 7199, number 5033.

their own health and prosperity, Jamaicans would demand that parish authorities make larger investments in public health.[35] Thus Washburn and his associates counted on the power of Jamaican opinion to force

[35] Ibid., p. 13. For the official view in Jamaica at this stage see AGR 1921, Medical Department, pp. 424–26. Also C. C. Wedderburn, *Four Decades of Advances in Health in the Commonwealth Caribbean* (Washington, 1979), pp. 18–25.

ILLUSTRATION 4.2. An improved latrine. *Source:* RAC, RF, RG Photographs, 437, Box 115, folder 7201, number 13281.

a parsimonious government to act. They wanted the people to become informed about disease risks for themselves and their communities. "A majority of the people do not understand anything at all about the nature of infectious disease. Many persons do not know that malaria is spread by mosquitoes" or how infectious diseases are transmitted.[36] In service of that goal, Gardner and Washburn adopted an intensive plan in which members of the hookworm unit would visit people in their villages and homes, "sound" them (i.e., use a stethoscope to listen to their hearts and respiration), and talk to them. From the first they invited people to express their opinions, to write letters and to make requests and demands.[37] As the report for October 1922 phrased it, the aim is to develop "a public conscience...in which the individual willingly subjugates his personal desire to the good of the entire community," not just about hookworm prevention but about public health in general.[38] Like Major Wood and Lewis A. Crooks, the Rockefeller agents believed that people could lift themselves out of poverty; they also believed that people could safeguard their individual health better and form a public health consciousness.

Rockefeller agents organized hookworm treatment, their part of the dual program of sanitating and treating, in a campaign moving from one locale to the next providing treatment and advice. Hookworm units, teams of 16 or 17 people led by the medical director, included microscopists who examined specimens in the field, nurses,[39] and clerks. The unit moved from district to district counting people and houses, checking how many people had latrines and whether they used them, calling on people to participate, and then collecting and testing fecal specimens. Microscopists examined the specimens, and nurses visited infected people in their homes, treated them, returned and collected new specimens, and re-treated as necessary, up to six times.[40] The units also propagandized about the dangers of soil pollution,

---

[36] BEW's report for 1920 in RAC, RF, RG5, Series 3, Box 180, folder 2246, p. 50.

[37] The United Fruit Company, which operated banana plantations in Jamaica and in Central America, also distributed a pamphlet on how to control hookworm and collaborated with the Rockefeller agent. See United Fruit Company, Medical Department, *Annual Report* (Boston, various years), e.g., the 1923 report, pp. 13 and 18.

[38] D. L. Sisco, Washburn's replacement during a leave of absence, wrote the October 1922 report: RAC, RF, RG5, Series 3, Box 181, folder 2247.

[39] Washburn selected mostly male school teachers and trained them to be nurses. When people under treatment became sick, sometimes from the treatments but more often from other causes, the nurses called in the medical director, who was a physician.

[40] Later, in 1926 or 1927, the hookworm units introduced a group system of treatment, in which nurses no longer went house to house but invited people who had tested positive to meet them at a central point in the district. Then they visited just the people who had not come. Under the group system they could treat three or four times more people in the same time. See RAC, RF, RG 5, Series 1, 437, Box 302, folder 3833, from Howard's report on his visit to Jamaica in 1927.

encouraged people to build and maintain latrines, and showed them how to construct proper pit latrines. At each site, team members lectured any crowd that could be collected, showing them lantern slides and specimens of hookworms and other parasites preserved in chemicals. They used a microscope to show eggs and larvae and showed a silent film, *Unhooking the Hookworm*.[41]

Washburn quoted from a letter from a resident of Spanish Town who had, before seeing the film, refused to complete her course of treatment: "Sir, I beg you forgit past foolishness and send me more medicine. I attend show last night and see what happen inside we and beg for more of the very good Govt. pill [spelling and punctuation preserved]."[42] Team members went house to house carrying an album with photographs made in the locale. Finally, the unit drew up a tally reporting the number of people enumerated, the number of people from whom specimens had been obtained, the number of positive specimens, and the count of people treated and re-treated. In most districts no one, or only one or two people, refused treatment.

By 1929 there were two sanitation units working to persuade people to build latrines, and two treatment units. That year, in June, a unit reached Ulster Spring in St. Thomas parish, surveyed the area's 1,736 houses and 8,962 occupants, and found a total of six sanitary latrines. They managed to persuade the residents to build 519 latrines in the year that followed, leaving 1,211 homes still without such facilities.[43] More progress was typically made in subsequent years, after the unit left, and in this way, locale by locale and depending chiefly on the goodwill of householders and their willingness to do the work necessary to build latrines, most of the island's homes were outfitted with pit latrines that prevented soil contamination and provided for the safe disposal of human waste. Parish sanitary inspectors then followed up to check that latrines were being maintained properly. The inspectors, hired and trained in a new program,[44] visited homes, businesses, and hospitals and other institutions to conduct inspections. By

---

[41] Made in 1920, this 10-minute silent film shows magnified pictures of hookworms and of a hookworm egg opening, the modes by which hookworms enter the human body, treatment, and approved latrines. RAC, RF, RG1, 100, Box 5, folders 40–43, provide information about the original script; translations into French, Spanish, and Portuguese; and, at length, about film making and costs. It may be viewed, as of July 8, 2004, at http://archive.rockefeller.edu/feature/hookworm.php.

[42] BEW's report for 1921 in RAC, RF, RG5, Series 3, 437, Box 181, folder 2247, p. 16.

[43] AGR 1930, Medical Department, p. 422.

[44] See below this chapter.

1931 the hookworm campaign, since taken over entirely by Jamaican authorities, had reached all but three of Jamaica's 14 parishes.

Scholars have usually judged the International Health Board's hookworm campaign on how far it succeeded in the goal of eradication and, since hookworm was not eradicated, they have sometimes described the campaign as a failure.[45] That interpretation overlooks the substantial degree to which hookworm was brought under control. It overlooks other goals and achievements of the campaign, which aimed more to control soil pollution and feces-borne disease rather than to eradicate hookworm. For Jamaica this judgment also overlooks the testimony of the people, especially working people, who reported in letters written to the medical director that after treatment they could work again and that they had gained weight and regained their appetites. "I was a sufferer for years with constapition tired feeling beatness of heart pain in the stomach sleppness debility and from since taken your hookworm medicine I am a new man with all those ailment [spelling and punctuation preserved]."[46] The doctors and nurses observed and people testified that successful treatment resulted in an almost immediate improvement, that people felt better, and that they had more energy and vigor. "With the removal of infection children begin to grow rapidly and become strong and healthy while their minds become alert and they are able to make good progress at school." Adults shed their "feeling of laziness," dizziness, heart palpitation, and shortness of breath, and could work better and harder and resist other diseases.[47]

In Jamaica the coordinated efforts of local health authorities and Washburn's units transformed a country where, in 1919, few households had latrines of any kind into one where most houses had approved pit latrines and people knew why they should use them. The hookworm campaign exposed people, at individual and household levels, to the idea of taking new steps in personal behavior for the sake of disease control and to formulating opinions about their need for public health services. Not only were people asked to build latrines and, if infected with hookworms, to take medicines that killed hookworms inside their bodies, but they were also asked to report particulars about household members, giving much the same information provided to

[45] E.g., Ettling, "Hookworm Disease," p. 788.
[46] RAC, RF, RG 5, Series 3, 437, Box 181, folder 2249. See also ibid., Box 180, folder 2246, Washburn's 1920 report, pp. 56–57; and ibid., Box 181, folder 2248, the 1925 report.
[47] Ibid., pp. 26–27, quote from p. 26.

census takers; to collect a feces sample from each person in the household in a small tin box; and to take those samples the next day to a hookworm unit, where they would be tagged and examined for evidence of hookworm eggs. Treatment in 1921 meant a preliminary purge the day before with jalap powder, then a capsule containing oil of chenopodium mixed with more jalap powder, in two doses, with the treatment being repeated a week later with a mixture of thymol and jalap powder. Follow-up treatments occurred at weekly intervals.[48]

In Jamaica as elsewhere the International Health Board asked for a matching investment and a gradual transfer of all costs and activities to parish authorities. It is not evident whether British or local authorities understood what they were committing themselves to by inviting the Rockefeller agents in. In particular, it seems unlikely that either the Central Board of Health, in Kingston, or the parochial boards understood how successful the hookworm campaign would be in persuading Jamaicans to demand more extensive public health facilities. There is no evidence of advance planning by either the central or parochial boards toward spending more on the public's health. But spending did rise, as the boards met their obligations to the Rockefeller agents and the demands made by their own residents.

To carry out their part of the bargain with the International Health Board, colonial authorities had to create a system of sanitary administration. The colonial government brought in a chief sanitary officer from Fiji, another British colony, and gave him the task of coordinating sanitation work with parish health boards. Although they would have preferred a centralized program, the Rockefeller people counted their work as a success when it resulted in local funding for a local public health operation. Thus Washburn reported whenever parish authorities appointed a medical officer of health, the term used for the director of sanitary services in the parishes, or a sanitary inspector.

By 1930 most parishes had appointed medical officers of health and all had sanitary inspectors checking latrines, food safety, drainage, and other matters. The corps of sanitary officials and the sanitary inspectors that emerged in the 1920s constituted a parallel health establishment larger than the DMO system but not as large as the entire system of medical practitioners, including those practicing privately and at

---

[48] BEW's report for 1921 in RAC, RF, RG5, Series 3, 437, Box 181, folder 2247, pp. 17–18 and 69–72. The treatment protocol changed from time to time, but thymol remained the principal vermicide.

hospitals, the asylum, and the DMOs. The sanitarians were mostly Afro-Jamaicans trained locally, whereas the medical establishment continued to be made up chiefly of doctors born and trained in Britain.[49]

"Adapted in rather remarkable degree to the educational level of the population," Washburn's hookworm and public health work created widespread enthusiasm for disease prevention, a popular demand for sanitation and better government sanitary services, and the public health–mindedness that Gardner and Washburn had hoped for.[50] It is at the very least an unexpected thing to notice also that Gardner and Washburn, two men from the American South, ended up creating a public health apparatus directed and staffed almost entirely by Afro-Jamaicans (Illustration 4.3).

Yaws. A disease associated with the tropics and poor hygiene, and most common in children aged 5–15 years, yaws has either the same causative agent as syphilis or a very similar agent but is transmitted through abrasions in the skin, usually on the legs. Most people with yaws recover without treatment in one to five years, although the disease may move into the joints and bones.[51] In Jamaica in the 1920s yaws afflicted large numbers of children in rural pockets where rainfall was heavy and the people notably poor. Children typically contracted the disease at ages of 7 to 9. In the first test area, centered on Bath in St. Thomas parish, nearly 80 percent of adults had had the disease.[52]

Attempts to identify Jamaicans suffering from this disease and to provide treatment began in the 1910s using the arsenic derivative Salvarsan as a treatment. DMOs, who were required to provide treatment for this disease, saw thousands of cases a year: in 1929 they treated 29,047 cases, but the following year there were thousands

---

[49] This is apparent from the photographs that Washburn took rather than from testimony about the racial identity of medical and public health officials. See esp. RAC, Special Collections, 1022, BEW Papers, Box 7, folder 1; and RAC, RF, Photograph Collection, Boxes 115 and 116, which contain photographs of Washburn posing with various members of the medical and public health establishment in Jamaica, successive classes of the School for Sanitary Inspectors, and treatment units in the field.

[50] Quote from Dr. E. O. Jordan, "Discussions of Health Conditions in Jamaica," probably 1932, in RAC, RF, RG5, Series 2, 437, Box 43, folder 263. Hector H. Howard, visiting Jamaica again in 1934, reported to the New York office: "The people have become public health minded." RAC, RF, RG 1.1, 437, Box 1, folder 5, p. 6.

[51] Don R. Brothwell, "Yaws," in Kenneth F. Kiple, ed., *The Cambridge World History of Human Disease* (Cambridge, 1993), pp. 1096–1100.

[52] RAC, RF, RG5, Series 3, 437, Box 180, folder 2244, Washburn's annual report for 1932, pp. 46–50 and two pages of photographs.

(a)

ILLUSTRATION 4.3a. Sounding (i.e., listening with a stethoscope). *Source:* RAC, RF, RG Photographs, 437, Box 115, folder 7199, number 5825.

more. The Jamaica Yaws Commission, organized in 1932 in a new agreement between the Rockefeller Foundation and British colonial authorities, carried out a five-year survey and introduced a new program of intensive treatment. The commission set up two treatment units, each led by a doctor accompanied by about 10 assistants. The units used two medications: neo-arsphenamine, which was more effective in healing lesions but took longer to apply, and a 10 percent solution of bismuth salicylate suspended in olive oil, which the doctors and nurses could apply to many more people each day and, in some circumstances, which had a longer effect. But the central and, for the time being, insurmountable problem was relapse, or reinfection, and the emergence each year of a new batch of these particularly susceptible seven-year-olds. The two units aimed to treat enough victims of the disease often enough to stamp out yaws or reduce its hold, but the commission did not succeed

(b)

ILLUSTRATION 4.3b. Taking hookworm medicine. *Source:* RAC, RF, RG Photographs, 437, Box 115, folder 7199, number 5827.

and turned its activities over to local authorities in 1937. Whereas hookworm control had reduced the proportion of the population that was infected while also promoting public health improvements, yaws treatment in this period was mostly palliative. Children continued to suffer and adults continued to experience secondary effects, including heart abnormalities and damage to the nervous system.[53]

Malaria. Malaria causes debilitating fevers that temporarily incapacitate a person, making the sufferer more susceptible to dying from other

[53] On yaws see also Washburn's later reports; the comprehensive reports of the two treatment units in RAC, RF, Series 3, 437, Boxes 186–187; and George M. Saunders' 1936 "Memorandum Concerning Yaws Control in Jamaica" in RAC, RF, RG 1.1, 437, Box 10, folder 131.

diseases. In Jamaica it was a major cause of death as well and had troubled the country for many decades. A survey done in 1928–29 found blood samples positive for three forms: *Plasmodium falciparum*, the most lethal strain; *P. vivax*, the mildest and generally the most common strain; and *P. malariae*, usually a mild strain. *P. falciparum* accounted for 90 percent of cases surveyed across the period 1929–39.[54] In 1910, at a time when quinine treatment was believed to promise malaria control, even potential eradication,[55] the Jamaican government began selling subsidized, measured doses of quinine at post offices and police stations. By the 1920s no public health authorities regarded quinine as sufficient for malaria management. It suppressed symptoms and reduced the lethality of malaria, but it did not cure the disease.[56] People were reluctant to take it in heavy doses because of unpleasant side effects and because, once treatment stopped, symptoms often returned.

Jamaican public health authorities put more faith in mosquito control, which emerged in the 1920s as the tactic widely regarded as most effective. They pressed people to install screens over windows, a suggestion most people resisted, and to prevent mosquito breeding by filling puddles, covering water barrels, treating ponds with chemicals, and interfering with breeding by other means. At the United Fruit Company's conference on health in the tropics, held in Kingston in 1924, J. A. LePrince wanted children to help out in killing mosquitoes inside the household, making it into a game, and urged householders to set out mosquito traps, which he described as treated boxes placed in shaded areas near breeding sites that would attract mosquitoes in daylight hours. He also wanted householders to make artificial breeding sites where they could collect eggs or treat the water to prevent the eggs from hatching. LePrince, a public health entomologist, reminded his audience that small fish eat mosquito larvae and that Paris green, a comparatively inexpensive arsenic compound mixed with a

[54] Boyd and Aris, "A Malaria Survey of the Island of Jamaica"; and Forest Ray Moulton, *A Symposium on Human Malaria, with Special Reference to North America and the Caribbean Region* (Washington, 1941), p. 14.

[55] Gordon Harrison, *Mosquitoes, Malaria and Man: A History of the Hostilities since 1880* (New York, 1978), pp. 169–76.

[56] The first treatment effective in killing the malaria parasite, chloroquine, was introduced in the United States in 1945; I have been unable to discover when it was first used in Jamaica. On quinine as a treatment, see Harrison, *Mosquitoes, Malaria and Man*, pp. 174–75.

suitable dust, would kill mosquito larvae while having low solubility in water.[57]

Dr. Mark F. Boyd of the Rockefeller Foundation directed a malaria survey of the island in 1928 and 1929, and a Malaria Commission with the task of coordinating disease control and mosquito eradication activities began operations in 1929.[58] From the late 1920s into the 1950s, children were examined for enlarged spleens.[59] The disease was rare at higher elevations but prevalent in the low-lying coastal plains, which were the most thickly populated parts of the country. In the years after 1929, authorities set up 14 control areas under the Medical Department and concentrated on dusting with Paris green, aiming to kill Anopheles larvae.[60] Only in the Kingston area were colonial officials willing to invest in drainage and land reclamation, lining ditches with concrete.[61] Thus mosquito control depended chiefly on the repeated dusting of breeding sites with Paris green.

In 1931 Washburn, just back from leave that had included course work at the London School of Tropical Medicine and some brief field work in Albania, reported that school attendance had risen in the areas being treated and that teachers said that their pupils, in better health, were doing better work. The proportion of children with enlarged spleens fell abruptly. The typical spike in malaria cases did not accompany unusually heavy rains that year. And the death rate in treated areas had declined.[62]

Thus mosquito control activities can be credited with assisting, and probably leading, the reduction in malaria mortality that began at the end of the 1920s, even though mosquito control had not yet moved

[57] J. A. LePrince, "Can We Get Better Anopheles-Control and More Malaria-Control at Less Cost?" *Proceedings of the International Conference on Health Problems in Tropical America held at Kingston, Jamaica, B.W.I., July 22 to August 1, 1924* (Boston, 1924), pp. 157–64.

A pigment for paints, Paris green was first used as an insecticide in the 1860s, but as a larvicide only much later.

[58] Boyd and Aris, "A Malaria Survey of the Island of Jamaica."

[59] G. E. Cumper, "Two Studies in Jamaican Productivity," *Social and Economic Studies*, 1 (1953): 3–83.

[60] Rupert Briercliffe, *Development and Welfare in the West Indies 1941–42, Public Health, Jamaica* (n.p., 1941), pp. 3–4.

[61] RAC, RF, RG 1.1, 437, Box 2, folders 23 and 31. The portion of the project dealing with Greenwich Pen, a new neighborhood in western Kingston, in 1934 is described by a drainage engineer who worked in Jamaica: E. H. Magoon, *Drainage for Health in the Caribbean Area* (n.p., 1945), pp. 88–93.

[62] RAC, RF, RG5, Series 3, 437, Box 180, folders 2242 and 2244.

ILLUSTRATION 4.4. Five men dusting with Paris green to kill mosquito larvae from a boat named "Maladie." *Source:* RAC, RF, Benjamin E. Washburn Papers, Box 7, folder 1, number 24.

beyond the areas of endemic malaria into those of merely seasonal cases. Health authorities called on Jamaicans to take part in mosquito control, but dusting with Paris green, which the Malaria Commission did, led the control effort. The chemical was effective as a larvicide, but it had to be applied and reapplied. Mosquito control with Paris green could never be more than temporary until all mosquito areas were treated more or less simultaneously in the larva season. Even without that, however, its effects were more powerful than quinine (Illustration 4.4).[63]

---

[63] Margaret Humphreys, *Malaria: Poverty, Race, and Public Health in the United States* (Baltimore, 2001), esp. pp. 108–12, attributes the rapid decline of malaria mortality in the American South in the latter 1930s to rural depopulation, speeded by federal programs aimed at relieving the Great Depression. These explanations do not apply to Jamaica, where most of the population continued to live in rural areas and close to Anopheles breeding sites. Nancy Elizabeth Gallagher, *Egypt's Other Wars: Epidemics and the Politics of Public Health* (Syracuse, NY, 1990), p. 93, reports that Paris green successfully eradicated *Anopheles gambiae* in Upper Egypt in seven months of intensive applications in 1945, duplicating an earlier success in Brazil.

Tuberculosis. Pulmonary or respiratory tuberculosis is a bacterial disease communicated from person to person through droplets coughed, sneezed, or spit by people with an active case of the disease. The droplets circulate in the air and are breathed in by other people. Many people who have been exposed become infected, and some of them go on to develop an active case, although the process of conversion to an active case is, even today, not well understood. Afro-Jamaicans in the 1920s differed from Europeans in converting to an active case more readily, after even a single exposure, in the more rapid progress of the disease, which came to a resolution within as little as six months, and in a higher lethality. Most of the tuberculosis cases in Jamaica were respiratory.[64] Once one member of a household had an active case, other members followed, so that "half of the members of the household may succumb to tuberculosis within a period of 2 years" of the onset of an active case in one household member.[65]

In the 1920s medical authorities in Jamaica believed that the disease was communicated through sputum, because they knew that bacilli in the sputum, which could be found through laboratory testing, showed that a case was active. Sputum samples from Afro-Jamaicans with tuberculosis showed higher bacillus counts than were found among whites or blacks in the United States, comparison populations often cited. A 1930 survey, which included tests for prior exposure to the bacteria and the first x-ray examinations of suspected cases, showed that tuberculosis infection was widespread.[66] By then about 1,200 new active cases were being reported each year.[67] These cases clustered in the Kingston area, chiefly because the disease was communicated more readily in the housing conditions of the city but also because some people with the disease and from other parts of the island went to Kingston for treatment.[68] People who had migrated to Kingston for work and

---

[64] Jamaican children did not often get bovine tuberculosis because few of them drank cow's milk.

[65] E. Joyce Saward, Persis Putnam, and Eugene L. Opie, *Studies on Tuberculosis* (Baltimore, 1941), p. 4; and the 1929 annual report written by Washburn's temporary replacement Paul S. Carley in RAC, RF, RG5, Series 3, 437, Box 179, folder 2239a.

[66] The first x-ray apparatus on the island was installed in 1921, but it failed to work and had to be returned to its manufacturer in England for adjustment. AGR 1921, p. 439.

[67] R. A. S. Cory, "Changing Trends in the Treatment of Pulmonary Tuberculosis in Jamaica," *West Indian Medical Journal*, 4 (1955): 5–8.

[68] Further information is provided by Eugene L. Opie, Persis Putnam, and E. Joyce Saward, "The Fate of Negro Persons of a Tropical Country, Jamaica, B.W.I., after Contact with Tuberculosis," in *Studies on Tuberculosis* (Baltimore, 1941), pp. 55–95;

contracted the disease were known to be returning to their rural homes and to be infecting household members there.

The treatment regime then recommended for tuberculosis was rest, fresh air, a diet with milk and fresh food, and consultation with a doctor. That was not a regimen most Jamaicans could afford, and one part of the 1930s campaign against tuberculosis was to make part of that regimen available to poor people. For the general population, physicians recommended the isolation of people with tuberculosis, meant to reduce the risk of their infecting others. But as late as 1927 isolation could not be provided by the island's hospitals. Most of the sick were treated at hospitals as outpatients, without additional provision being made by the medical establishment for isolation, rest, or diet.[69] Doctors believed that they could manage the disease if treatment started early enough but considered later-stage cases to be incurable.[70] The Rockefeller Foundation sent Eugene L. Opie to Jamaica in 1928 to conduct a survey in preparation for a treatment campaign for the disease claimed to be the leading cause of death in Jamaica and the cause of about half of all deaths at ages 20 to 40.[71]

A campaign against the disease was also launched in 1928. The Anti-Tuberculosis League, formed that year, opened a dispensary in 1929 in Kingston, and a second in Spanish Town, and hired two public health nurses to visit patients in their homes and to furnish food to indigent patients. Washburn, directing the Jamaica Tuberculosis Commission, had already written articles about tuberculosis in his monthly *Jamaica Public Health*, urging people attending the sick to disinfect or bury the sputum of their patients. The campaign aimed to identify people with the disease and warn those in contact with the sick, recommending rest and a better diet. But it was difficult to get patients to stay in bed or to eat the foods recommended, which many could not afford. An x-ray lab was opened in January 1931, and in September a mobile x-ray unit began operations. Schoolchildren were given tuberculin tests, which distinguished people previously exposed to the disease and therefore at elevated risk to develop an active case. What campaign leaders most

and successive reports from the Medical Department in AGR, various years, 1910s–1940s.

[69] RAC, RF, RG5, Series 1, 437, Box 302, folder 3833.

[70] See BEW's 1926 memo on tuberculosis in RAC, RF, RG5, Series 1, 437, Box 302, folder 3836.

[71] RAC, RF, RG 1.1, 437, Box 2, folders 27–29. Farley, *To Cast Out Disease*, p. 186, provides a critique of Opie.

ILLUSTRATION 4.5. House in Kingston with a shed added for a household member with tuberculosis. *Source:* RAC, RF, RG Photographs, 437, Box 116, folder 7210, number 20561b.

wanted to do – i.e., isolate the sick – was still not practical. In the meantime they asked people to do what they could. If the household could not provide a separate sleeping room for a sick member, perhaps they could build a separate hut outside the house to accommodate a sick person (see Illustration 4.5). In any case, children should live elsewhere, with relatives or friends. Isolation protected the associates of the sick person from infection, and rest converted many life-threatening cases into a milder form.[72]

The league raised money for a 50-bed hospital that opened in 1935, which provided both isolation and rest. Meanwhile separate accommodations were being built at most of the island's hospitals. A larger sanatorium opened in 1940, and by 1941 there were 450 beds available for isolation of cases, in addition to separate but less satisfactory accommodations in the poor houses.

An extensive survey done in 1938 using tuberculin testing, x rays, and physical exams and the taking of clinical histories showed that most

[72] The campaign can be followed in BEW's annual reports (e.g., the 1936 report in RAC, RF, RG5, Series 3, Box 184, folder 2292), and, in much more detail, in the monthly reports of different units. In addition, the Tuberculosis Commission studied the disease at the mental hospital, giving the tuberculin test to new patients and testing a vaccine on negative cases. See esp. RAC, RF, RG 1.1, 437, Boxes 4–9.

of the population had been exposed to tuberculosis: 82 percent of the Kingston population, 76 percent of adults in small towns, and 65 percent of adults in rural areas.[73] The lowest rate of positive reactions in tests occurred in young children, the proportion of people testing positive rose steadily with age, and in Kingston infection was nearly universal in people aged 30 years and above. Although Afro-Jamaicans had more severe cases of tuberculosis than did Britons, tuberculin tests showed that similar proportions of people in the two countries had been exposed to the disease. In Britain, where tuberculosis mortality may have been declining from the 1840s and was certainly declining from the 1870s, the death rate from this disease diminished long before the introduction of medications effective in its treatment, and long before there was any shrinkage in the proportion of the population that had been exposed to the disease.[74]

Mortality from tuberculosis declined in Kingston from the late 1920s and in the island as a whole during and after the 1930s. In Kingston, this decline was under way well before the isolation hospital opened in 1935, or the sanatorium in 1940. Antibiotics effective in treating this disease were introduced in Jamaica in the late 1940s, two or three years after their introduction in the United States and well after the tuberculosis death rate was already much reduced.[75] By 1940 tuberculosis mortality in Jamaica had declined to a level similar to that in the United States or northern Europe.[76]

Some explanations for the decline of tuberculosis in Britain and elsewhere before the introduction of medications effective in its treatment apply to Jamaica: less crowded housing, the isolation of the sick, and perhaps also better nutrition for the sick under treatment. Other explanations – higher incomes and better nutrition in the populace at large – simply do not apply to Jamaica. Health authorities there made concerted efforts to teach people how to reduce the chances of catching tuberculosis from someone else in the household by isolating that

---

[73] C. W. Wells and H. H. Smith, *The Epidemiology of Tuberculosis in Kingston, Jamaica, B.W.I.* (Kingston, 1938), pp. 12 and 43; and E.W. Flahiff, *The Epidemiology of Tuberculosis in Large Towns, Small Towns and Rural Areas of Jamaica* (Kingston, 1938), p. 13.

[74] See F. B. Smith, *The Retreat of Tuberculosis, 1850–1950* (London, 1988); and Linda Bryder, *Below the Magic Mountain: A Social History of Tuberculosis in Twentieth-Century Britain* (Oxford, 1988).

[75] Cory, "Changing Trends," reports the delay of several years but does not give the year in which streptomycin was first used in Jamaica.

[76] See Opie's 1940 report in RAC, RF, RG 1.1, 437, Box 4, folder 54.

person, where possible, and by getting that person to sneeze and spit into handkerchiefs or rags that would then be burned, boiled clean, or disinfected. Moreover, the public was warned against spitting and against exposure to a diseased person who coughed or spat. By the 1930s public health nurses also supervised known cases in their homes.[77] These individual-level changes in behavior coincide so closely with the sudden retreat of tuberculosis mortality in Jamaica that they appear – in concert with less crowded housing, isolation of the sick, and better nutrition for tuberculosis patients – to explain that retreat.

The campaigns against hookworm, yaws, malaria, and tuberculosis all find their origins in the activities and concerns of British colonial health authorities in the 1910s. In each case physicians sent to Jamaica by the Rockefeller Foundation devised and implemented more aggressive plans for action. Although most of those physicians had trained in medical schools and hospitals, in Jamaica they adopted an approach more closely identified with public health than with formal medicine, taking their campaigns to the people. Two of the four diseases, hookworm and yaws, could be cured, albeit temporarily, with medicaments available at the time, and the symptoms of malaria could be managed with doses of quinine. For tuberculosis, in contrast, there was no effective medicine until the late 1940s. But all four campaigns relied less on medicines than on arming people with the knowledge they needed to protect themselves against these diseases.

SANITARY IMPROVEMENTS

British cities pioneered the control of waterborne diseases through providing safe water and controlling the disposal of human waste, and Britain's colonies tried to follow in the same path. In Jamaica, investments in improved sanitation occurred mostly in Kingston. Water filtration had been introduced in parts of the city in the 1871–76 period, and by 1882 the system could provide filtered water to 4,800 houses.[78] Construction of a waterborne sewage removal system was begun during the 1890s, and by 1905 nearly 2,000 houses, about one in six in the city, were connected.[79] That system deteriorated, presumably because of the 1907 earthquake, and the 1908–21 period was one of especially

[77] *Jamaica Public Health*, vol. 4, no. 12 (1929).
[78] *Handbook of Jamaica for 1882* (Kingston, 1882), p. 218.
[79] Clarke, *Kingston, Jamaica*, p. 43.

high mortality in Kingston from waterborne diseases. The colonial government added a bacteriologist in 1920,[80] made improvements to the water supply system in 1922–24 and in the same period began to test for bacteriological contamination of water, expanded chlorination in 1928–30, and made improvements to the filtration and sewage systems in 1931–34.[81] In 1932 a new laboratory was built to test water for bacterial contaminants, and in 1938 sewage treatment facilities underwent a major expansion.[82] The death rate from waterborne diseases in Kingston fell in the late 1920s, even though sanitary facilities had not yet been extended to working-class and poor neighborhoods.

However, less than 10 percent of the island's population lived in Kingston. Spanish Town, the old capital just a few miles from Kingston with a 1921 population of 8,700, also introduced water filtration and chlorination in the late nineteenth century, and by 1930 there were waterworks in at least nine towns, although the provisions for disposing of human waste had not been modernized beyond latrine building. Most people lived in rural villages and still took water for drinking, cooking, and bathing from streams, wells, springs, and reservoirs, or they collected rainwater in tanks.[83] Nevertheless mortality from waterborne diseases diminished throughout Jamaica in the 1920s. Since most households outside Kingston lacked piped water or toilets hooked up to sewage systems, and thus any possibility of controlling waterborne diseases through water filtration, chlorination, or sewage treatment, the reduction of mortality from waterborne disease cannot be accounted for by sanitary improvements on the British model. Such improvements certainly helped in Kingston and, less so, in other cities, but they did not serve enough people so as to have been leading factors.

[80] In seven months of activity in 1920 the bacteriologist tested 3,136 specimens, the largest share being blood samples tested for enteric fever (typhoid). See AGR 1920–21, p. 480.

[81] The Rockefeller Foundation contributed an expert on water supply systems in 1930, E. H. Magoon, who for several years advised on filtration, bacteria counts, and the distribution system in general. See RAC, RF, RG 5, Series 3, 437, Box 180, folder 2244, the 1933 annual report; and ibid., RG 1.1, 437, Box 1, folder 31.

[82] On the improvements see W. Kirkpatrick, *A Short History of the First One Hundred Years of the Public Water Supply in the Kingston and Liguanea Area, 1849–1949* (Kingston, 1949). The first waterworks was built in 1849. Also Jamaica Archives, Water and Sewerage Board, Second Annual Report, mimeo, 1935, Printed works, Box 7. Working-class neighborhoods received water from standpipes, which ran continuously.

[83] See the discussion of techniques in northern Manchester parish in AGR 1930, Medical Department, pp. 430–31.

Extensive information is available about sanitary practices, and especially about how people dealt with human waste, which is one of the important elements in waterborne diseases. The evidence comes from DMOs, who were alert to changes in the incidence of diarrheal diseases in their districts; school inspectors, who, since the government had begun in 1910 or 1911 making grants to schools to improve sanitary facilities, reported about schoolchildren's toilet practices at home and at school; and visitors, including Rockefeller agents. In the 1910s and 1920s, when more and more Kingston households were installing water closets, people living in other regions disposed of waste in several different ways. Reports for 1921 show that the *least* common technique was the pit latrine, which was coming to be favored by public health experts as the best way to dispose of waste because properly constructed pits prevented contamination of groundwater, assured no further human contact with waste, and controlled the housefly population by sealing off the waste. (Houseflies can be important vectors for some diarrheal diseases, especially typhoid fever.) Such latrines involved digging a pit at least six feet deep, installing a seat with a seal and devices to control the access of houseflies to the pit, and building over it an outhouse for privacy. After being used for a time the pit was to be filled in with dirt and perhaps lime, a new pit dug, and the outhouse moved to the new location.

In 1921 the medical officer from St. Ann parish reported that the "better class" of people used surface latrines, but small farmers mostly used "the bush." The only fly-proof latrine in the parish was at the public hospital. The Grange Hill medical officer wrote, "Waste matter is thrown on adjacent land [to the household] or allowed to rot." In villages across the island, most people used surface latrines. Children deposited their solid waste here and there, without using any disposal system.[84] When H. H. Howard visited in 1915 to explore the possibility of extending the Rockefeller hookworm campaign to Jamaica by making a survey of hookworm prevalence, he observed human waste in areas where people walked barefoot, and inferred that hookworms were passed from person to person by contact with waste deposits.

In Port Antonio, a town with a population of about 7,000 in 1927, most people used the bucket system before the sanitation unit arrived, meaning that they deposited waste in buckets that were then collected twice a week by licensed night soil removers. The contents

[84] See these reports in AGR 1921, quotes from pp. 329 and 335.

were dumped into the sea. In practice, however, the system often broke down, removals being less frequent and some householders not obeying the law. And in any case, human waste collected along the seafront.[85]

Detailed annual reports from the hookworm campaign show that people changed their toilet habits in the 1920s. Even in the cities, but especially in rural areas, they dug pit latrines and built outhouses. Washburn reported a telling assessment in 1932: in 1919, at the start of the hookworm campaign, only 4 percent of the houses in Clarendon parish had had any type of latrine; but in 1932, in districts not yet sanitated, such as Westmoreland parish, already 23 percent of the houses had latrines, most of the approved type. Thus by 1932 latrine building was preceding the hookworm campaign and the Central Board of Health program to persuade people to build pit latrines.[86] Mortality from diseases associated with human feces fell sharply decades before most of the populace had access to waterborne sewage disposal and before most people had piped water in their homes.

By 1925, implementing a program begun in 1922, there were 105 sanitary inspectors looking for shortcomings in public, business, and household sanitation. In St Mary parish in 1930 the seven sanitary inspectors visited 40,712 buildings (some more than once), 38,076 of them private dwellings, and issued 4,525 notices. By the end of that year, 95.8 percent of those sites had sanitary latrines, this after the inspectors had demanded that 2,799 latrines be improved and 1,180 be built.[87] An area that had had only a handful of latrines in 1910 was almost universally outfitted by 1930. The first Jamaican school medical inspectors were appointed in 1925, when also the first dental clinics were introduced; two years later, school sanitary inspectors were appointed.[88]

Jamaicans controlled the spread of diseases associated with human waste by modifying their habits, disposing of waste in pit latrines rather than in unsanitary latrines or casually on the surface of the ground. By making these improvements they reduced the importance of water filtration and treatment. Properly sited and constructed pit latrines posed little or no threat of water contamination, and the use of latrines rather than a waterborne toilet system meant that drinking and cooking

---

[85] RAC, RF, RG 5, Series 3, Box 181, folder 2250.
[86] BEW's 1932 report in RAC, RF, RG 5, Series 3, 437, Box 180, folder 2244, p. 8.
[87] AGR 1930, Medical Department report, pp. 445–46.
[88] AGR 1926, Medical Department report.

water was not used in disposing of human waste and therefore was not contaminated in the first place.

HYGIENE AND INDIVIDUAL KNOWLEDGE ABOUT DISEASE HAZARDS

Heightened interest in hygiene and public health in Jamaica is said to date from the hookworm eradication campaign begun in 1919 or from Major Wood's 1922 report on conditions in Jamaica in which he recommended that sanitation and hygiene be added to the school curriculum. In fact concern about these issues had begun to develop earlier. Calls for closer attention to public health issues, and specifically for better management of human waste and the control of mosquitoes and other insect vectors of disease, began to be heard around 1910.[89] After the colonial government began to make grants for the construction of new latrines in schools, in 1910 or 1911, school authorities called for instruction in hygiene and began to describe students as agents who would carry this information home to their parents.[90]

In 1921, by which time the Rockefeller hookworm program had begun activities in only two or three parishes, J. D. Lucie-Smith, a colonial civil servant who was then private secretary to the governor of Jamaica, edited *A Text Book for Teachers of Hygiene, Malaria, Hookworm*. This booklet of 51 pages, less than half the length of McFarlane's book, aimed specifically at elementary school teachers.[91] Having decided to add health and hygiene education to the elementary school curriculum, the colonial government in 1919 sponsored a prize competition inviting essays directed at children aged about 14 years. Lucie-Smith selected parts from a number of the essays submitted, like McFarlane combining elements of filth and germ theory, explaining the role of germs in disease, the dangers of unpleasant smells, why the sick should be isolated, and other lessons. Children were to learn about personal

---

[89] In 1910 Rubert W. Boyce, promoting mosquito control in order to reduce the incidence of yellow fever, described it as the duty of colonial administrators, medical people, local community leaders, journalists, and the public itself to educate themselves in the modern doctrine of sanitation. See his *Health Progress and Administration in the West Indies* (London, 1910), pp. 41–48.

[90] Jamaica, Education Department, *Annual Report of the Education Department for 1914–15* (Kingston, 1915), pp. 8–9.

[91] J. D. Lucie-Smith, ed., *A Text Book for Teachers of Hygiene, Malaria, Hookworm* (Kingston, 1921).

hygiene, including the reasons for daily bathing with soap; the role of germs in disease and of houseflies in germ transmission; the healthiness of fresh air and sunshine; why to filter or boil pond or river water; how and why to build a latrine; when and where to use household disinfectants; and why to isolate sick people living in the household. Children were also to be urged to press their parents to build a latrine for the household if it lacked one.[92]

Lucie-Smith expected schoolchildren to learn how to use locally available materials, many of which did not have to be purchased, to avoid, prevent, and manage infectious diseases. Whereas McFarlane organized *Hints on Hygiene* with sections on diseases of leading importance, Lucie-Smith made personal action the motif of his book. For example, to make a latrine, dig a hole at least two feet deep and free from surface water, deposit excrement in it, and cover it with dirt each time, adding white lime if available. When the hole has been filled to within 6 inches of the surface, fill it completely and start a new latrine. Keep the latrine ventilated, and wipe the seat and floor with a disinfectant solution once a week.[93] To the suggestion to boil pond or river water, Lucie-Smith added the alternative of filtering it. People should build houses on dry and airy locations, away from swamps, and use a rosemary bush to repel mosquitoes. On many issues Lucie-Smith repeated advice that had appeared in McFarlane's *Hints on Hygiene*, but he put nearly all of his main points in the first 15 pages or so of the booklet. Taken separately or together, these two books provided practical, valid, and accessible advice about the prevention and control of diseases of major importance in Jamaica, with attention being concentrated on diarrheal diseases, including hookworm, malaria, tuberculosis, and some other common childhood infections.

The Schools and the Child-to-parent Campaign. "Sanitary homes will finally result from sanitary schools," proclaimed the Education

---

[92] Ibid. Essayists had been asked to write for children aged 14 years, the highest age of elementary schooling. That request may have had in mind students or teaching assistants, who were students who finished the entire five elementary grades, many of whom went on to train to be elementary teachers. On teacher recruitment see Erna Brodber, The Second Generation of Freemen in Jamaica, 1907–1944, unpublished Ph.D. thesis, University of the West Indies, Mona, 1984, p. 109. The Kingston medical officer recommended in 1921 that individual households that could afford them use Pasteur filters to purify drinking water, or boil water for at least 20 minutes. See the report of the medical department in AGR 1921.

[93] Lucie-Smith, ed., *Text Book for Teachers of Hygiene*, p. 9.

Department in its 1915 report.[94] According to the Hygiene and Sanitation Department report for 1922, "schools ought to become the chief agency in the health campaign and the teacher the chief agent."[95] The original idea was that children, mastering these and other health lessons in school, would not merely learn how to protect their own health but also carry the information home to their siblings and parents. Later was added the further idea that the schools, outfitted with running water and sanitary facilities, would be sites for instructing children in sanitary behavior and in the desirability of having such facilities in their own homes.

The school-based public health campaign conceived in the 1910s and carried out in the 1920s and 1930s itself depended on earlier developments in education. Most of the schools operating in the 1910s were still government-aided denominational schools run chiefly by Baptists, Anglicans, and Methodists. They provided up to five years of schooling, which students usually began at age seven. Few children completed five years, and very few went on to the mere handful of secondary schools in Jamaica. (In 1929 there were 25 secondary schools with 2,677 students.[96]) Among students who continued beyond primary school, many went directly to either a teachers college – Mico College for men and Shortwood for women, both located in Kingston – or one of the two other training colleges.[97] In 1930 Jamaica's four teacher-training colleges enrolled 180 students.

According to the 1921 census, 52.1 percent of adults could read and write, and a further 8.8 percent could read. In 1911 a few more females than males aged 10 years and above were unable to read or write; by 1921, 35 percent of males but only 32.7 percent of females

[94] AGR 1915, Education Department report, p. 8.
[95] AGR 1922, p. 84.
[96] Gisela Eisner, *Jamaica 1830–1930: A Study in Economic Growth* (Manchester, 1961), p. 336. Errol Miller, "Church, State and Secondary Education in Jamaica 1912–1943," in Ruby Hope King, ed., *Education in the Caribbean: Historical Perspectives* (Kingston, 1987), p. 131, gives statistics on secondary school enrollment for 1912–38. See also Verene Shepherd, The Education of East Indian Children in Jamaica, 1879–1949, unpublished seminar paper, UWI, 1983, for its information on schools for Indian children and attitudes of Indians toward Afro-Jamaicans and vice versa.
[97] On secondary schools see Miller, "Church, State and Secondary Education." On the teacher colleges see Millicent Whyte, *A Short History of Education in Jamaica* (London, 1977); and Vincent Roy D'Oyley, *Jamaica: Development of Teacher Training through the Agency of the Lady Mico Charity from 1835 to 1914* (Toronto, 1964).

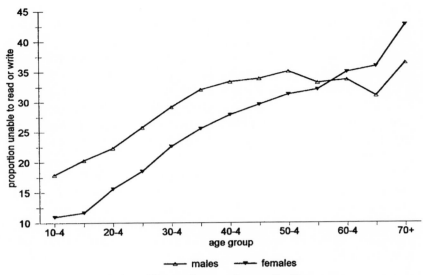

FIGURE 4.3. Illiteracy in 1943. *Sources:* See Figure 4.1.

could neither read nor write. Higher levels of literacy were recorded in 1943, and the average duration of schooling completed had risen to six years. The 1943 census first reports, by age and sex, the proportion of people who could neither read nor write (Figure 4.3). Each age group in Figure 4.3 represents a cohort that began its schooling about five years earlier than the next younger cohort; thus the 10–14 cohort began schooling around 1938, the 15–19 cohort around 1933, and so forth. Projecting backward in that way it becomes evident that illiteracy among males began to decline for ages less than 40–44, thus after about 1908. For females, however, the 1943 census does not reach back far enough to find a period when literacy was flat. For females therefore literacy seems to have been improving as early as the 1880s, a period in which church-run primary schools were first given financial assistance by the state. It may be especially significant that the first public primary schools were organized in 1885, joining the already sizable number of denominational schools. School fees were abolished in 1892 (leaving parents to pay for books, uniforms, transport, and lunch).

The number of children enrolled in primary schools rose steadily across the entire period from 1868 to 1960, without much change in average annual attendance, which until the 1940s was stuck at about

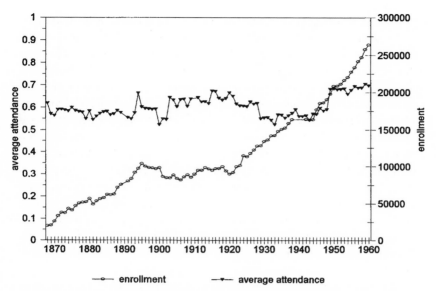

FIGURE 4.4. Primary school enrollments and attendance, 1868–1960. *Sources:* See Figure 4.1.

60 percent of those enrolled (Figure 4.4).[98] Gains in literacy therefore derived from larger numbers of children enrolling and from a rising share of the age group gaining access to a few years of schooling. The proportion of children enrolled in school rose from about two-thirds in 1880 to something approaching universal enrollment in the 1920s.[99]

Inspectors visited the primary schools at least once a year and reported to the Education Department. Their detailed reports are reproduced in the Education Department annual report for the 1910s and 1920s up to 1927. In the 1920s the inspectors looked for many things: the students needed to be taught well enough to recite upon the inspectors' visits; the teachers needed to offer a model of cleanliness and enthusiasm, to inspect their students' health, and to exclude those with infectious disease (presumably applying lessons learned from McFarlane

[98] AGR 1938, Education Department, pp. 372–73, reports that attendance was then compulsory in the towns, where an average of 63.2 percent of students attended, but not in villages, where an average of 56.1 percent attended.

In 1994 primary school attendance was 71 percent. Sharmaine Elaine Hutchinson, Health, Nutrition and Social Determinants of School Achievement in Rural Jamaican Primary School Children, unpublished M.S. thesis, UWI, Mona, 1996, p. 25.

[99] These are rough estimates, made necessary by the broad range of ages to which school was open.

in the recognition of infectious maladies); and the school managers, a grandiose title for the people whose task it was to clean and maintain the schools, needed to keep the latrines tidy and attend to their other duties. In the 1910s school inspectors complained tirelessly about how teachers needed to instruct students in using latrines, but they also noticed some improvements: more latrines were being built, McFarlane's *Hints on Hygiene* and illustrated cards issued by the Central Board of Health were being used, and some students were passing on what they learned to their parents. The best schools, called first class, made the earliest progress toward teaching hygiene. Initially the inspectors described schools as being poorly outfitted with sanitary devices and students and teachers as inadequately prepared to practice hygiene. By 1920 they found that the teachers had taught hygiene lessons, because the students could recite satisfactorily on the inspectors' visits. But too few students practiced what they had learned; they needed practical illustrations.

The 1921 Education Department report mentioned that sanitary facilities had not yet been improved in many schools where hygiene lessons were being given. But by 1924 the inspectors reported much improvement. More schools had been outfitted with improved latrines. Students, who had been memorizing lessons in hygiene since early in the decade and who initially had not put theory together with practice, had learned to use the latrines in approved ways. Teachers, who before had not closely monitored either the students or the manager in charge of school maintenance, had begun to supervise the latrines, their use, and their cleanliness. In some schools in 1928 teachers kept cards on which they recorded their students' daily health practices: whether they used the latrine at their regular time and then washed their hands, bathed three times a week, washed their hands before meals, used a handkerchief when they coughed or sneezed, and so forth.[100] By 1929, when 128,000 children were enrolled in elementary schools throughout the island, at least the children attending school had learned important lessons about the prevention of diarrheal disease.[101]

Health Propaganda. Social science studies done since about 1980 in developing countries usually show that the children of parents with more years of schooling themselves have a better chance of survival,

---

[100] AGR 1928, Medical Department report, p. 239.
[101] Average attendance in 1929 was reported at 80,000, or 62 percent of enrollment. AGR 1930, Education Department report.

with the mother's education showing a stronger association than the father's.[102] Better-educated parents are able to protect their children from health hazards much better than parents with fewer years of schooling or with none. In this instance it is important to decide whether such an association may have existed in Jamaica by the 1920s. Did effects operate from parents to children, as has been typical in findings about poor countries in the late twentieth century? Did they operate directly on the students? Or did they operate from schoolchildren to their parents, as the people leading the school health campaign hoped? Could the schools teach lessons useful for personal and community health to students enrolled for only three or four years? Did the schools try to teach plausible lessons using material appropriate for teachers and students?

Preston and Haines, who studied the United States around 1900, found an association but one much weaker than has appeared in studies of developing countries in the 1970s and 1980s, and suggested that the capacity of education in parents to assist child survival was only beginning to emerge.[103] Other scholars studying circumstances in Europe and the United States have found a stronger association in the nineteenth century.[104] What is not yet clear from these cases is whether, in this early period, education marks higher socioeconomic position or, instead, something associated directly and exclusively with schooling, which could include information about health or the greater social confidence associated with literacy or with more years of schooling.

That the capacity of parental education to improve the survival prospects of children may have been strengthened in the early twentieth century in some countries makes much sense, given changes under way

---

[102] J. C. Caldwell, "Education as a Factor in Mortality Decline: An Examination of Nigerian Data," *Population Studies* 33 (1979): 395–413; John Hobcraft, "Women's Education, Child Welfare and Child Survival: A Review of the Evidence," *Health Transition Review*, 3 (1993) 159–75; and John G. Cleland and Jerome K. van Ginneken, "Maternal Education and Child Survival in Developing Countries: The Search for Pathways of Influence," in John C. Caldwell and Gigi Santow, eds., *Selected Readings in the Cultural, Social, and Behavioural Determinants of Health* (Canberra, 1991), pp. 79–100.

[103] Samuel H. Preston and Michael R. Haines, *Fatal Years: Child Mortality in Late Nineteenth-Century America* (Princeton, 1991), pp. 177–98 and 201–2.

[104] George Alter, "Infant and Child Mortality in the United States and Canada," in Alain Bideau, Bertrand Desjardins, and Hector Perez-Brignoli, eds., *Infant and Child Mortality in the Past* (Oxford, 1997), pp. 91–108; and Ólöf Gardarsdóttir, *Saving the Child: Regional, Cultural and Social Aspects of the Infant Mortality Decline in Iceland, 1770–1920* (Umeå, 2002).

around 1900 in the things that mothers and fathers could do. These included giving children pasteurized milk and adopting the strategies of parenting associated with the mothercraft campaigns of the early years of the century. The early part of the century also saw lessons being distilled from the filth and germ theory in terms that made them accessible to the general public, in Jamaica as represented by the books by McFarlane and Lucie-Smith. But until the latter 1920s most of the effort to teach hygiene in Jamaica was directed toward primary school children.

Then, in 1926, Benjamin Washburn formed the Bureau of Health Education for the purpose of supplying health information to the general public as well as to teachers and the schools.[105] With government underwriting for printing costs and distribution, Washburn published a monthly bulletin called *Jamaica Public Health* in an initial run of 5,000 copies and distributed it without charge to the schools, teachers, ministers, doctors, and anyone who asked for it.[106] The five issues of 1926 discussed typhoid fever, smallpox vaccination, malaria and its control, tuberculosis, houseflies as disease vectors, and other topics. Washburn, who had learned Jamaican English and sometimes used a little of it in his bulletin, wrote short essays directed at adults, stories meant to be read aloud to students, poems, and plays suitable for performance by elementary students. Short stories featured fictional characters who understood the new lessons and acted on them: "Thomas Ezekiel Brown attends a health lecture."[107] Mindful of the unceasing flow of students into the schools, later bulletins tirelessly repeated essays about familiar topics and introduced new elements, such as the 1929 typhoid vaccination campaign. The bureau also distributed films dealing with health

[105] From that point on, Washburn styled his activities as "cooperative public health work" between the International Health Division of the Rockefeller Foundation and the Jamaican government. He was careful to cultivate colonial officials and to share credit for public health successes.

    Health education, in Washburn's sense, which is the sense used here, should be distinguished from medical education, which refers to the training of health practitioners.

[106] The National Library of Jamaica holds an incomplete series beginning with Vol. 4, No. 12, Dec. 1929. A set lacking only Vol. 4 may be found in RAC, BEW Papers, Box 2. By 1930 the Central Board of Health funded this bulletin, while the Rockefeller Foundation underwrote some other Board of Health Education activities. On purposes and activities see especially Washburn's 1927 report in RAC, RF, RG 5, Series 3, 437, Box 179, folder 2238.

[107] Washburn collected material from his monthly in *Jamaica Health Stories and Plays* (Kingston, 1929); and *The Health Game* (London, 1930). The quote comes from p. 2 of *The Health Game*.

issues.[108] By 1927 more than 10,000 copies of *Jamaica Public Health* were being distributed each month, and by 1930 the circulation rose to 19,750 copies, which went mostly to Jamaica, though also to Britain, the United States, and some British colonies in Africa.[109] Beginning in 1927 those lessons were taught with the assistance of a health week during which children performed plays from *Jamaica Public Health*.[110]

Washburn reported major improvements in home sanitation since 1919, but lamented that too few homes as yet had latrines of the most advanced kind. (Better latrine designs were introduced during the 1920s, so that the pit latrines promoted in 1921 seemed, by the end of the decade, to be unsatisfactory, chiefly because improved techniques for fly control had been introduced but also because the preferred pits of the late 1920s were deeper and the outhouses more solidly built. (See Illustration 4.1.)) Nevertheless, the number of people who tested positive for hookworm had dropped sharply, as had levels of infestation. Washburn, who wanted faster progress, turned in 1929 to an attempt to vaccinate against typhoid. But that campaign failed because too few people returned for their second and third shots and because of the limited effectiveness of the vaccine.[111]

The bureau also distributed pamphlets on leading diseases and their prevention, proper latrine construction, infant care, and other topics. By 1930 it operated a prenatal division, which sent a series of nine letters to expectant mothers and served as an intermediary for the growing number of health agencies and commissions, informing one about the activities of the other.[112] Washburn also organized a School for Sanitary Inspectors, which opened in 1927 and trained people to be sanitary and food inspectors, supplying most of the men serving parishes from 1928 onward. And together with one or two dentists, Washburn formed school hygiene units. Initially the units included a doctor who gave the children physicals, and a dentist and hygienist who examined and cleaned teeth and repaired caries (Illustration 4.6).[113]

---

[108] B.E. Washburn, "Report of the Co-operative Public Health Work in Jamaica during 1926," extract from the *Jamaica Gazette*, supplement, Vol. 70, No. 3, May 12, 1927.

[109] AGR 1927, esp. p. 361 and p. 274; AGR 1930, Medical Department report, p. 438.

[110] Jamaica, Ministry of Education, *Annual Report of the Ministry of Education for 1934* (Kingston, n.d.).

[111] The campaign is described in *Jamaica Public Health*, 5, no. 1 (1930).

[112] AGR 1930, Medical Department report, p. 438.

[113] School health services in metropolitan Kingston are discussed in interesting detail in Dahlia Whitbourne, "History of the School Medical Services, Kingston, Jamaica (1934–1959)" *West Indian Medical Journal*, 14 (1965): 167–79.

ILLUSTRATION 4.6. Graduates of the fourth session of the School for Sanitary Inspectors, 1929, with instructors. *Source:* RAC, RF, RG Photographs, 437, Box 116, folder 7206, number 25091b. *Instructors:* (Seated) – H. T. Thomas, Inspector of Police; Rabbi Solomon, Meat Inspector for Kingston; Dr. G. C. Strathairn, S. M. O. H. of Jamaica; Dr. B. M. Wilson, S. M. O. of Jamaica; Dr. B. E. Washburn; Dr. E. E. Murray, M. O. H. of Kingston; Major M. A. Simms, Director of Public Works of Jamaica; (Standing at right) – E. Glen Campbell (with hat), Chief Sanitary Inspector of Kingston; Dr. L. A. Crooks, M. O. H. of St. Andrew.

In 1930 Washburn published in book form a collection of material from *Jamaica Public Health*, explaining that this "bulletin is issued to meet the demands of the people for definite and practical information on health subjects. The teacher of a rural school, for example, inquires how measles is spread, a social worker asks what can be done to control tuberculosis, or a planter desires to know the cause of chronic leg ulcers among his labourers; answers to such questions form the basis of the articles."[114]

The information provided in *Jamaica Public Health* differed little from what was already available in McFarlane's *Hints on Hygiene* or

The Rockefeller Foundation later helped organize a center for training health personnel, including public health nurses, lab technicians, and health educators, for Jamaica and the British West Indies. See RAC, RF, RG 1.1, 437, Box 3, folders 38–43.

[114] Washburn, *The Health Game*, p. v.

Lucie-Smith's *Text Book for Teachers of Hygiene*, except of course that much more was said about hookworm. Washburn's essays resembled the earlier publications, too, for their accessibility, although he took even greater care in *Jamaica Public Health* to find ways to convey information on terms that the audience would find not just accessible but appealing. Washburn's bulletin also put more emphasis on responsibilities of the individual to the community in isolating the sick from the healthy.

Washburn turned the Bureau of Health Education over to colonial authorities in 1937, after which its activities slowed somewhat. When he was interviewed about this in 1970, Washburn apparently believed that things had fallen apart. In reality the bureau continued in operation, publishing issues of *Jamaica Public Health* at least as recently as 1971, and kept Washburn's activities going, distributing films and promoting public awareness of health issues. Jamaicans no longer needed either Washburn or the colonial government to carry these activities forward. What is more, a new organization formed by Jamaicans, called Jamaica Welfare, also commissioned material designed to inform schoolchildren and the public about health issues while also promoting adult education and literacy.[115] Lilian Price's 14-page booklet, *A Healthy Home in Healthy Surroundings*, distributed since 1943 by the Jamaica Social Welfare Commission (JSWC), successor to Jamaica Welfare, illustrates this work. Promoting the filth and germ theory alike, Price urged readers to provide fresh air and sunlight; to purify or boil water where necessary; to clean the bath, hand basin, and sink with a disinfectant cleanser; and to teach children to wash with soap and water. "Germs breed in dirt and love to get into unclean homes so that they spread far and wide." She also introduced readers to Jamaica's public health nurses and referred readers to other JSWC brochures, including one on how to make a pit latrine. Price aimed this advice at parents, who were meant to instruct their children.[116] The pamphlets

---

[115] Jamaica, Ministry of Education and Social Welfare, *A Review of the Developments in Education and Social Welfare in Jamaica during the Period 1944–1954* (Kingston, 1954), p. 25.

[116] Lilian Price, *A Healthy Home in Healthy Surroundings* (Kingston, 1943), quote from p. 3. See also the anonymous *Home Care of the Sick*, also published in 1943 and distributed by the JSWC, which explains the principles of home care for a patient with a communicable disease. This pamphlet provides much the same information as found in longer treatments with the same title published in the United States, e.g., by Amy Elizabeth Pope in 1911, Clara Dutton Noyes in 1924, and Norma Selbert in 1929. But the same points are made in many fewer pages and in more accessible prose.

in this series, brief and written in accessible language, used illustrations featuring Afro-Jamaicans rather than people of European origin.

The Island Medical Department contributed Cynthia Murray's 1941 pamphlet of 20 pages, *Maternal and Infant Care*.[117] Murray urged readers to use the antenatal clinics at welfare centers, gave advice about a mother's diet and exercise, proposed that infants should be breastfed for at least six months, and explained how to prepare food supplements: mix boiled water with strained orange juice from six weeks, avoid pacifiers because they introduce germs, and bathe the infant daily and clean his/her mouth.

Even though formal education remained largely a matter of elementary schooling, the early expansion of schools in Jamaica created children and adults, especially the children of the 1920s and 1930s, who were attuned to health issues and who were the first generation of Jamaicans instructed in the principles of filth and germ theory. The ideas about health and health education originated outside Jamaica, but students and teachers were overwhelmingly Jamaican, and Jamaicans wrote some of the curriculum materials. Washburn, an American, led the Bureau of Health Education, but nearly everyone else associated with its activities was Afro-Jamaican. Jamaicans led Jamaica Welfare and its successor, JSWC. Jamaicans adopted these ideas and, in agreement with British authorities and other outside agents, decided that they were useful for the well-being of the general public.

Instruction: Methods, Content, and Effects. Lacking libraries and other equipment, outfitted with ill-suited desks and benches, often led by untrained teachers, and combining all ages in a single room, Jamaican schools relied heavily on drill.[118] Teachers recited things they wanted students to learn, asked the students to repeat those things aloud, and then conducted verbal tests.[119] In the nineteenth century the lessons dealt with reading, writing, sums, the catechism, moral education, and hymns.[120] By 1920 there was less religious content, and a more varied curriculum including lessons on health and hygiene.

---

[117] (Kingston, n.d.).

[118] AGR 1930, Education Department report, pp. 226–27, on facilities and equipment deficiencies. In 1930, 33 graduates of the teacher training colleges began teaching, and so did about 150 untrained teachers. Ibid., p. 227.

[119] Anthony C. Winkler, *Going Home to Teach* (Kingston, 1995), pp. 242–44, describing the classroom in 1975 and recalling his own experience in such classrooms from the 1940s.

[120] *Handbook of Jamaica for 1882* (Kingston, 1882), p. 236.

In a good school, in the eyes of the school inspectors, teachers repeated lessons and students responded with some enthusiasm. Students understood well enough what the lessons meant, so that they could answer the inspector's questions about their lessons or, in the case of latrine use, apply a lesson by using the latrine in an appropriate way.

Education Department officials nevertheless complained about this mode of instruction. According to the 1930 report, "it is to be feared that the hygiene taught in the majority of Elementary Schools is mainly repetition," though in some schools drill was supplemented by articles read from the monthly *Jamaica Public Health* and by plays on health topics taken from the same source.[121] The school curriculum was being modified to local needs in the 1920s and 1930s. These modifications began with instructional material on gardening and hygiene introduced in the 1910s, so that for a time students continued to learn British history and geography while they were studying how to grow vegetables and fruits in Jamaica and what to do to protect themselves from health threats in their own environment. Then in 1939 a revised curriculum was introduced giving history, natural history, and other material based on the West Indies. In the meantime the curriculum at the teacher-training colleges was also being reformed. By 1930 female teachers in training studied first aid along with needlework, cookery, and academic subjects, and they operated a practice school.[122]

How Little Schooling is Enough? One of the distinctive features of Jamaican experience with health and hygiene education in the 1920s lies in the brevity of the schooling received by most students. On average the children who attended primary schools completed three or four years, during which they learned to read but probably not well enough to read McFarlane's *Hints*, Lucie-Smith's *Text Book*, or *Jamaica Public Health*. In the census, the people being enumerated evaluated a degree of literacy, and authorities accept the idea that Jamaicans overstated their ability to read and write. The key question therefore is not whether the people producing health propaganda were able to simplify printed material well enough to reach these primary school students directly yet preserve useful content, for it is apparent that in general they did not. That question is instead whether the health propaganda was simplified enough to reach the teachers, who themselves had completed

---

[121] AGR 1930, Education Department report, quote from p. 235.
[122] AGR 1930, Shortwood Training College report, pp. 192–96.

primary school plus two or three years at the teacher's college, and the many teaching assistants, who had merely completed primary school or distinguished themselves in the years of schooling they had completed. Some modern research suggests "that even fewer than four years of formal schooling in the most inadequately equipped school" may be enough to make a difference in people's later ability to protect their children from health hazards.[123]

The Education Department's Evaluation. Despite the changes that had taken place since 1910, Education Department authorities in the 1930s usually took the position that hygiene and health instruction in the schools remained inadequate. According to the 1930 report, "it cannot be reported that the importance of education for health is fully realized by the teacher, and much remains to be done before it can be said to occupy the place it deserves in Jamaican education." Hygiene lessons had not yet been incorporated into science instruction (it being a trend-setting idea at that time that hygiene should be taught along with science rather than separately).

At best a text book knowledge is acquired, of little interest, carrying little conviction, and of small effect, if any, in forming the habits of health, or in reinforcing the effort in Health Education now being made in the Island. The sanitary conditions in many schools must daily discredit the hygiene lesson.... The remedy lies with the teachers and their training.[124]

Moreover, the schools had latrines, but never enough of them, and they rarely provided sanitary paper or facilities for students to wash their hands after toileting.[125]

The bar had been raised. In the 1910s education authorities complained that the schools lacked latrines altogether, that lessons did not include any material on health and hygiene, and that the teachers lacked any preparation for teaching hygiene. It is telling to notice that the schools were outfitted with surface, and then pit, latrines before they were provided with running water. But it is also important to notice

[123] D. T. Slaughter-Defoe, W. A. Addae, and C. Bell. "Toward the Future Schooling of Girls: Global Status, Issues, and Prospects," *Human Development*, 45 (2002): 34–53, quote from p. 35.

[124] AGR 1930, Education Department report, quotes from p. 235. For more disparaging comments on hygiene instruction in the schools, see *Annual Report of the Jamaica Schools Commission, 1938* (Kingston, n.d.), p. 4.

[125] AGR 1930, Education Department report, p. 233.

that Education Department officials remained unaware of the contents of another 1930 report, this one from the Medical Department, which highlighted that year for having the lowest overall mortality and the lowest infant mortality in Jamaica's history, no serious outbreak of epidemic disease, and a definite decline in enteric fever and dysentery.[126] School authorities in Kingston could not say whether the schools had contributed to these gains because they did not inquire about death rates or because they did not associate health education in the schools with lower death rates.

The Medical Department report also commented on health education in the portion of Manchester parish that the hookworm campaign reached in 1929:

The people on the whole show the results of educational campaigns by a general lively interest in all matters concerning health. It is a pleasure to talk with individuals and to note the genuine gratification they will display when given an opportunity to show their knowledge on health matters.[127]

In the 1940s Jamaican schools still contended with many of the problems they had confronted in the 1910s: enrollment rates were higher but attendance remained about 60 percent; students left after a few years; teachers were poorly paid, and many of them had little or no training and worked in teaching for only a few years;[128] the facilities and equipment were inadequate and overcrowded; the schools or the teachers had a few books, but students did not; only a few students could hope to move on to secondary schools or find places at university.[129] Health education also figured less prominently in the curriculum and in the concerns of educational leaders than it had in the 1920s and 1930s. By 1947 health education had been incorporated into the instruction

---

[126] AGR 1930, Medical Department report, p. 385.

[127] AGR 1930, Medical Department report, p. 431. The educational campaigns referred to are those of the Bureau of Health Education.

[128] AGR 1938, Education Department report, p. 391, gives statistics on the training status of secondary and primary school teachers.

[129] These are only the main points of a critique. For more detail, see Eric Williams, *Education in the British West Indies* (Port of Spain, 1950), pp. 29–56. The Medical Department report for 1938 mentioned that the most overcrowded school in Kingston had only 3.4 square feet per student. AGR 1938, Medical Department, p. 436. Diane J. Austin, *Urban Life in Kingston, Jamaica: The Culture and Class Ideology of Two Neighborhoods* (New York, 1984), pp. 17–18, explains that private primary and secondary schools used by the elite give their children preferential access to higher education and positions of authority in Jamaican life.

given to girls in domestic science.[130] Boys no longer received any formal instruction, and the subject was accorded less time.

A 1939 curriculum reform made physiology and hygiene compulsory subjects, but it used a British syllabus with no reference to tropical conditions, and instruction that was chiefly theoretical.[131] Ronald Lloyd Douglas in a text published in the 1950s was content to urge cleanliness and a well-balanced diet but to limit himself to vague homilies, providing much less specific information on health and hygiene than either McFarlane or Lucie-Smith.[132] His book was not nearly as useful as the pamphlets published in earlier years by the Bureau of Health Education or Jamaica Welfare.

In Jamaica as in many other countries the intensive effort to instruct primary school students in hygiene and health was temporary. It exposed 20 or 25 years worth of students to health lessons. By the end of that period, in Jamaica as elsewhere, the lessons being taught – about soil pollution, latrine building, unsafe drinking water, the need to avoid insect vectors, control of sputum from tuberculosis patients, and so forth – were no longer so vital, because the diseases associated with these measures and behaviors had been largely brought under control. Moreover, people had evidently absorbed these lessons. When instruction in health education was curtailed to being a part of the girls' lessons in domestic science, there is no indication that the diseases reappeared or that mortality increased. Nor is there any indication that the school authorities, who revised the curriculum to incorporate hygiene lessons into physiology, reducing their content and making the lessons nonspecific, ever drew any connection between these lessons and population health.

On the basis of this evidence, it is difficult to allocate responsibility for educating the public in these basic lessons about health and to decide whether the schools did more or less than the Jamaica Hookworm Commission, the Bureau of Health Education, Jamaica Welfare, or JSWC. Too much of their work overlapped. Certainly the primary schools and the health propaganda directed at the adult public tried to teach people lessons that would allow them to reduce risks associated

[130] Jamaica, Ministry of Education, *Annual Report of the Ministry of Education for 1947* (Kingston, n.d.).

[131] Jamaica, Ministry of Education, *Annual Report of the Ministry of Education for 1939–40* (Kingston, n.d.), p. 3.

[132] Ronald Lloyd Douglas, *General Science with Health and Hygiene for West Indian Schools* (Kingston, n.d.).

with diarrheal diseases. The most unambiguous success came in the installation of latrines, which houses and schools alike had lacked in the 1910s. By 1940 most houses and schools had latrines of an improved kind, capable not just of disposing of human waste safely but also of limiting the opportunity for houseflies to breed.

The evidence about how much children and adults learned from health and hygiene lessons and health propaganda has some uncertain qualities. The sources have much to say about what people were taught but little to say about what people learned. Nevertheless there is an obvious contrast between the early twentieth-century Jamaican, who knew little or nothing about filth or germ theory or about how to control disease risks, and the 1940s-era Jamaican, who had mastered enough information so as no longer to need health education or an active adult health propaganda campaign to control diarrheal diseases and to limit risks associated with mosquitoes and malaria and with tuberculosis.

The most telling evidence is circumstantial. Mortality from the diseases about which people were being taught declined in the 1920s and 1930s along with the instruction. If other explanations for that decline could be suggested, then schooling and health propaganda would merely be listed as contributory factors. But most Jamaicans still did not see doctors, who were too few to attend the general population, much less to have been agents for instructing people in health behavior. In 1950, most Jamaicans still did not have piped water or waterborne means of waste disposal in their homes. Other explanations cannot be suggested, and their absence elevates health education to the position of a leading factor in the control of diarrheal disease and an important factor in the control of other communicable diseases.

POLITICAL AND COMMUNITY DEVELOPMENT

Lord Sidney Olivier, former governor of Jamaica and a Fabian socialist, failed to understand how much the economic contraction of the 1920s and 1930s had hurt working Jamaicans, and in 1936 he still regarded Jamaica preeminently as "the blessed island."[133] His was nevertheless one of the British voices speaking out to encourage Britain to invest in economic and community development projects in Jamaica. W. M. Macmillan, who also published an important book in 1936, warned

[133] Sydney Haldane Olivier, *Jamaica: The Blessed Island* (New York, 1936).

about an army of landless and unemployed people in the British West Indies, called for development spending, and made an appeal: "colonial democracy must be helped to its birth."[134] Progressive thinkers in Britain were preparing for a near-term future in which British investments would stimulate employment and economic opportunity in Jamaica and in which Jamaicans would become more widely involved in governing themselves. The last major reform of the political system, but for admission of some women to voting privileges in 1919, had occurred in 1895, and much had happened since then in Jamaican and British attitudes toward how broad political participation should be.

Along a parallel course, Jamaicans, too, were planning a different future. Britain figures much less prominently in their plans than in those of Olivier and Macmillan, for Jamaicans saw, beginning in the 1920s, the opportunity to attract investment capital from North America. They were less interested, too, in waiting for the British to provide leading ideas about political and social development. It is important to notice the timing of things. The British began actually to make changes in 1940 and the period 1940–46 was one of modifications in the relationship between mother country and colony. Jamaicans had begun to revamp things earlier, from 1937 and 1938. While the British thought about voting rights, participation in government, and economic development projects, Jamaicans thought, beside these things, about community development led locally, the need for jobs, political organizations including parties, health education and propaganda, and more generally about social development.

The most conspicuous event of this period was the labor revolt that began in May 1938. A new sugar factory was opened at Frome in Westmoreland parish, and people traveled there in the hope of getting a job. The demand for jobs far surpassed the supply, leading to unrest and violence among disappointed job seekers, which quickly spread. Dockworkers and public employees in Kingston and banana and sugar plantation workers across the island joined in, and the unrest came to a head in the last week of May. The British especially were shocked by how quickly labor unrest spread, how angry people were, and how widespread discontent was in the West Indies.[135] They organized the

---

[134] W. M. Macmillan, *Warning from the West Indies: A Tract for Africa and the Empire* (London, 1936), esp. pp. 196–97, quote from p. 201.

[135] Ken Post, *Arise Ye Starvelings: The Jamaican Labour Rebellion of 1938 and Its Aftermath* (The Hague, 1978). See also Maurice St. Pierre, "The 1938 Jamaica Disturbances: A Portrait of Mass Reaction against Colonialism," *Social and Economic*

Moyne Commission and began to experiment with economic development programs and to promote a move toward political autonomy.[136] Working-class unrest forced political reform and more urgent British interest in economic development.

A Political and Social Transition toward Autonomy. Sociologists examining cultural and political leadership in Jamaica detect a series of transitions in the twentieth century. At the beginning of the century a traditional class of British plantation owners controlled the political apparatus of the island, most wealth, and most leadership roles in political, social, and cultural affairs. Their position was undermined first in the 1890s by a sharp decline in sugar exports, and then by the declining profitability of sugar cultivation as producers in the British Caribbean found themselves unable to compete with U.S. rivals in Cuba. Many of the British planters, who had dominated sugar output, sold out and moved away. Their place in the economy was taken chiefly by British and North American corporations. Independent Jamaican farmers gained more leadership positions in politics and more wealth, and, especially in the 1930s, the Jamaican middle class grew in scale and authority. The adoption of universal suffrage in 1944 consolidated the power of the middle class, composed of independent farmers, merchants, and professionals, and the middle class gained control of the two political parties, the Jamaica Labour Party and the Peoples National Party. Both parties favored higher levels of public spending on education and health. The size of the public sector grew in the period 1930–50, with government revenues rising from 8 percent of GDP in 1930 to 14 percent in 1950, and, a point already made, spending on health and education rose sharply in the same period (Figure 4.1).[137]

The programs and ideas that emerged in the 1930s and 1940s also reveal something important about Jamaican ideas about political

Studies, 27 (1978): 171–96; and, on the Caribbean context, Richard Hart, "The Labour Rebellions of the 1930s," in Hilary Beckles and Verene Shepherd, eds., *Caribbean Freedom: Society and Economy from Emancipation to the Present* (Kingston, 1993), pp. 370–75; and Arthur Lewis, "The 1930s Social Revolution," in idem, pp. 376–92. Elizabeth McLean Petras, *Jamaican Labor Migration: White Capital and Black Labor, 1850–1930* (Boulder, 1988), p. 257, suggests that returning labor migrants may have contributed to the 1938 revolt, having learned about labor movements in Panama and Cuba.

[136] The recommendations appear in West India Royal Commission 1938–39, *Statement of Action Taken on the Recommendations* (London, 1945).

[137] Carl Stone, *Class, State and Democracy in Jamaica* (New York, 1986), esp. 19–32.

economy. Jamaican Welfare, the JSWC, and the two political parties favored using a combination of public funds and volunteers to promote community development. Both parties also adopted economic policies that favored free trade and entrepreneurship. As early as the 1930s, but more obviously in the 1940s, it is possible to identify a Jamaican political economy that mixed social democratic ideas for community development with capitalist ideas about economic development, and high public spending on health and education with stronger individual responsibility for taking advantage of the opportunity for schooling and of health and hygiene education.

Jamaicans – mostly people from Africa but also those from India and China – had long staffed the primary schools of the island, in most cases a single teacher to a school. By the 1910s Afro-Jamaicans also taught at Mico, Shortwood, and the other teachers colleges and at the technical schools created in that decade. Before 1900 some Afro-Jamaicans served as DMOs; they dominated the sanitation and public health apparatus created in the 1920s. The Kingston police force, long made up chiefly of Afro-Jamaicans in the ranks, began to accept those men as officers in 1921. This may have occurred because so many men, about 7,500, had served in the British army during World War I, acquiring training appropriate to the police force.[138]

Another important element of social transition lies in the creation of a large and important area of Jamaican authority operating sometimes in collaboration with British colonial authorities and sometimes independently. Although outsiders, first British planters and then British and North American corporations, continued to exercise economic power, locals moved into controlling positions in political, social, and cultural affairs from the 1910s onward, and with special vigor in the 1930s and 1940s. Well before independence in 1962, Jamaicans formulated public policy and staffed most public sector jobs. They had also created private associations dedicated to social welfare and formulated popular policies of intervention in health, education and the dissemination of information, charity, and other areas. The Women's Social Service Association (WSSA), organized in 1918, represents the traditional attempt by private individuals to promote social welfare. The WSSA aimed to better the health of women and children by advocating and teaching parent craft, lobbying for better housing, setting up free clinics, and providing visitors for newborn children. Its members

---

[138] Brodber, The Second Generation of Freemen in Jamaica, p. 110.

were the more fortunate women of the community, and its intended beneficiaries the less fortunate.

That style of community engagement was pushed aside in the late 1920s and during the 1930s with the creation of many new health and educational organizations led and staffed by Jamaicans, which paralleled the movement for self-government and black nationalism led by Marcus Garvey, Bustamante's trade unionism, Pentecostalism, and other popular movements.[139] Especially in the aftermath of 1938, Jamaicans formulated their own plan of social development, one that emphasized self-help, community engagement, and the use of public and private money to fund such specific local projects as improvements to water supply, cooperatives, community centers, and an expansion of tomato cultivation. The ideas behind this movement can be associated, at least in some measure, with the declaration by the People's National Party in 1938 of a social democratic platform similar to that pursued by the British Labour Party. In 1937 Norman W. Manley assumed leadership of Jamaica Welfare (JW), using its funding from North American banana companies to pay for local projects aimed at developing rural Jamaica and to "serve the general interests and the social and economic betterment" of Jamaicans. JW made grants to build community centers; promoted the formation of village organizations, including cooperatives, credit unions, cooperative house building, and improvement projects; and distributed information about village improvement. It promoted the organization of 4-H clubs, introduced in 1940 on the U.S. model, for rural primary schools, the students being intended to learn by doing in the areas of cooperative action, habits of healthful living, improved farming practices, and self-help.[140] Pioneer clubs drew youths, aged 18 years and above, and provided a transition from 4-H to adult cooperatives, the pioneer clubs being places to teach farming technique and cooperative work on house building and preparing land for planting. (Recognizing Jamaica as a pioneer in community development programs, UNESCO trained personnel there in the 1950s.[141])

---

[139] Tony Martin, "Marcus Garvey, the Caribbean, and the Struggle for Black Jamaican Nationhood," in Hilary Beckles and Verene Shepherd, eds., *Caribbean Freedom: Society and Economy from Emancipation to the Present* (Kingston, 1993), pp. 359–69; and Rupert Lewis, *Marcus Garvey: Anti-colonial Champion* (Trenton, NJ, 1988).

[140] Williams, *Education in the British West Indies*, p. 42.

[141] Sybil Francis, "The Evolution of Community Development in Jamaica (1937–1962)," *Caribbean Quarterly*, 15 (1969): 40–58.

In 1938 JW programs were under way in 10 villages; by 1949 the number had grown to 229 villages, many with several organizations. JW also organized a mass education program in nutrition, trying to correct problems uncovered by the nutrition surveys carried out in 1945 and 1946. It also formulated the 3F program, Food for Family Fitness, which provided nutrition education.[142] During World War II, when the banana companies could no longer fund these activities, government contributions took their place and JW evolved into the Jamaica Social Welfare Commission (JSWC). Although JW and JSWC hired and trained a staff, their activities centered on the dissemination of information about useful programs and the means to engage in them.

Self-help organizations had a much longer history, but in their earlier forms, such as friendly societies and the City Dispensary set up in Kingston in 1876, they directed activities chiefly toward paying members. In the new form, Jamaicans sought to find cooperative ways to promote general welfare.[143] The friendly societies still flourished, providing their members with compensation for part of wages lost during sickness episodes and with burial benefits.[144] The trade union movement, which began in the 1930s, continued to grow in the postwar period with union membership rising from less than 1 percent of the wage labor force in 1941 to 21 percent in 1950.[145]

The Moyne commission members, meeting in 1938 and 1939, concluded that people had turned to violence in 1938 because there were

---

[142] See H. W. Howes, *Fundamental, Adult, Literacy and Community Education in the West Indies* (n.p., 1955).

[143] Patrick E. Bryan, *Philanthropy and Social Welfare in Jamaica: An Historical Survey* (Kingston, 1990), pp. 38–39, 43, and 53–58; Francis, "The Evolution of Community Development"; Norman Girvan, ed., *Working Together for Development: D.T.M. Girvan on Cooperatives and Community Development, 1939–1968* (Kingston, 1993); and Roger Marier, *Social Welfare Work in Jamaica: A Study of the Jamaica Social Welfare Commission* (Paris, 1953), p. 17, quoting the memorandum of association. For an explanation of why the cooperative movement did not persist, see E. R.-M. Le Franc, "The Co-operative Movement in Jamaica: An Exercise in Social Control," *Social and Economic Studies*, 28 (1979): 21–43.

[144] Beverley Joy Anderson, The Decline of Friendly Societies of Jamaica: A Traditional Voluntary Association in a Developing Society, unpublished Ph.D. dissertation, Boston College, 1985, p. 168. The decline began around 1964.

[145] Stone, *Class, State and Democracy in Jamaica*, p. 106; O. W. Phelps, "Rise of the Labour Movement in Jamaica," *Social and Economic Studies*, 9 (1960): 417–68; and O. Nigel Bolland, *The Politics of Labour in the British Caribbean: The Social Origins of Authoritarianism and Democracy in the Labour Movement* (Kingston, 2001).

too few jobs to be had and that people with jobs had joined in because their earnings were too low. The commission recommended the creation of a welfare fund to relieve distress, the legalization of trade unions to allow labor to bargain collectively, a minimum wage, and an economic reorientation toward smallholdings and small farms with more diversified crops. But the commission opposed the creation of new industries, specifically rejecting the idea of building a cement factory in Jamaica to supply construction materials, and therefore opposed the most obvious steps that might have been taken to create new jobs. Moreover, in order to attract support to its proposals for economic and social development, the commission advised constitutional reform and a vast expansion of the electorate, which numbered about 63,000 in 1937 but more than 600,000 after the 1944 reforms.[146]

The commission report led to a 1940 parliamentary act making £5 million available annually for grants to Jamaica and other British colonies for social and economic improvement. Jamaican projects began in 1940, when Frank Stockdale was appointed Comptroller for Development and Welfare. Stockdale and his assistants, Rupert Briercliffe for public health, S. A. Hammond for education, and T. S. Simey for social welfare, formulated expansive plans. Briercliffe's 1941 memorandum assessed public health requirements and planned what could be done with the larger Colonial Development and Welfare Act grants that would become available on the conclusion of World War II. Much was deficient in public health and medical care, but Briercliffe's recommendations would revive and expand familiar programs rather than beginning anew. For example, after Washburn's departure, the Bureau of Health Education had become less active, and Briercliffe proposed to revive it with a full-time health education officer as well as assistants.[147] Jamaica needed more of nearly everything, and greater attentiveness to maintaining existing programs, but Briercliffe believed that the proper initiatives were already under way.

---

[146] Trevor Munroe, *The Politics of Constitutional Decolonization: Jamaica, 1944–62* (Mona, 1972), pp. 32–36.

[147] Briercliffe, *Development and Welfare in the West Indies 1941–42*, p. 6. Also see Stockdale's reports: Frank Stockdale, *Development and Welfare in the West Indies, 1940–1942* (London, 1943); and idem, *Development and Welfare in the West Indies, 1943–44* (London, 1945); as well as the further series *Development and Welfare in the West Indies*; and West India Royal Commission 1938–39, *Statement on Action Taken on the Recommendations*. From 1938 the colonial government also published an *Annual Report on the Social and Economic Progress of the People of Jamaica* (London, from 1939), giving upbeat testimony about achievements.

When the sociologist Simey published *Welfare and Planning in the West Indies* in 1946, he argued that solutions to Jamaica's problems lay in self-help programs.[148] What is especially curious about Simey's published ideas is how little they reflect familiarity with the self-help activities that had blossomed in Jamaica since the 1920s. Simey, who saw himself as a witness privileged to be on hand at the beginning of an experiment in reshaping the lives of West Indian people, expected Jamaicans and West Indians to be able to make improvements through British actions that would lay the groundwork for self-sufficiency. What he thought he knew about West Indian people came chiefly from reading academic works, especially the studies of an American scholar, Melville J. Herskovits, who had studied the African origins of West Indian culture.[149] Simey had little confidence in Jamaican leaders or in what Afro-Jamaicans could do for themselves. He wanted Jamaicans to learn social mores from the British and was keen on the idea that Jamaican families should have dinner together in the manner of the British bourgeoisie.[150]

George Beckford and Michael Witter describe the period 1938–1962 as an era of mulatto petit-bourgeois leadership fostered by the Moyne commission report, which urged land reform and self-government with adult suffrage.[151] Land reform transferred small plots, often with poor quality soil, into the hands of formerly landless farmers. Intentions aside, Michael Manley could still describe the situation in 1969 as one in which 45 percent of arable land was owned by 0.2 percent of the farmers.[152] Jamaicans of African and European background alike held two visions of the island's future in the 1930s. The dominant vision, which did not eventuate, foresaw a rural land of small farmers and landowners. Thus, for example, Olivier, writing in 1936, struggled with the problem whether Jamaica had enough land to be able to turn its people into smallholders, and he solved it with the suggestion that crown lands be sold off in five-acre plots and other uncultivated,

---

[148] T. S. Simey, *Welfare and Planning in the West Indies* (Oxford, 1946). Simey visited Jamaica during World War II and urged British colonial authorities to join in promoting self-help initiatives, which he studied in Girvan's training courses in 1943–44.

[149] Simey, *Welfare and Planning*, pp. 30–35.

[150] Ibid., p. 91.

[151] George Beckford and Michael Witter, *Small Garden...Bitter Weed: The Political Economy of Struggle and Change in Jamaica* (Morant Bay, Jamaica, 1982), pp. 61–62.

[152] Michael Manley, *Up the Down Escalator: Development and the International Economy: A Jamaican Case Study* (Washington, DC, 1987), p. xi.

privately owned land be put to the same use.[153] As late as 1952 a team from the World Bank promoted the same vision, recommending agricultural development and better preparation of the populace to fill unskilled handicraft jobs by reducing the duration of schooling to four years and emphasizing practical skills.[154]

The individual actions of Jamaicans show that they held another vision, one that looked to the schools as an avenue of social and economic mobility, hoped for better schools and higher wages, and looked to the future to offer new sources of employment outside farming, sugar and banana plantation work, higglering, and domestic service. H. P. Jacobs, who led the survey of the rural parish of St. Mary after the labor revolt of 1938, found general resentment toward declining revenues from banana cultivation, and a general wish for higher wages.[155] Jamaicans imagined a future of more and better jobs. These things are the featured elements of the standard Jamaican history of the 1930s and 1940s. They are inaccurate only in failing to include, in fact to emphasize, the part played in political and community development by health education, the control of major communicable diseases, the creation of a Jamaican public health organization, and the other things that reduced mortality risks. Jamaicans first worked together, sometimes in association with their British colonial masters or Rockefeller agents and sometimes on their own, in the business of disease control.

CONCLUSION

A transformation of health and life expectancy in Jamaica began in the 1920s. Sanitary improvements on the British model were made in Kingston and a few towns via water filtration and chlorination and, less often, waterborne sewage disposal, but those improvements reached only a small fraction of the population. The island's system of dispersed medical care, created in the 1860s, expanded slightly in the period 1920–50, adding a few doctors, hospitals, and clinics. Smallpox vaccinations had been general enough in Jamaica for decades before 1920 to make smallpox and the related disease alastrim insignificant causes of death. Doctors could successfully treat hookworm and yaws

---

[153] Olivier, *Jamaica: The Blessed Island*, esp. pp. 274–86 and 349–54.

[154] International Bank for Reconstruction and Development, *The Economic Development of Jamaica* (Baltimore, 1952).

[155] Claus F. Stolberg, ed., *Jamaica 1938: The Living Conditions of the Urban and Rural Poor: Two Social Surveys* (Kingston, 1990), p. 14.

and could manage malaria with quinine, but they could not prevent the reoccurrence of hookworm or malaria and could do little or nothing to cure most of the other diseases from which Jamaicans suffered. The comparatively extensive health system in place by 1920 had not yet managed to reduce mortality. Antibiotics and other effective medicines and vaccinations did not begin to reach Jamaica until the end of the 1940s. Nor can it be said that between 1920 and 1950 the standard of living improved, incomes rose, people ate better, or conditions of life improved much. Yet mortality declined rapidly in Jamaica in these three decades.

The leading explanations for this rapid improvement in life expectancy lie in public health, education, and individual behavior. The public sector spent more on health and education, and this investment was complemented by the engagement of the Rockefeller Foundation in a series of campaigns against specific diseases. In the 1920s Jamaica created a new island-wide cadre of public health and sanitation workers who made inspections and enforced good sanitary practice. Beginning in the 1910s and 1920s schoolteachers indoctrinated students in lessons about safeguarding health and preventing disease. From 1926 the Bureau of Health Education propagandized the adult public in the same lessons. Through indoctrination, rote learning, and the repetition of a few selected lessons, children and adults discovered how to protect themselves from diarrheal diseases, malaria, tuberculosis, and other important causes of death. People learned these things as children reciting lessons about health in their schools, hearing stories about good health practices, and learning how to use and also how to build latrines, and they learned them as adults exposed to health propaganda in the visits of hookworm and yaws units to their villages, in the broad dissemination of health lessons, and in the work of organizations promoting community action. The essential background for these developments lies in the prior development of primary schools and teacher-training schools, widespread acceptance of the value of educating children, the high regard Jamaicans had for education as a path of individual advancement, and the training of teachers in health education.

There is also the important stimulus provided by the steps taken by McFarlane and Lucie-Smith to synthesize filth and germ theory into pithy lessons about what Jamaicans could do for themselves, and by the appearance of agents from the Rockefeller Foundation's International Health Board, who had concrete and proven ideas about how to engage people at the household, village, and neighborhood level in disease control. The result was a transformation from a people who, around 1910, knew very little indeed about how diseases common to their experience were transmitted or how they might be avoided, into a people who could do much to protect themselves. As Washburn wrote, "progress in improving the public health depends on the conduct of the individual."[156] Among the people the British regarded as willful and disobedient, the essential steps were taken by self-reliant Jamaicans, who decided to become better informed about hygiene and health and to have their children learn about these things, who agreed to build latrines with locally available materials, and who cooperated with the new public health authorities and modified their own behavior in many ways.

China took an approach to disease control in the 1950s that has some similarities to the earlier Jamaican approach. In the absence of adequate medical or public health personnel or facilities, and strapped financially, China turned to a mobilization of the populace, one much more overt than anything attempted in Jamaica. In the Patriotic Hygiene Campaign Chinese peasants were called on not just to learn how to protect themselves against disease, but also to help cleanse the country of disease vectors and filth.[157] As in Jamaica in the 1920s and 1930s, so in China in the 1950s rapid gains in survival occurred.

The methods of disease prevention and avoidance that Jamiacans learned consisted chiefly of actions that individuals could take without any substantial cost: building latrines and safely disposing of human waste, isolating the sick, interfering with housefly and mosquito breeding, recognizing tuberculosis and learning how to reduce the chances of infection when someone in the household contracted the disease, and changing personal behavior in ways that protected against other diseases. Mortality from diarrheal diseases, malaria, and tuberculosis, the three leading causes of death at the beginning of this period, fell sharply between 1920 and 1950, mostly before the introduction of new means of control or treatment, such as DDT for malarial mosquitoes and streptomycin for tuberculosis. In the 1940s more extensive maternal and child health care, provided in clinics and by public health nurses, also contributed to the reduction of mortality.

[156] Washburn's 1926 report, RAC, RF, RG 5, Series 3, Box 181, folder 2249, p. 5.
[157] Peter Heller, "The Strategy of Health-Sector Planning," in Myron E. Wegman, Tsung-yi Lin, and Elizabeth F. Purcell, eds., *Public Health in the People's Republic of China: Report of a Conference* (New York, [1973]), pp. 62–107, esp. 74–76.

Most of the medical and public health ideas that made this transformation possible came from the outside. So, too, did much of the practical assistance necessary to initiate public health programs and campaigns against particular diseases, in which the Rockefeller Foundation played a leading part. Outsiders showed a deep interest in the health of ordinary Jamaicans, which impressed Jamaicans. By themselves, however, these things from the outside could not have reduced mortality so dramatically. The essential allies were the Jamaicans who saw the benefits offered by the new ideas about disease control and prevention, and the Jamaicans who worked as public health officials. Jamaicans acted on the possibilities before them at two levels. In the household they changed their ordinary ways of doing things enough to reduce the disease risks they faced. And at the community level they organized themselves in ways that made it easier and more efficient to act on health advice.

It may be that intervention from the United States, and therefore from outside the British colonial system, played a key role. Even though the Rockefeller Foundation agents never wrote that they wanted to champion the interests of Afro-Jamaicans over British authorities or over whites in Jamaica, there is enough indication of tension between these agents and the British to infer that Washburn and the others found Afro-Jamaicans better allies for their work than they did the British in Jamaica. Certainly it is difficult, even impossible, to imagine either so much higher spending on public health in the 1920s and 1930s or the creation of an Afro-Jamaican-dominated public health establishment without Rockefeller intervention. It is equally difficult to imagine so much success if the iterative campaigns against hookworm, yaws, malaria, and tuberculosis had not employed Afro-Jamaicans as nurses, microscopists, or clerks, and in other roles. At first glance the most important effect of the intervention from the United States might seem to be the introduction of energy, well-defined plans, talented medical people, and some funds. But the more important effect may instead have been the alliance that Afro-Jamaicans struck with the Americans. Hookworm, malaria, and tuberculosis could not have been controlled to the substantial degree that they were by colonial medical authorities or Washburn and the other Americans working alone. In the final analysis, success depended chiefly on Jamaicans themselves.

It is interesting to notice that these successes in health and survivorship began to appear in the 1920s, before one can detect overt signs of a demand coming from Jamaicans for political autonomy, which emerged in the 1930s. Jamaicans asked their parish authorities to do more in public health and responded in a mostly cooperative way to the things that parish authorities did, even to the intrusive sanitary inspections. This suggests, in the degree to which Jamaicans took up and took over the effort to improve health, that a demand for social and local autonomy appeared before there was a demand for national autonomy and that a demand for social autonomy emerged in the same period as Marcus Garvey's call for black majority rule and in advance of an open demand for political autonomy.[158] In turn the new health initiatives led to more people getting experience in administrative tasks, especially operating government programs and running cooperatives, and to collaboration in community tasks. Like the trade unions, but unlike Revivalism and Pentecostalism, the organization of community effort toward health objectives set attainable this-worldly goals and moved toward them.

As colonizers, the British were adept at building institutions; there were many schools, churches, government offices, hospitals and clinics, prisons, police units, and other organizations to be staffed. By 1950 Jamaica possessed a class of people experienced in the operation of small and large organizations and capable of carrying them forward on their own. Photographs from the period, such as the 1931 group picture of the Church of England synod,[159] the initial medical class at the University of the West Indies in 1948, and employees of the Kingston sanitation department, show the mixed-race composition of people filling these many positions, although the whites remained in control of most of the highest posts and offices.

[158] In 1929 in the United Negro Improvement Association manifesto launching the People's Political Party, Garvey included a provision encouraging the creation of clinics with trained nurses to make home visits in rural districts to demonstrate sanitation and health. See Lewis, *Marcus Garvey*, pp. 212–13. But there seems to have been little or no overlap between public health activities that had emerged while Garvey was in the United States and Garvey's activities on his return to Jamaica.

[159] See *Handbook of Jamaica for 1931* (Kingston, 1931), opposite p. 308, for a photograph of the synod in 1931.

5

THE GOOD YEARS: 1950–1972

Jamaica's health transition continued through the 1950s and 1960s with life expectancy at birth rising from 54.6 years in 1950 to 69 years in 1972, at a still rapid pace of 0.65 years gain per year of calendar time. Table 5.1 shows age-specific death rates at the beginning and end of this period. Reductions occurred in every age group, with the age group 5–44 leading.[1] Some elements of the cause-of-death pattern can be picked out from the available documentation, but the task grows more difficult because of the greater importance of noncommunicable diseases, which are typically more poorly identified than communicable diseases. Through 1962, official sources report deaths by cause in two categories, certified and uncertified, but afterward report only for certified causes. Most authorities deal with this problem by discussing only certified deaths, which, in 1950, made up 57 percent of the total. The large volume of deaths reported without certified causes means that there is much room for error in this way of proceeding, but there is also no choice. It is necessary also to report deaths from one cause as a proportion of all certified deaths rather than death rates.

Table 5.2 gives a crude idea about the changing importance of some diseases. Tuberculosis, malaria, and most other communicable diseases

---

[1] Death rates are available for most ages for 1970 but not for 1971. G. Edward Ebanks, *Infant and Child Mortality and Fertility: Trinidad and Tobago, Guyana, and Jamaica*, World Fertility Survey, No. 75 (Voorburg, 1985), p. 48, estimates infant mortality for males and females together in 1970 at 43 per 1,000. World Bank, *World Development Indicators 2002*, CD-ROM (Washington, 2003), gives an estimate of 47.8. Sex-specific estimates are available for ages 0–4, including those from United Nations, *Demographic Yearbook, Historical Supplement 1948–1997*, CD-ROM (Washington, 2000), but the estimates of infant mortality from this source are too low.

TABLE 5.1. *Age-specific death rates in 1949–51 and 1970*

	Females			Males		
	1949–51	1970	Percent change	1949–51	1970	Percent change
IMR*	73.7	n.a.		86.2	n.a.	
1–4	9.4	n.a.		10.9	n.a.	
5–9	2.3	0.6	−73.9	2.6	0.5	−80.8
10–14	2.2	0.4	−81.8	1.4	0.6	−57.1
15–19	3.9	0.8	−79.5	2.3	0.8	−65.2
20–24	4.4	0.9	−79.6	5.6	1.5	−73.2
25–34	5.0	1.6	−68.0	5.2	1.9	−63.5
35–44	7.6	3.4	−55.3	8.3	3.3	−60.2
45–54	11.4	6.5	−43.0	14.8	8.5	−42.6
55–64	19.2	14.0	−27.1	25.2	19.9	−21.0
65–74	38.9	34.6	−11.1	54.6	44.0	−19.4
75–84	83.6	71.6	−14.4	119.7	86.0	−28.2
85+	203.2	168.3	−17.2	252.6	210.0	−16.9

*Infant deaths in the year divided by births in the year.
n.a. = not available.
Sources: Kalman Tekse, *Population and Vital Statistics: Jamaica, 1832–1964: A Historical Perspective* (Kingston, 1974), pp. 34–36 for census data, from which population estimates for 1950 were derived by interpolation, and pp. 170–73 for births and pp. 258–67 for deaths in 1949–51; and United Nations, *Demographic Yearbook: Historical Supplement 1948–1997* (New York, 2000), pp. 804–807, for death rates at ages 5–9 through 85 and above for 1970.

diminished further in importance, although diarrheal diseases causing death mostly in children did not. Diseases associated with aging and organ deterioration – heart and circulatory diseases, diabetes, and neoplasms – came further to the fore, partly because by 1970 a larger proportion of deaths were certified and assigned to one of these causes, but mostly because people were dying at older ages and thus more people lived long enough to die from these causes. In 1950, 45.5 percent of deaths occurred at ages 45 and above, rising to 66.8 percent in 1970. Further reductions came in mortality in the category "fevers," to which many deaths probably due to malaria and tuberculosis were assigned (Figure 5.1). As a diagnosed cause of death, malaria did not lose importance until the early 1960s, when it was virtually eradicated. But the curve for fever mortality in Figure 5.1 suggests that the process of malaria (and tuberculosis) control was an achievement mostly of the 1930s and early 1940s.

TABLE 5.2. *Leading certified causes of death in 1950 and 1970*

	1950	1970
Diseases of the heart and circulatory system	13.7 percent of all deaths	34.9 percent of all deaths
Respiratory tuberculosis	8.5	0.4
Neoplasms	7.1	11.4
Pneumonia	6.7	6.5
Gastroenteritis (in 1970, enteritis and other diarrheal diseases)	5.0	6.8
Vascular lesions of the central nervous system*	5.0	Not listed
Accidents and violence	4.7	3.5
Malaria	4.5	0.008
Nephritis	4.0	0.9
Diabetes mellitus	1.5	4.3
Avitaminosis and other nutritional deficiency diseases	Not listed	4.1

* This category probably included deaths from syphilis.
Source: Jamaica, *Annual Report of the Registrar General's Department* (Kingston, 1951), pp. 48–53; and Jamaica, Statistical Institute of Jamaica, *Statistical Yearbook of Jamaica 1982* (Kingston, 1983), pp. 140–45.

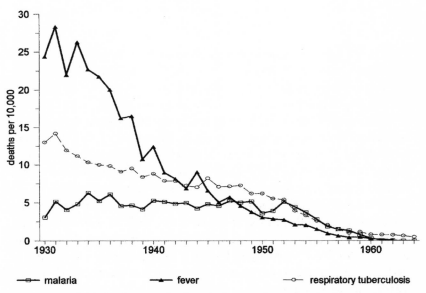

FIGURE 5.1. Malaria, fever, and tuberculosis mortality, 1930–64. *Source:* Jamaica, *Annual Report of the Registrar General's Department* (Kingston, various years).

TABLE 5.3. *Death rates in Jamaica and the United States in 1950*

	Jamaica	U.S. total	U.S. whites	U.S. nonwhites
0–1 per 1,000 births	80.0	33.0	29.9	53.7
1–4 per 1,000	10.2	1.4	1.2	2.5
5–14	2.0	0.6	0.6	0.9
15–24	3.4	1.3	1.1	2.5
25–34	5.1	1.8	1.5	4.4
35–44	7.9	3.6	3.1	8.1
45–54	13.1	8.5	7.7	17.1
55–64	22.0	19.1	18.0	33.7
65–74	49.6	40.7	40.2	46.0
75–84	98.3	93.3	94.2	80.4
85+	220.5	202.0	206.8	144.7

Source: Kalman Tekse, *Population and Vital Statistics: Jamaica, 1832–1964: A Historical Perspective* (Kingston, 1974), pp. 34–36, 258–59, and 264–65, interpolating between censuses to estimate the population at risk after infancy; and United States Department of Health, Education, and Welfare, *Vital Statistics of the United States 1950*, 3 vols. (Washington, 1954), I, 157–61.

In 1920–24, life expectancy at birth in Jamaica totaled 35.9 years against 58.2 in the United States, a gap of 22.3 years. By 1950 Jamaicans had an expectation of 54.6 years and Americans 68.4 years, so that the gap had been cut by a third. Table 5.3 shows age-specific death rates in the two countries in 1950, distinguishing rates for whites and all others in the United States. The Jamaican rates lagged the overall U.S. rates at all ages and rates for nonwhites in the United States at most ages except 35–64. By 1972 Jamaica had narrowed the gap in life expectancy to somewhere between 2 and 4 years and moved decisively ahead of non-whites in the United States.[2]

By 1950 Jamaica already possessed greater human resources, in the sense meant by Jere Behrman, than most other low-income countries of that day. It already had comparatively high life expectancy and its people already had more years of schooling. If human resources are an important precondition for economic growth, Jamaica was poised for growth.

---

[2] The World Bank estimates Jamaican life expectancy in 1972 at 69 years, which may, for reasons discussed earlier, be as much as two years too high; U.S. life expectancy that year was 71.2 years, and for nonwhites in the United States it was 64.7 years. World Bank, *World Development Indicators 2002*, CD-ROM (Washington, 2003).

POVERTY, POOR NUTRITION, AND UNEMPLOYMENT

The people who had made such rapid gains in survival in the preceding three decades remained, in 1950, a people living in poverty. Edith Clarke documented poverty as a side issue in the famous *My Mother Who Fathered Me*, a study of household and family structures in three villages based on fieldwork done in the 1940s.[3] Clarke found poverty to be associated with single-parent households, usually maternal, and with landlessness and tenancy rather than landownership. Most Jamaicans had enough to eat, but they ate mostly an unbalanced diet comprising starchy foods spiced with small quantities of salt fish.

Surveys of food availability made in the 1960s suggested a plentiful supply of calories, at about 2,600 per person per day, but found pockets of undernutrition or malnutrition that occurred most often in infants and children aged 12–35 months, in people whose diet was deficient in animal protein, and in population pockets where people lacked enough food. The school feeding program was expanded in the 1950s to 1,100 primary schools and infant centers.[4]

Infant malnutrition remained a common cause of or contributor to mortality into the 1970s amid general improvements in nutrition, as seen from comparative studies of height and weight of elementary school children and surveys showing better nourishment of young children between weaning and age 3.[5] A new program distributed free milk to children between ages 1 and 2 in an attempt to improve nutrition, especially after weaning. But children who particularly needed better nutrition were less likely to get this milk because of factors associated with the families and households: their mothers were poorer, they had less education, and they were less likely to attend maternal clinics.[6] Many households did not take advantage of the program. It was not

---

[3] Edith Clarke, *My Mother Who Fathered Me: A Study of the Family in Three Selected Communities in Jamaica* (London, 1966), pp. 25–26 and passim. See also Fernando Henriques, *Family and Colour in Jamaica*, 2nd ed. (London, 1968), for the situation around 1950.

[4] Jamaica, Ministry of Education, *Annual Report of the Ministry of Education 1958* (Kingston, 1961), p. 15.

[5] Jacques M. May and Donna L. McLellan, *The Ecology of Malnutrition in the Caribbean* (New York, 1973), esp. pp. 118–25; and Arthur H. Furnia, *Syncrisis: The Dynamics of Health: An Analytic Series on the Interactions of Health and Socioeconomic Development XX. Jamaica* (n.p., 1976).

[6] Herman I. McKenzie et al., "Child Mortality in Jamaica," *Milbank Memorial Fund Quarterly*, 45 (1967): 303–20, reporting results from a 1962–63 study.

enough to create institutions offering milk, day care for the infants of working mothers, and maternal/child health services. The need was to find better ways to draw people into those services, made difficult by the practical realities of working mothers and single-parent families.[7]

Using census data, Owen Jefferson estimates unemployment at 25.1 percent in 1943 and 13.5 percent in 1960, with the improvement being assisted by emigration to Britain and the United States, higher rates of attendance at secondary schools (which effectively raised the age of work entry to above 14 years), and the creation of many new jobs in manufacturing.[8] But unemployment rose after 1960 to 17 percent in 1969 and to 23 percent in 1972, so that Jamaica returned to its customary position of having about a quarter of the potential labor force out of work.[9] In Jamaica in 1970, as in 1950, poverty was marked by unemployment and underemployment, single-parent households, few household assets and thus nothing to fall back on in harder times, and, for some, also poor nutrition.

ECONOMIC GROWTH, THE STANDARD OF LIVING, AND SOCIAL PLANNING

Jamaica's economy began to expand in the early 1950s, motivated largely by new activities in bauxite mining, which met the growing world demand for aluminum after World War II, and by tourism.[10] Bauxite and exports of bauxite processed into alumina jumped from zero in 1950 to J$70.6 million in 1965, and tourist spending rose from J$6.6 million in 1950 to J$46.4 million in 1965 (current values). In the mid-1950s Jamaica adopted an overt model of industrial modernization, Industrialization by Invitation, a policy widely followed at the time by poor countries trying to attract foreign capital and to build a manufacturing sector, and one adopted in Jamaica on a model taken from Puerto Rico.[11] Both the Moyne Commission and the 1945 Economic Policy Committee had resisted the idea of stimulating

---

[7] Ann Ashworth and J. C. Waterlow, *Nutrition in Jamaica, 1969–70* (Kingston, 1970).

[8] Owen Jefferson, *The Post-war Economic Development of Jamaica* (Kingston, 1972), pp. 27–28.

[9] Derick A. C. Boyd, *Economic Management, Income Distribution, and Poverty in Jamaica* (New York, 1988), p. 9.

[10] Frank Fonda Taylor, *To Hell with Paradise: A History of the Jamaica Tourist Industry* (Pittsburgh, 1993), pp. 156–88, discusses the postwar growth of tourism.

[11] Intermediate-term plans for economic development were formulated in 1947, 1951, and 1957, and Jamaican authorities also consulted outsiders. International Bank for Reconstruction and Development, *The Economic Development of Jamaica*

manufacturing within Jamaica to produce goods already imported from Britain. The economist Arthur Lewis attacked that stance in a 1944 essay in which he identified the main economic problem as unemployment and the solution as government actions to replace imports with locally made goods.[12] The government response, formulated in the early 1950s, paired a timid effort at government sponsorship of local manufacturing with a more aggressive attempt to attract foreign capital, especially into manufacturing.

This was an important period in economic policy making because the decision in 1944 to move toward political independence implied also a decision to leave Jamaicans in charge of their own economic policy. Without any particularly vigorous debate, Jamaica opted for a free enterprise system. In a period when Britain was creating a mixed economy, Jamaica elected to maintain a capitalist system, at least in its economic policies, trying, with weak tools, to draw private enterprise in preferred directions.[13] Jefferson explains this orientation as the result of a basic weakness in Jamaica's position and the continuing control of policy from London. Lacking sufficient capital within the country to build manufacturing on its own, Jamaica could only appeal to foreign capital and accept its terms. Moreover, as the Moyne Commission had made clear, the United Kingdom did not wish to encourage Jamaica to manufacture the goods that it exported to the island.[14] Whereas the colony laid out a plan in the 1950s for political independence, the economic plans made led toward continuing dependence. The government spoke in favor of an economic policy of job creation, but it practiced policies that contributed little to that goal.[15]

The Industrialization by Invitation policy remained in place from about 1955 until the mid-1970s. By mid-1950s the PNP began to talk more openly about broader government intervention in the economy,

(Baltimore, 1952), gives the report of a World Bank team that visited the island in 1952.

[12] Jefferson, *Post-war Economic Development*, p. 6.

[13] This decision has prompted criticisms from economists looking back. In addition to Jefferson, *Post-war Economic Development*, see Shirley J. Smith, Industrial Growth, Economic Opportunities, and Migration within and from Jamaica, 1943 to 1970, unpublished Ph.D. dissertation, University of Pennsylvania, 1975, pp. 59–63 and passim; and Boyd, *Economic Management*.

[14] Jefferson, *Post-war Economic Development*, p. 9.

[15] "Westminster export philosophy was...profoundly suspicious of state involvement in economic ownership." Edwin Jones and Gladstone E. Mills, "The Institutional Framework of Government," in Rex Nettleford, ed., *Jamaica in Independence: Essays on the Early Years* (Kingston, 1989), pp. 105–30, quote from p. 107.

but when Norman Manley came to power in 1955 he maintained the laissez-faire model. The PNP did negotiate higher revenues from bauxite producers, and then invested the proceeds in public projects, health, and tourism. The Jamaican middle class, thinking largely in harmony with imperial authorities, preferred conservative economic policies and a gradual movement toward independence.[16]

The 1950s and 1960s were also a period of important changes in employment opportunities. People who got work in bauxite extraction and processing gained higher pay than was available in most other sectors, but manufacturing jobs, too, paid better than farming.[17] Thus the wage sector saw much sharper differentiation than had existed earlier, with bauxite workers at the top of the hierarchy. Agriculture contracted, but people who left farming generally moved into occupations with higher earnings.

Agriculture's contribution to gross domestic product declined from a historical level of about 40 percent to 31 percent in 1950, and to only 8 percent in 1980, and mining grew from nothing in 1950 to a peak of 13 percent in 1974. Manufacturing, construction, distribution, and finance all remained close to their 1950 proportions throughout the period 1950–75. Thus manufacturing (and these other sectors) expanded apace with the Jamaican economy; most of the new manufacturing facilities created in these years were capital- rather than labor-intensive, but they included plants where workers assembled final products from components manufactured elsewhere.

Table 5.4 and Figure 5.2 report Jamaica's per capita GDP in the period 1950–98 expressed in 1990 international or purchasing power parity (PPP) U.S. dollars and in 1995 U.S. dollars.[18] The PPP

[16] Trevor Munroe, *The Politics of Constitutional Decolonization: Jamaica, 1944–62* (Mona, 1972), pp. 106 and 113.

[17] Elsie Le Franc, "The Bauxite Labour Force in Jamaica: A High Wage Sector in a Dual Economy," *Social and Economic Studies*, 36 (1987): 217–68.

[18] See also Jefferson, *Post-war Economic Development*, who reports GDP at factor cost in constant 1956 J$, and World Bank, *World Development Indicators 2002*, CD-ROM (Washington, 2003), which reports GDP at basic prices in 1995 U.S.$ PPP. The factor cost approach, used in the British Commonwealth, treats subsidies and taxes on factors of production differently. Jefferson (pp. 40–41) cautions that his estimates, which presumably provide the basis for all others for the 1950s, omit production for home use, which in the 1950s averaged perhaps 8 percent of personal consumption and was declining.

    Jeanette Bethel, "Some National Income Aggregates for Jamaica: At Constant Prices," *Social and Economic Studies*, 10 (1961): 128–56, also provides GDP estimates.

TABLE 5.4. *Two estimates of GDP per capita, 1950–2000*

Year	GDP per capita (1990 U.S.$ PPP)	GDP per capita (1995 U.S.$)	Year	GDP per capita (1990 U.S.$ PPP)	GDP per capita (1995 U.S.$)
	Maddison	World Bank			
1950	1,327		1976	3,564	1,805
1951	1,412		1977	3,451	1,743
1952	1,504		1978	3,439	1,735
1953	1,691		1979	3,336	1,684
1954	1,858		1980	3,121	1,566
1955	2,020		1981	3,162	1,584
1956	2,190		1982	3,150	1,577
1957	2,468		1983	3,188	1,583
1958	2,458		1984	3,128	1,543
1959	2,541		1985	2,952	1,453
1960	2,654	1,387	1986	2,972	1,460
1961	2,702	1,404	1987	3,176	1,564
1962	2,722	1,399	1988	3,247	1,605
1963	2,757	1,420	1989	3,445	1,701
1964	2,904	1,504	1990	3,605	1,773
1965	3,070	1,600	1991	3,584	1,889
1966	3,129	1,632	1992	3,643	1,908
1967	3,178	1,634	1993	3,679	1,927
1968	3,284	1,699	1994	3,716	1,925
1969	3,480	1,756	1995	3,746	1,924
1970	3,849	1,936	1996	3,697	1,888
1971	3,803	1,968	1997	3,584	1,842
1972	3,858	2,256	1998	3,533	1,819
1973	4,130	2,092	1999		1,801
1974	3,908	1,986	2000		1,785
1975	3,845	1,953			

Sources: Angus Maddison, *The World Economy: A Millennial Perspective* (Paris, 2001), p. 290; World Bank, *World Development Indicators 2002*, CD-ROM (Washington, 2003).

adjustment tries to capture differences across countries in purchasing power. Per capita GDP increased from 1950 to peak in 1972 or 1973, giving the appearance of rapid gains in well-being across the population with the most rapid improvement coming in the 1950s amid rising fertility, declining mortality, and rapid population growth. Gains were not evenly distributed. Jamaicans in the upper 20 or 30 percent of the income distribution, not people in general, acquired substantially larger

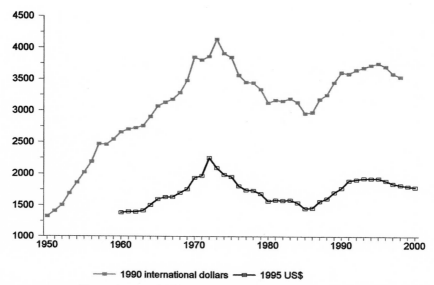

FIGURE 5.2. Two estimates of GDP per capita, 1950–2000. *Source:* Angus Maddison, *The World Economy: A Millennial Perspective* (Paris, 2001), p. 290; World Bank, *World Development Indicators 2002*, CD-ROM (Washington, 2003).

resources than they previously had.[19] Expressed in 1990 U.S. dollars adjusted for purchasing power parity, average per capita income rose from about $1,300 in 1950 to a plateau of roughly $3,000–3,500 in the mid-1970s.

By the late 1950s Jamaica was one of the richest poor countries in the world. But the gains in economic activity were concentrated in certain regions and limited to certain segments of the population, especially those linked closely to bauxite and tourism. The prosperous and modern elements of the economy stood side by side with a large impoverished group of people who most often earned their meager livings through working smallholdings and, increasingly, by casual labor in unskilled jobs in the towns.

Figure 5.3 shows government expenditures as a share of GDP in Jamaica and, for comparison, the United Kingdom and the United States. Around 1950, government spending totaled about 13.5 percent of GDP. It held on that level through 1957 and then began to increase, rising to 21.0 percent in 1972 (Figure 5.3), and then in 1975 jumped up suddenly to a proportion (above 35 percent) seen often in

[19] See below this chapter for discussion of income distribution.

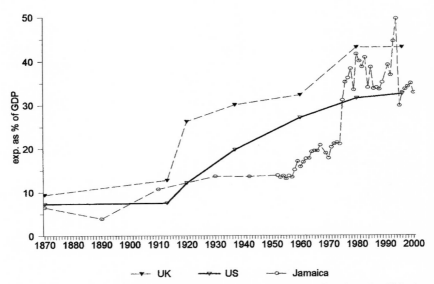

FIGURE 5.3. Government expenditures as a share of GDP in Jamaica, the United Kingdom, and the United States. *Source:* Gisela Eisner, *Jamaica 1830–1930: A Study in Economic Growth* (Manchester, 1961), pp. 118–23; Owen Jefferson, *The Postwar Economic Development of Jamaica* (Kingston, 1972), p. 251; World Bank, *World Development Indicators 2002*, CD-ROM (Washington, 2003); Jamaica, Planning Institute of Jamaica, *Economic and Social Survey Jamaica* (Kingston, various years); and, for the U.K. and U.S. estimates, Vito Tanzi and Ludger Schuknecht, *Public Spending in the 20th Century: A Global Perspective* (Cambridge, 2000), p. 6.

developed countries, especially social democracies, but rarely in poor countries. Once more the absence of gains in spending power by lower-income Jamaicans was compensated partly by rising levels of government spending on public services of broad benefit to ordinary people, especially education and health. Spending in these two areas rose from 19.5 percent of total government expenditures in 1950 to 28 percent in 1960 and then leveled off, closing the period in 1972 at 24 percent (Figure 4.1).

In the 1920s and 1930s a certain style of Jamaican social planning emerged in the mixture of practical activities led by Washburn's Bureau of Health Education; Jamaica Welfare and its successors; the public health, medical, and education establishments within the colonial government; the *Daily Gleaner*; school teachers and the teacher-training schools; and elsewhere. It was still an ad hoc style, although one marked by a particularly Jamaican combination, which paired higher public sector investments in health and education with more individual and personal responsibility for schooling, individual awareness of health hazards and their control, labor organization, and other things. In 1947 Jamaican authorities formulated the Ten Year Plan of Development, which, like its successors of 1957 and 1963, set economic and social goals. The social goals were usually explicit and specific, although the economic goals often were not. Thus the 1947 plan proposed to expand the educational system, provide better housing, improve health services, furnish safe water to more households, and broaden the welfare program. It also proposed to develop agriculture and to provide more jobs, reducing unemployment. The latter economic goals are explicit enough; the problem was a lack of concrete ideas about what would be done to achieve them. High unemployment persisted; farming remained less productive than other activities, and earnings for small farmers remained meager.[20]

The social goals proved to be more attainable. Per capita spending on government health services nearly quadrupled, rising from J$6 in 1946 to J$23 in 1970 in constant prices, while the number of physicians in government service rose from 130 to 307.[21] In the preceding period the colonial government had concentrated on building hospitals in underserved areas and enlarging the supply of beds. Hospital expansion continued in the 1950s and 1960s, but at a slower pace and commanding a smaller share of resources. Public health nurses, sanitary inspectors, and health visitors were trained in rising numbers at a school established in 1944, and expanded in 1957 as the West Indian School of Public Health.[22] In 1948 the initial class of 33 medical students began training at the medical school of the University College of the West Indies. The 1950s government also began building new clinics while staffing and outfitting them more extensively. In 1961 Jamaica had 73 health centers and 67 dispensaries.[23]

The Ten Year plans for social development formalized an orientation of public sector spending that had been adopted earlier. During 1950–70, health and education continued to receive a rising share of public resources.

---

[20] Jefferson, *Post-war Economic Development*, gives the most detailed picture of economic gains and problems in the period 1945–68.

[21] G. E. Cumper, "Jamaica: A Case Study in Health Development," *Social Science & Medicine*, 17 (1983): 1990.

[22] Affette McCaw-Binns and C. O. Moody, "The Development of Primary Health Care in Jamaica," *West Indian Medical Journal*, 50 (2001, suppl. 4): 8.

[23] *Handbook of Jamaica for 1961* (Kingston, 1961), p. 511.

THE DISTRIBUTION OF STATUS AND INCOME

The transfer of power from British to Jamaican hands between 1944 and 1962 coincided with the emergence of a new Jamaican middle class, one comprising not clerks and teachers claiming a marginal place in the lower ranks of the bourgeoisie but people working in the professions and the higher ranks of government service. Afro-Jamaicans came to hold more positions of influence and many more Jamaicans earned middle-class incomes. But it cannot be said that Jamaica moved very far or very aggressively toward a self-perception of an egalitarian society. Nancy Foner, who studied villagers in St. Ann parish in the late 1960s, found that most people living in that parish regarded themselves as poor, lower class, and rather powerless, attitudes she linked to the long period of colonial rule.[24] Foner also found that, in postindependence Jamaica, villagers in her study area tended not to cross social barriers. Children of parents with more years of schooling were themselves the most likely to attain equal or greater schooling, and parents with little or no education were likely to raise children without much education. Nevertheless, villagers displayed remarkable faith and enthusiasm for education, which they saw both as a way to break the status boundaries so strong during British rule and a means to gain social and economic advancement for their children.[25] Only one section of the area Foner studied, where about 3,500 people lived, had piped water; the first health clinic had been organized in 1962; and electricity was still unavailable to many residents. Thus signs of underdevelopment, compared to Kingston and to Jamaican towns, were manifest and visible. The lives of rural Jamaicans were changing more slowly than those of people living in cities or in mining districts.

In the two-tier labor force created by bauxite mining and alumina production and the development of trade unions, one group comprising perhaps 30 percent of the labor force earned higher wages and began to enjoy unprecedented prosperity in the 1950s, whereas the larger group benefited much less. Wage rates grew much more slowly in agriculture than in manufacturing and mining, or even in services.[26]

---

[24] Nancy Foner, *Status and Power in Rural Jamaica: A Study in Educational and Political Change* (New York, 1973).

[25] Ibid., esp. pp. 47, 51–52, and 59.

[26] Jefferson, *Post-war Economic Development*, p. 37.

E. Ahiram did the first formal investigation of income distribution in 1958, and his findings have remained the benchmark against which later distributions are compared. Drawing on expenditure and labor force surveys from 1957 and 1958, Ahiram placed Jamaica in the upper tier of countries in the skewness of its income distribution, just above Mexico.[27] Selecting the Gini coefficient as an index,[28] Ahiram rated the inequality of household income at 0.53 and of individual income at 0.57 on a scale of 0 to 1, compared to 0.35 in the United States in 1950 and 0.33 in Britain in 1951–52. (A higher score indicates a more uneven distribution; across time, nearly all countries have fallen within the limits 0.2 to 0.7.) Jamaican households ranking in the top 20 percent in income commanded 61.5 percent of income, and those in the bottom 20 percent only 2.2 percent. By the early 1970s the distribution was slightly more skew.[29] Rastafarianism gained followers in the 1950s and 1960s, especially among the poor of Kingston who could not find jobs.[30]

If about 30 percent of the population actually enjoyed rising incomes, then their incomes rose faster than the national average. This segment of the population could make many new spending decisions, including some with implications for health. But across the period of economic growth, most of the population could not. If the rising tide of incomes played a significant part in life expectancy gains in the 1950s and 1960s, then those gains, too, would have been bifurcated. The much more prosperous 30 percent should have gained more than the remaining 70 percent. But there is scant evidence of such a pattern. The parishes

---

[27] E. Ahiram, "Income Distribution in Jamaica, 1958," *Social and Economic Studies*, 13 (1964): 313–69. See also Jerry Cromwell, "The Size Distribution of Income: An International Comparison," *Review of Income and Wealth*, Series 23, No. 3 (1977): 291–308; and G. E. Cumper, "Incomes of Upper 2.5 per cent and 8.5 per cent of Income Tax Payers in Relation to National Income, Jamaica, 1951–65," *Social and Economic Studies*, 20 (1971): 362–68. G. E. Cumper, *The Economy of the West Indies* (Kingston, 1960), p. 18, suggests that the distribution was yet more skew at the 1943 census.

[28] The Gini coefficient provides a convenient gauge of income distribution by measuring the difference between a completely even distribution, in which each quintile of the population has an equivalent share of income, and the actual distribution.

[29] Boyd, *Economic Management*, 1988, p. 11; and Charles E. McLure, Jr., "The Incidence of Jamaican Taxes, 1971–72," *Social and Economic Studies*, 29 (1980): 101–33.

[30] M. G. Smith, Roy Augier, and Rex Nettleford, *The Ras Tafari Movement in Kingston, Jamaica* (Mona, 1960), pp. 15, 23, and 26.

differed from one another in median incomes, on which estimates were collected in the censuses of 1943 and 1960, but infant mortality did not vary with those income levels in these years.[31] Nor, as we have seen, did life expectancy rise in the hesitant way suggested by the existence of a small leading segment of the population and a trailing majority. Strong inequality in the distribution of income had not prevented gains in life expectancy between 1920 and 1950, and it did not prevent further gains up to 1972.

Wendell Bell's survey done around 1961 showed that Jamaicans, even members of the elite, shared a desire for greater equality in the distribution of incomes, within limits.[32] Michael Manley promoted the idea that every person "will start with an equal chance."

An egalitarian system must rest upon the possession by every man of the minimum means of self-support, the economic security without which family life is impossible, and an education system that puts all the children in one stream where they can compete equally for the benefits of the educational system.[33]

But, as was reported above, these sentiments were not acted upon before 1972. In fact Jamaica shifted from a largely unified system of schools around 1950 to a dual system with private schools for the better-off, with little movement between the public and private school systems.[34] Jamaica's income distribution remained skew, to the dismay of economists, among them especially George Beckford, who argued that the uneven distribution was a legacy of the old plantation system and a serious hindrance to economic development.[35] Michael Manley's government would address this issue, but that is a topic of Chapter 6.

There were, nevertheless, some areas of improvement in the lives of the 70 percent of Jamaicans who shared little or nothing of the gains

---

[31] Smith, Industrial Growth, 1975, p. 87, provides index numbers for median income, and Kalman Tekse, *Population and Vital Statistics: Jamaica, 1832–1964: A Historical Perspective* (Kingston, 1974), pp. 186–7 and 198–9, data for births and infant deaths. The association is positive for 1943 and negative for 1960, but not statistically significant for either year. Of course it would be preferable to have individual level data to examine this association.

[32] Wendell Bell, "Equality and Attitudes of Elites in Jamaica," *Social and Economic Studies*, 11 (1962): 409–32.

[33] Quoted by Foner, "Status and Power," p. 46, from the *Daily Gleaner*, June 5, 1969.

[34] Compare Fernando Henriques, *Family and Colour in Jamaica*, 2nd ed. (London, 1968), p. 64, describing schools around 1950, with Adam Kuper, *Changing Jamaica* (London, 1976), p. 71, reporting about 1972–73.

[35] George L. Beckford, *Persistent Poverty: Underdevelopment in Plantation Economies of the Third World* (London, 1973).

in income. Successive household expenditure surveys show that, in greater Kingston, the share of spending on food and housing dropped slightly between 1955 and 1963–64, creating an opportunity for more discretionary spending.[36] By the early 1960s nearly every household in Kingston had piped water, although only 40 percent of the rural population did.[37]

ADAPTING IN POVERTY

Higglering as a Stopgap. Weekly markets in Jamaica date from the era of slavery, slave entrepreneurs taking what they had grown on their provision lots to the market to sell. Individual-scale trading, called higglering, persisted into the twentieth century, its focus becoming the daily markets in towns and cities and stalls scattered here and there along roads and byways where entrepreneurs sold fruits and vegetables. In the 1950s women dominated, selling agricultural goods, inexpensive manufactured items, and cooked foods. Up to the 1970s higglering continued to center on fruit and vegetable sales, patronized by the growing number of city residents who had little or no opportunity to grow any food of their own. Such activities belong for the most part to the informal economy.

Households headed by women had long dominated family life in Jamaica, a characteristic associated with the strong, independent Jamaican woman. Although she lived in poverty and often had a male partner in the household but was unmarried, this woman raised her children and fed and clothed them with no more than occasional help from others, sent them off to school, and provided a model of competence in adversity.[38] Rather than being an avenue of upward mobility, higglering served as a way for a family – most often a family headed by a single parent, a mother – to earn a living or to supplement other sources of income. Le Franc reports that "folk legend and verandah

---

[36] Jamaica, Department of Statistics, *Expenditure Patterns of Working Class Households* (Kingston, 1967), p. 14.

[37] A. Curtis Wilgus, ed., *The Caribbean: Its Health Problems* (Gainesville, 1965), pp. 104–5.

[38] "Omniscient, resilient and resourceful" in the words of Maxine Henry-Wilson, "The Status of the Jamaican Woman, 1962 to the Present," in Rex Nettleford, ed., *Jamaica in Independence: Essays on the Early Years* (Kingston, 1989), pp. 229–53, quote from p. 231. Henry-Wilson examines this image in the context of female unemployment and access to social services. See also Benjamin Washburn's remark about public health work: "[T]he women were and still now are the leaders." RAC, RF, RG 13, Washburn interview, Sept. 15, 1970, p. 8.

chatter" tell of children "who owed their life's achievements to their strong higgler mothers."[39]

Cohabitation rather than marriage, which women often called the "sweetheart life," has remained the most typical form of male–female bonding. The children of such unions had significantly lower survival prospects in the 1960s, when the issue was investigated extensively, than the children of parents who were married, but it remains unclear whether their poor prospects arise more from poverty or from other elements of family life.[40]

Many commentators have praised Jamaican women for adapting to the circumstances of temporary conjugal unions, female-headed households, lower wages, and other difficulties. Errol Miller and Barry Chevannes point out, however, that the counterpart of female adaptation has often been male marginalization, or even a cultural preference for women.[41] As adults, in fact from adolescence on, males on average earn more, but they fare more poorly than females on many indices, the most important of them being education. Females outnumber males in the secondary schools, and by a huge margin in higher education. In the late 1990s, 76 percent of the enrollment at the Mona campus of the University of the West Indies was female, and the teacher-training colleges enrolled mostly women.[42]

---

[39] Elsie Le Franc, "Petty Trading and Labour Mobility: Higglers in the Kingston Metropolitan Area," in Keith Hart, ed., *Women and the Sexual Division of Labour in the Caribbean* (Kingston, 1989), p. 100.

[40] George W. Roberts and Dorian L. Powell, *Recent Population Movements in Jamaica* (Paris, 1974), pp. 107–12.

[41] Errol Miller, *Marginalization of the Black Male: Insights from the Development of the Teaching Profession* (2nd ed., Mona, 1994), attributes marginalization to a gender shift in which, between 1900 and 1930, females came to dominate Jamaica's primary schools and the teaching profession. Barry Chevannes, *Learning to Be a Man: Culture, Socialization and Gender Identity in Five Caribbean Communities* (Kingston, 2001), esp. pp. 49, 67, and 204, prefers a more immediate explanation in an expectation within Jamaican culture that boys should grow up early and as independent people. See also Carolyn Sargent and Michael Harris, "Bad Boys and Good Girls: The Implications of Gender Ideology for Child Health in Jamaica," in Nancy Scheper-Hughes and Carolyn Sargent, eds., *Small Wars: The Cultural Politics of Childhood* (Berkeley, 1998), pp. 202–27. Bob Marley's mother explained things in yet another way: "From an early age Jamaican girls are taught responsibility – to cook, clean and sew; the boys, on the other hand, are usually just loved and let loose to romp." Cedella Marley Booker and Anthony C. Winkler, *Bob Marley, My Son* (Lanham, MD, 1996), p. 49.

[42] On UWI enrollment see Heather Ricketts, Equity Issues as Highlighted by the Jamaican Survey of Living Conditions (JSLC) and Other Data Sources, unpublished paper, July 2000 (available at SALISES). Walter Nugent suggests that this may be

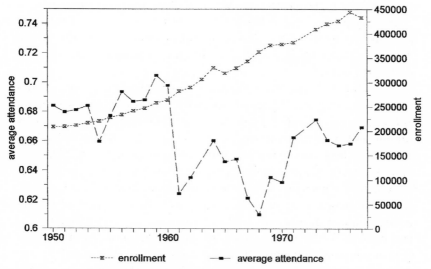

FIGURE 5.4. Primary school enrollments and attendance, 1950–77. *Source:* See Figure 4.1.

EDUCATION

Between 1943 and 1960, literacy levels improved for both males and females, even among people who had already passed the school-leaving age in 1943, who were reached through new programs in adult education. Throughout, the emphasis remained on elementary school instruction. By 1960, 73.7 percent of the 20–24 age group had completed at least four years of elementary school, but only 8.6 percent had completed secondary school, and 0.1 percent, university.[43] Enrollments rose sharply with population growth in the 1950s and 1960s (Figure 5.4), while attendance fluctuated between 60 and 70 percent.[44]

As had been true for a long time, expenditures on education had to rise sharply merely to maintain the existing level of opportunity. A

partly an effect of higher levels of male than female migration for work. Males and females comprised much the same share of population at ages through 10–14, but for 20–24 through 35–39 females have outnumbered males. See Tekse, *Population and Vital Statistics*, pp. 30–33, for the period 1881–1960.

[43] Tekse, *Population and Vital Statistics*, pp. 12, 81, 86–97, and 161. See also the more detailed information in Jamaica, Department of Statistics, *Census of Jamaica, 7th April 1960*, 2 vols. (Kingston, n.d.), Vol. II, Part 9, pp. 2–49 and 2–61.

[44] Sonja A. Sinclair and Barbara M. Boland, "Characteristics of the Population," in *Recent Population Movements in Jamaica* (Paris, 1974), p. 19, show that the 1970 census is not entirely reliable on educational attainment.

study by the sociologist C. A. Moser showed that the population of 7- to 14-year-olds had increased from the 1930s into the 1950s at a pace just about equal to school building; Jamaica began the period with 603 places for every 1,000 children of school age and ended it with 595 places.[45]

Errol Miller characterizes the period 1953–78 as an era of "expansion and development" marked especially by the creation of secondary and vocational schools.[46] In the 1950s the government opened a new training college with a one-year course, aimed at experienced but untrained teachers. And in the 1960s the government built new secondary schools as part of a program to extend schooling beyond the primary grades. The University of the West Indies, located in the Kingston suburb of Mona and opened in 1948, also absorbed part of the education budget. In the early 1950s, 72 percent of education spending had gone to the primary schools, which accounted for about 95 percent of school enrollments. By the late 1960s their spending share had dropped to half. In the meantime, primary school enrollments rose by about 150,000, passing 400,000 in 1973, and secondary school enrollments by about 20,000. In 1968 the primary schools officially provided spaces for 247,300 students, but 363,900 were enrolled.[47] Thus little money was available to build anything more than the least expensive structures, to provide equipment, to stock libraries, or otherwise to improve the schools. A 1972 estimate based on a survey done 10 years earlier suggested that about 400,000 people were functionally illiterate.[48] That is, in the early 1960s, about a quarter of the population of an age to have learned to read and write could not in practice do so.

Anthony Winkler, a Jamaican writer who had been teaching in the United States, returned in the mid-1970s to teach for a year at one of the teacher-training schools in its two-year program. At the end of the school year Winkler and his colleagues visited the primary schools where students finishing their training were practice-teaching.

---

[45] C. A. Moser, *The Measurement of Levels of Living with Special Reference to Jamaica* (London, 1957), p. 12. These are planned spaces and have little to do with actual attendance.

[46] Errol Miller, "Educational Development in Independent Jamaica," in Rex Nettleford, ed., *Jamaica in Independence: Essays on the Early Years* (Kingston, 1989), pp. 205–28, quote from p. 210.

[47] Jefferson, *Post-war Economic Development*, p. 273n51. Ibid., pp. 270–71, provides annual figures on education spending for 1952–53 to 1967–68.

[48] UNESCO, *Jamaica: National Literacy Programme: Project Findings and Recommendations* (Paris, 1976).

The first school I visited turned out to be indistinguishable from the second or the third or any of the other score of schools [visited]. . . . It was a cinder-block concrete building upended over the dead air of a gully, a sullen and grimy structure with a flat roof, louvreless windows, and no interior walls or partitions. It squatted low-slung and ugly in the middle of trampled and grassless grounds looking as if it had been flattened into the earth by a giant thump. Its outer walls were painted a dreary grey [sic] stained with splotches of mud and grime. Because the building had no interior walls, the classes within were separated merely by the arrangement of desks. . . . Within the single cavernous room seven or eight classes were so separated by the arrangement of desks and benches and by blackboards placed to serve as crude partitions.

It was not the repelling aesthetics, the overall grimy and airless ugliness of the concrete building or even the dimly lit and stiflingly cramped conditions that wore on your nerves and grated all livelong day at the teachers and students. It was simply that without walls to physically separate the different classes you could not hear yourself think.[49]

Winkler concluded that his year had been wasted because he had not known, or not remembered, what the schools were like. "You could not effectively teach pupils who couldn't hear you, and that was that." He had spent his time teaching writing and literature when the teachers-in-training needed to be learning about how to cope with the circumstances in which they would be teaching.[50]

In the period 1950–72 the development of secondary and university education and expanded teacher training added to the ranks of Jamaican physicians, dentists, professors, and teachers. More people learned to read and write, including adults who had missed out in their childhood, and more people stayed in school longer. Instruction in health and hygiene, and health propaganda aimed at the general population, was narrowed rather than broadened with health classes being offered to girls and a few boys under the heading of domestic science but no longer in separate class sessions and no longer with as much publicity or enthusiasm as had accompanied it in the 1920s and 1930s. According to the World Bank team that visited in 1952, teachers

---

[49] Anthony C. Winkler, *Going Home to Teach* (Kingston, 1995), pp. 242–43.

[50] Charles E. Asbury, the U.S. consul in Kingston, in "The Public School System of Jamaica," *United States Bureau of Education Bulletin*, 49 (1919): 35, reports similar conditions in the 1910s:

The first impression of a Jamaica school room is likely to be one of hopeless confusion. Each of the three divisions [lower, middle, and upper] may be reciting at the same time, to the teacher, the assistant, and a pupil-teacher. It is remarkable what good results are obtained, however, in some schools.

still told their students why and how to boil water to make it safe, but that was not enough to prevent water contamination.[51]

PUBLIC HEALTH, MEDICINE, AND HEALTH CARE

Activities of the Bureau of Health Education, now operating under the Ministry of Health, were revived in the latter 1940s and in nearly an identical form as had existed in the 1930s. During the 1950s and 1960s the bureau published its quarterly bulletin and, through it, promoted a series of health campaigns. Thirty-two squads with 149 sprayers, working under the parish public health inspectors, used DDT to reduce the mosquito population and complete the control of malaria as a cause of sickness and death. The bulletin alerted readers to the signs and symptoms of polio, discussed diabetes, fostered the idea of mental illness as a treatable condition, and promoted safe driving and limited alcohol use, all new topics. It also refreshed memories of older topics: infant and child care, food safety, tuberculosis and BCG vaccination, the public health nursing system, and the Anti-Tuberculosis League. In the malaria eradication program of the late 1950s, inspectors went from house to house to find cases for treatment and to identify areas needing spraying. The yaws campaign, under way more or less continuously since the early 1930s, was brought to a successful conclusion at the end of the 1950s when the two yaws units started using penicillin to treat cases and for the first time had a really effective therapy. The bureau still lent public health films from its library, dispatched health education lecturers on request, collaborated with school teachers in identifying children needing treatment for yaws, promoted latrine building and repair, and distributed booklets and pamphlets. It led a campaign to vaccinate children against smallpox; diphtheria, whooping cough, and tetanus; polio; typhoid fever; and tuberculosis. And in the 1960s the bureau helped promote family planning.[52]

The sulfonamides and penicillin, streptomycin, and other antibiotics revolutionized the treatment of many bacterial diseases and infections in Jamaica as elsewhere. Although toxic, sulfapyridine worked

[51] International Bank for Reconstruction and Development, *Economic Development of Jamaica* (Baltimore, 1952), pp. 263–64. On the content of the curriculum see Jamaica, Ministry of Education, *Annual Report of the Ministry of Education 1952* (Kingston, 1954), p. 15.

[52] *Jamaica Public Health*, Vols. 33–38, and the special issue of 1968–70 on family planning; and Jamaica, Ministry of Health, *Report of the Medical Services of Jamaica and Its Dependencies for 1955* (Kingston, n.d.).

effectively in many types of pneumonias, gonorrhea (for a few years, until resistant strains appeared), bacillary dysentery, and staphylococcal infections. Penicillin, the use of which began in the United States and Britain during World War II and in Jamaica after the war, also successfully treated some pneumonias, gonorrhea, and staphylococcal infections, as well as many diseases, including syphilis, scarlet fever, diphtheria, rheumatic fever, yaws, and erysipelas, usually without toxic side effects although some people could not tolerate the drug. Streptomycin, introduced at the end of the 1940s in Jamaica, worked against tuberculosis. Other antibiotics, and variants on the earliest ones, treated typhus, *E. coli* and salmonella infections, and a number of other diseases.[53]

Among diseases that appeared directly as causes of a substantial number of deaths or as contributory factors in Jamaica in the late 1940s and 1950s, the new drugs had their principal effect in controlling tuberculosis, which could be treated effectively by streptomycin but not cured, and syphilis. Each of the other diseases mentioned in the preceding paragraph figured less prominently in the Jamaican cause-of-death profile, but their collective disappearance mattered.

New immunizations were also introduced in the 1950s and 1960s, for the most part after the diseases in question had become infrequent causes of death in Jamaica. Neither the typhoid vaccine of the 1890s nor the influenza vaccine introduced during World War II proved effective, and the yellow fever vaccine, first made in 1936, appeared long after that disease had ceased to be a significant cause of death. Vaccines for polio, measles, and rubella, and the BCG vaccine, which is effective in preventing some forms of childhood tuberculosis, all contributed something to the retreat of mortality in Jamaica.

For antibiotics and the new immunizations alike, the principal issue was access. Jamaica already had an island-wide system of clinics and hospitals and thus the capacity to provide treatment and vaccines to most people.

Britain granted Jamaica independence in 1962, and the elections that year returned the more conservative Jamaica Labour Party to power, ousting the PNP. No significant changes occurred in public policy until the end of the 1960s, when public sector employment began to rise. In

[53] Joel Shapiro and Harry Diakoff, *Antibiotics in Historical Perspective*, David L. Cowen and Alvin B. Segelman, eds. (n.p., 1981), pp. 125–225, passim links specific medications to the diseases against which they were effective.

the meantime new hospitals were built and existing facilities expanded, with some 1,200 beds added. About four new primary health care centers were opened each year, and usage rose sharply (the number of visits to health centers doubled).[54] In the early 1960s there were 73 health centers and 67 dispensaries, the latter providing more elementary services than the health centers.[55] By 1972 the reporting health centers (82 of 97) and dispensaries (21 of 57) attended 674,277 patients and administered 519,965 vaccinations.[56]

Even though 1,200 beds were added to Jamaican hospitals, the supply of beds rose at a slower rate than the population. Pressed by the higher cost of hospital facilities, government spending favored primary health services, and the orientation of the public sector in health began to move toward primary care. The supply of registered doctors, including graduates from the new medical school at the University of the West Indies, which graduated its first class in 1954, rose faster than the population and at a more rapid pace than previously (Figure 4.2). In 1950 there were 4,028 people per doctor; by 1972 the number had declined to 1,632. The number of nurses and other medical personnel also increased at a faster pace than the population, although the number of dentists did not.

DDT, introduced to Jamaica in 1944, worked far better to control mosquitoes than did the larvicides in use before, and malaria mortality and morbidity diminished further with its use. Filtered and chlorinated water was supplied to more rural households in the 1950s and 1960s. Smallpox immunizations continued, and to them were added new government-sponsored programs to immunize against other childhood diseases. Fertility rose sharply in the period 1945–60, peaking at a level higher than any previously attained and giving rise to worries about excessively rapid population growth (Figure 5.5).[57] But then, in the years immediately after independence, Jamaica began a rapid fertility transition that continued to the century's end, a brief interruption in the early 1990s notwithstanding. New family planning programs, sponsored by the government and by foreign agencies, made fertility reduction easier to achieve. Meanwhile the proportion of deliveries in

54 Carol Gayle, "The Political Economy of Health Care in Jamaica: An Historical Analysis, 1962–1983," typescript, 1985, pp. 11–12.
55 Handbook of Jamaica for 1961 (Kingston, 1961), p. 511.
56 Jamaica, Department of Statistics, Statistical Abstract 1973 (Kingston, 1974).
57 Judith Blake, Family Structure in Jamaica: The Social Context of Reproduction (New York, 1961), p. 7 and passim.

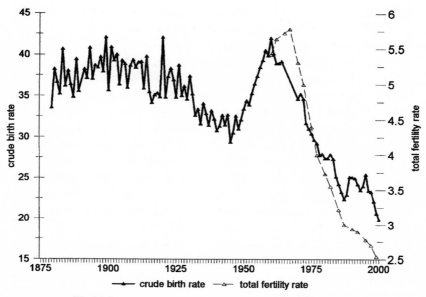

FIGURE 5.5. The birth rate, 1879–2000. *Sources:* For the crude birth rate, Kalman Tekse, *Population and Vital Statistics: Jamaica, 1832–1964: A Historical Perspective* (Kingston, 1974), pp. 176–81 for 1879–1964; and for the later period and total fertility rate, World Bank, *World Development Indicators 2002*, CD-ROM (Washington, 2003).

hospitals rose to about 60 percent,[58] and public policy warmed further to the idea that better prenatal care and the provision of opportunities for births in hospitals would redress some of the deficit faced by single mothers, whose infants and children died more often than did those of two-parent families. Maternal mortality declined sharply, falling from about 60 deaths per 10,000 live births in 1938 to about 21 in 1960.[59]

CONCLUSION

The leading characteristic of the period 1950–72 lies in a shifting emphasis, in which self-reliance and individual action toward disease control waned in importance while health institutions and public sector

[58] Cumper, "Jamaica: A Case Study in Health Development," p. 1991.
[59] Affete McCaw-Binns, "Jamaica, 1991–1995," pp. 123–130 in Marjorie A. Koblinsky, ed., *Reducing Maternal Mortality: Learning from Bolivia, China, Egypt, Honduras, Indonesia, Jamaica, and Zimbabwe* (Washington, 2003). McCaw-Binns reports further that maternal mortality decreased from about 21 in 1960 to 10.8 in the early 1980s, but then leveled off.

spending on health gained importance. Antibiotics and DDT were introduced in the latter part of an ongoing decline in mortality from bacterial diseases and malaria, so that they consolidated and sustained improvements already under way. Jamaica began to train its own physicians and more nurses and public health personnel, and the numbers of trained medical and public health workers rose toward the ratios found in rich countries. The hospital system struggled to keep up with population growth and, behind the scenes, government policy began to favor primary care, seen to be a more efficient way to provide health care. An attendance in a system of dispensaries and clinics cost much less than one at hospital, whatever the relative merits of the treatment. The education ministry struggled to keep up with sharply higher demand for classroom seats accompanying rising fertility while also building new high schools and opening the Mona campus of the University of the West Indies. Health education in the schools favored physiology over hygiene, which became a much less important part of the curriculum than it had been in preceding decades and something limited to domestic science classes.

Up to 1972 Jamaica provides a classic example of how misleading per capita income may be as an assessment of well-being within a population. Behind the appearance of economic growth lies the reality of an uneven distribution of income and wealth. Some 30 percent of the population enjoyed most of the economic gains of the period 1950–72, leaving most people nearly as poor in 1972 as their counterparts had been in 1950. In 1950–72, as in 1920–50, the inability of most of the population to spend more money on housing, medical care, schooling, and other things associated with better health was compensated for partly by higher levels of public sector provision, with the main difference that in 1950–72 there were so many more health workers. Things weighing against the further decline of mortality, such as the ongoing poverty of the many, high levels of unemployment in the formal economy, and single-parent households and higher mortality for children in such households, did not turn the tide of mortality reductions. Survival rose. The peculiarly Jamaican political economy that had appeared in the 1920s and 1930s in a mixture of wider-scale government action with self-help continued to mark programs, policies, and individual behavior associated with health and survival in the years 1950–72, even though self-reliance played a lesser part and public health institutions a growing part. The public health apparatus created in the 1920s and 1930s remained in place. It had singular success in eliminating indigenous cases of malaria and in maintaining protection against a broad array of communicable diseases.

In terms of human resources and their potential contribution to economic growth, Jamaica in 1950 seems to have been poised for growth. The relationship that Behrman found in most Latin American countries in the period 1965–90, in which higher levels of schooling and health care and better survival coincided with higher rates of economic growth despite marked inequality in income distribution, might explain some of Jamaica's prosperity in the period 1950–72, and it might also lead to the expectation of continuing growth.

6

AGAINST GROWING ODDS: 1972–2000

In 1972 Jamaica stood close to the top of countries in its region in gross domestic product per capita but by 2000 had fallen far back. In 1973 the country entered a protracted period of trying to adjust to economic shocks from the outside world and to decisions made elsewhere. The first shock came in the price of oil, which Jamaica uses not just to operate motor vehicles but also to generate most of its electricity. The main outside decisions came from the International Monetary Fund (IMF), the World Bank, and the Reagan administration in the United States, which instructed, jawboned, and wheedled the country toward economic and monetary policies it would not have adopted on its own, at least not at the times these policies were proposed.

Jamaica initiated two economic transformations in the 1970s, the first being a shift toward greater equality in the distribution of consumption than had previously existed and the second being a sharp rise in the scale of government activities. Although outside agencies pushed Jamaica toward free market policies, smaller government, and less indebtedness, Jamaica actually adopted a mixed set of policies that included higher government spending and a larger public sector. The effect was to create a mixed economy with some capitalist and some socialist features, something that grew out of the Jamaican political economy formed in the 1930s and 1940s that blended social democratic ideas for community development with capitalist ideas about economic development, and high public spending on health and education with stronger individual responsibility for taking advantage of the opportunity for schooling and of health and hygiene education. Government spending rose from about 15 percent of the gross domestic product in the 1960s to about 35 percent in the 1980s and early

1990s before falling back to about 30 percent in the late 1990s. The economy remained open, and people continued to move back and forth between the formal and informal sectors of the domestic economy and to migrate outside Jamaica to exploit job opportunities and then to return. A brief period in which some enterprises were nationalized was followed quickly by reprivatization. Outside agencies tried to push Jamaica back toward purer free-market policies and especially to reduce the scale of government activity. Domestic political and economic realities gave Jamaica's political leaders little option but to adopt social democratic policies with a larger public sector.

The economic stagnation that set in during the early 1970s and the move shortly thereafter toward enlarging the public sector alarmed the international agencies and foreign observers that wanted to preserve Jamaica as an open economy with a stable monetary system and keep it a safe place for investment. That reaction in turn aggravated concern among observers of Jamaica's political, economic, and social circumstances, who became more anxious about the country's well-being. The economic situation also threatened Jamaica's standing as a poor country with good health. Would mortality – especially that sensitive indicator, infant mortality – begin to rise in the economic downturn and in the face of the structural adjustment policies that the IMF and other agencies urged the government to adopt? Were Jamaica's pre-1973 gains in survival at risk? How would Jamaica fare in the face of sustained economic trauma?

The approach used to this point in this book, comparing age-specific mortality and causes of death at the beginning and end of periods, falters now because the information is of poorer quality (death rates) or simply unavailable (age-specific causes of death). Nevertheless, it is important to make what use can be made of the available statistics and estimates.

Death rates continued to decline in most age groups in the period 1970–2000, but at a slower pace (Table 6.1). Those more gradual changes are common to all countries that have achieved a life expectancy of about 70 years, as Jamaica had by 1977, and they should be attributed, at least in part, to the greater difficulty of reducing mortality at higher ages rather than to a faltering health infrastructure. For males aged 15–34 years mortality increased, chiefly because of higher numbers of violent deaths, and for females aged 20–34 years it diminished very little. But mortality declined at older ages, which is

TABLE 6.1. *Age-specific death rates, 1970 and 2000*

	Females			Males		
	1970	2000	Percent change	1970	2000	Percent change
IMR	n.a.	n.a.		n.a.	n.a.	
1–4	n.a.	0.7		n.a.	0.8	
5–9	0.6	0.3	−50.0	0.5	0.3	−40.0
10–14	0.4	0.2	−50.0	0.6	0.4	−40.0
15–19	0.8	0.3	−62.5	0.8	1.1	+37.5
20–24	0.9	0.7	−22.2	1.5	2.0	+33.3
25–34	1.6	1.4	−12.5	1.9	2.5	+31.6
35–44	3.4	2.3	−32.4	3.3	3.2	−3.0
45–54	6.5	4.7	−27.7	8.5	5.9	−30.6
55–64	14.0	10.8	−22.9	19.9	13.0	−34.7
65–74	34.6	22.6	−34.7	44.0	28.7	−34.8
75–84	71.6	51.8	−27.7	86.0	66.9	−22.2
85+	168.3	136.8	−18.7	210.0	146.8	−30.1

n.a. = not available

Sources: United Nations, *Demographic Yearbook: Historical Supplement 1948–1997* (New York, 2000), pp. 804–07, for death rates at ages 5–9 through 85 and above for 1970; A.D. Lopez et al., *World Mortality in 2000: Life Tables for 191 Countries* (Geneva, 2002), pp. 294–95, for estimated death rates at ages 1–4 and above.

noteworthy, and Jamaicans shared in the old-age segment of the health transition experienced by rich countries in the same period. For gains in life expectancy the period 1972–2000 is not as momentous a phase as 1920–50 or 1950–72. In this later period the main issues deal with how Jamaica managed to sustain and add to its already high level of life expectancy.

One assessment of changes in causes of death is provided by the Pan American Health Organization's summaries, which appear in Table 6.2. Communicable diseases continued to shrink in importance, so that more and more people lived to older ages and died of cardiovascular diseases, cancers, and diabetes. In the years 1979–82, the four leading causes of death were "cerebrovascular disease, heart disease, malignant neoplasms, and hypertensive disease," and diseases of the heart and circulatory system accounted for 35 percent of all deaths.[1] Clinics and hospitals continued to treat many cases of

[1] Jamaica, Ministry of Health, *Annual Report of the Chief Medical Officer 1984* (Kingston, 1986), quote from p. 21 concerning data from p. 25.

TABLE 6.2. *Deaths from certain causes as a share of all certified deaths, 1970–99*

Year	Deaths from communicable diseases	Deaths from neoplasms	Deaths from diseases of the circulatory system
1970	18.9	12.1	37.1
1984	9.8	17.6	41.4
1999	4.0	16.0	31.0

Source: PAHO, *Health Statistics from the Americas: Mortality since 1960* (Washington, 1991), pp. 247–49; PAHO, *Health in the Americas* (Washington, 2002), II, 366–67.

gastrointestinal disease and fever, but those patients seldom died.[2] Infant mortality declined across 1972–2000 even though it remained significantly higher than suggested by the registered births and registered infant deaths that contributed to official estimates.

Jamaica's shift in the early to mid-1970s into economic stagnation and then toward a larger public sector make a counterpoint to the transformation of the Soviet Union that began in 1989, which combined political realignment, a move toward a smaller public sector, and protracted economic stagnation or decline. Whereas death rates in Russia and other countries formerly part of the Soviet Union rose, most sharply among adult males, and life expectancy deteriorated, Jamaica escaped those effects. Jamaica's death rates continued to decline amid further progress in reducing infant mortality and controlling communicable diseases. Since so many observers expressed concerns about Jamaica's health indicators, the following questions arise: Did Jamaicans escape damage to their survival, or has that damage merely been deferred? Was the economic stagnation misleading, so that in fact Jamaicans were not really as much at risk as estimates of GDP per capita would suggest?

HARD TIMES

After two-and-a-half decades of rapid growth, the Jamaican economy faltered in 1973, just ahead of the international oil price shock. The oil crisis that began in early 1975 created a serious problem because of Jamaica's dependence on imported oil and the lack of alternative sources of energy. Then aluminum prices dropped in the 1980s and

[2] Ibid., p. 41.

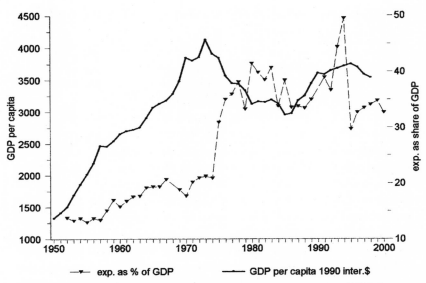

FIGURE 6.1. Per capita GDP overlaying government spending as a share of GDP. *Sources:* See Table 5.4 and Figure 5.3.

bauxite production dropped by half between 1983 and 1985, leaving Jamaica to depend more heavily on tourism as a source of hard currency and employment. From 1973 there followed 12 years of shrinking output, then a hopeful but brief recovery, a period of stability, and another contraction. Figure 6.1 shows the course of GDP per capita overlaying a curve showing government spending as a share of GDP. The years of economic growth and the popular unhappiness about the uneven distribution of income still evident in 1972 encouraged the government to expand its role in economic life; government spending as a share of domestic economic activity doubled between the mid-1960s and the early 1980s, moving upward sharply in 1975 as employment in the public sector grew.

That trend, and rising indebtedness to domestic and foreign lenders, worried outside observers. The U.S. government, the IMF, and the World Bank all pressed Jamaica to adopt supply-side policies and to reduce the scale of government activity. The sense of urgency felt at the IMF was compounded by the rhetoric of Michael Manley, who led the People's National Party into power in the 1972 elections and who in 1974, on the occasion of Julius Nyerere's visit, launched a campaign for democratic socialism. Manley's rhetoric and his policies, and the inspiration he drew from Cuba, alienated the business community inside Jamaica and alarmed many outside observers.[3]

But, as recent investigations have underscored, Manley's eight years in power, in which he did nationalize some businesses, were followed by a repudiation of some of his policies, including reprivatizations, but maintenance of the revolution he had engineered in the scale of government activity. Becoming prime minister in November 1980, Edward Seaga announced that his government would follow the IMF lead toward structural adjustment and a reorientation toward economic policies in place before Manley took power. Just as Manley had talked of democratic socialism more fiercely than he had implemented its policies, Seaga talked about free-market capitalism but in practice consolidated the higher scale of government activity that had emerged under Manley.[4] When Manley returned to power, in 1989, he kept most of Seaga's program in place.

In the 1950s economic planners contended with the reality of Jamaica's status as an exporting country and therefore necessarily as an open economy in which imports of manufactured goods made it difficult to build up domestic manufacturing. Infant industries in Jamaica could rarely compete with foreign rivals. In addition, much of the investment capital necessary for new initiatives had to come from the outside. Those problems remained in place in the 1970s, intensified somewhat by the rising importance of trade in global economic activity.[5] These were joined by new problems: higher levels of inflation in consumer prices; a bigger debt and higher spending on debt service; higher unemployment, which peaked in 1982 at 27.6 percent; growing dependence on foreign aid; and the deteriorating position of the Jamaican dollar.[6] In the 1950s the dollar traded at J$.71 to U.S.$1.00 and in 1980 on the free market still at J$2.50 to U.S.$1, but it fell

[3] Evelyne Huber Stephens and John D. Stephens, *Jamaica's Democratic Socialist Experience* (Washington, 1985); and EPICA Task Force, *Jamaica, Caribbean Challenge: A People's Primer* (Washington, 1979).

[4] Damien King, "The Evolution of Structural Adjustment and Stabilisation Policy in Jamaica," *Social and Economic Studies*, 50 (2001): 1–53.

[5] Imports and exports together rose from 72.4 percent of GDP in the 1960s to 114.0 percent in the 1990s. World Bank, *World Development Indicators 2002*, CD-ROM (Washington, 2003).

[6] Year-to-year changes in financial and economic indicators may be followed in International Monetary Fund, *International Financial Statistics Yearbook* (Washington, various years); and in World Bank, *World Development Indicators 2002*, CD-ROM (Washington, 2003).

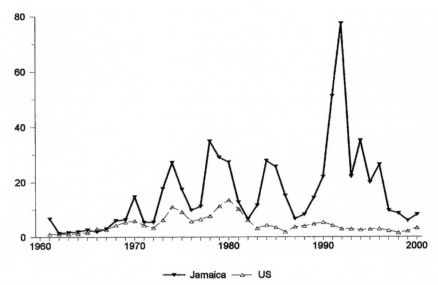

FIGURE 6.2. Annual change in consumer prices in Jamaica and the United States, 1961–2000. *Source:* World Bank, *World Development Indicators 2002*, CD-ROM (Washington, 2003).

thereafter to J$ 37.10 to U.S.$1.00 in 1998. Figure 6.2 plots the annual change in consumer prices in Jamaica in comparison to those in the United States. In a seemingly random pattern, some years brought extraordinary instability in prices, with price change peaking at 77.3 percent in 1992. The central government debt rose rapidly in the early 1980s, along with aid from outside sources, although both of those diminished in the 1990s.

Economic hard times aggravated the sense many Jamaicans had of being trapped in a situation beyond their control and of aspirations that could not be achieved, an outlook captured by Michael Manley in his 1987 book *Up the Down Escalator.*[7] There Manley argued, in agreement with dependency theory, that imperialism had created a world economy biased in favor of the imperial powers, which were also the industrial powers, leaving other world regions to play the role of producing raw materials and basic goods. More recently Kari Leavitt has iterated this view: "Jamaica is in the position of a drowning man, treading

[7] Michael Manley, *Up the Down Escalator: Development and the International Economy: A Jamaican Case Study* (Washington, 1987).

water to keep afloat, but slowly drifting offshore."[8] Carlene Edie denounces the political order for its dependence on external forces, and for "a party system based on clientelist patronage."[9] Trevor Munroe expresses discouragement about the absence of a meaningful democracy, the ongoing threat of anarchy, and growing corruption.[10] In everyday conversation Jamaicans arrive quickly to the point of expressing frustration about poverty, unemployment, violence, and corruption in the police force and among political leaders. The newspapers reinforce this frustration by reporting so many of such examples; the Jamaican press is free and well informed enough to contribute to the national mood of pessimism and frustration. And, indeed, it is true that there is too much poverty, unemployment, violence, and corruption.

Intellectual leaders and ordinary citizens often describe Jamaica's position as one of helplessness. The principal laments are the following:[11]

- Foreign interests, usually corporate, own too much of Jamaica's productive capacity.
- Jamaica is too dependent on foreign loans and aid, debt relief in 1991 notwithstanding.
- High levels of violence, especially that associated with criminal activity and the narcotics trade, which expanded rapidly in the 1970s,[12] deprive ordinary Jamaicans of a sense of security. The autonomy that rose during the decades-long run up to independence in 1962 and remained high from 1962 until the late 1970s or early 1980s waned in the face of this violence, giving way to a sense of powerlessness and a belief that the police and the political parties are tied to criminal activity and therefore will not take useful steps to suppress violence.

[8] Used as an epigraph by Marcel Bayer, *Jamaica: A Guide to the People, Politics and Culture* (New York, 1993), p. 31.
[9] Carlene J. Edie, *Democracy by Default: Dependency and Clientelism in Jamaica* (Boulder, 1991), p. 3.
[10] Trevor Munroe, *Renewing Democracy into the Millennium: The Jamaican Experience in Perspective* (Kingston, 1999), pp. ix, 8, 90–91, and 114.
[11] For elaboration of one or more of the points that follow see also Carl Stone, *Class, State, and Democracy in Jamaica* (New York, 1986); and Edie, *Democracy by Default*. S. Jacqueline Grant and Toby Shillito, "Island in a Turbulent World," in Deepa Narayan and Patti Petesch, eds., *Voices of the Poor from Many Lands* (New York, 2002), pp. 429–60, update these laments from experience in nine selected communities in the period 1999–2000.
[12] Adrian Boot, *Jamaica: Babylon on a Thin Wire* (London, 1976), captures elements of life on the edge in the 1970s in a photographic essay.

- Unemployment is too high.
- The poor are too numerous.
- Jamaica exports raw and partly processed materials, chiefly baux-ite, sugar (which revived in the early 1990s), and bananas, but im-ports oil, technical goods, manufactured goods, consumer goods, and expertise, making it a dependent economy.
- The population growth rate is too high (even though it has dropped sharply since the 1960s).
- Corruption is too widespread.
- The political parties operate by a patronage system rather than through a marketplace-of-ideas approach to selecting policies.

In the period 1973–2000, Jamaicans refined a pessimistic vision of life and came to expect things to get worse.

STRUCTURAL ADJUSTMENT

In the aftermath of the oil crisis, the IMF pushed Jamaica toward struc-tural adjustment and economic liberalization, as it did also many other developing countries. In Jamaica, IMF pressure in favor of such poli-cies began to build in 1976, upon the reelection of Michael Manley's government.[13] Manley devalued the Jamaican dollar, removed many price controls, restricted wage increases, and raised taxes. The IMF involved itself because Jamaica's balance of payments position was de-teriorating, the Fund demanding a change in policies in return for a loan that would provide support. By 1978 the IMF had become more deeply engaged in Jamaican policy, demanding sharp reductions in the gap between revenues and expenditures. Manley and his government felt threatened by IMF intervention because the Fund condemned its specific policies and its general philosophy. Whereas the IMF wanted to make Jamaica a healthier place for businesses to operate, Manley wanted to improve the material conditions of life for poorer people. The period 1950–72 had delivered strong economic growth and a good climate for business but little improvement in the living conditions of most people, and these circumstances led to Manley's election.

Many analysts find that IMF policies aggravated the hard times. An effective statement of the case against IMF policies is provided by a

---

[13] On structural adjustment and its effects, see also Robert E. Looney, *The Jamaican Economy in the 1980s: Economic Decline and Structural Adjustment* (Boulder, 1987).

collection of essays edited by Elsie Le Franc.[14] There the argument is made that the overall effect of those policies was substantial and negative: demand contracted, the public sector shrank, income distribution shifted away from the poor, and employment rose only in services and the informal economy. These authors argue that structural adjustment policies were actually implemented on a broad front. Many initiatives in education were undercut by the conditions imposed by the IMF: the student-to-teacher ratio rose, education's share of central government spending fell, and schools, in poor condition to begin with, received even less maintenance.[15]

In contrast Derick Boyd finds that economic hardship should be attributed not to the IMF and structural adjustment but to policy decisions made in the 1950s and 1960s, arguing that a key policy failure consisted of allowing Jamaica to remain dependent on imports. Moreover, Boyd argues, government policy allowed the distribution of income in Jamaica to become more concentrated in the elite even though the public sector became much larger between 1950 and 1970. Thus economic growth in that period did little for the poor, especially small farmers. Not until Seaga's "adjustment at a more human pace" in 1985 did the government attempt to cushion the effect of its policies on poorer Jamaicans. Thus Boyd describes the plight of the Jamaican poor as serious, real, and more attributable to failed government policies than to structural adjustment.[16] Boyd's view can be faulted for his failure to see the longer-term rise in government spending on health and education, which cushioned some aspects of life for poorer people, and in shortchanging the Manley government's social policies favoring the poor. The merit of his case lies in its restatement of the position Arthur

---

[14] Elsie Le Franc, ed., *Consequences of Structural Adjustment: A Review of the Jamaican Experience* (Kingston, 1994). See also Michael Witter and Patricia Anderson, The Distribution of the Social Cost of Jamaica's Structural Adjustment 1977–1989, unpublished paper, 1991 (at SALISES); the discussion of economic trends in Planning Institute of Jamaica, *Human Development Report 2000* (Kingston, 2000), pp. 9–13; and Edward Seaga's views when prime minister in Jamaica, *The Social Well-being Programme: A Programme for Social Development* (Kingston, 1988), pp. i–iii. George Stiglitz, *Globalization and Its Discontents* (New York, 2002), also attacks the IMF for the uniformity of its advice to countries struggling with different problems.

[15] Errol Miller, "Educational Development in Independent Jamaica," in Rex Nettleford, ed., *Jamaica in Independence: Essays on the Early Years* (Kingston, 1989), pp. 214–16.

[16] Derick A. C. Boyd, *Economic Management, Income Distribution, and Poverty in Jamaica* (New York, 1988), esp. pp. 83–92.

Lewis had taken in the 1940s, which insisted that Jamaica needed to build its own manufacturing capability.

Looking specifically at health care, George Cumper argues further that shortcomings in the Jamaican health system could better be attributed to defective planning and management than to structural adjustment policies. In the face of shrinking revenues, policymakers tried to go ahead with plans to expand the health care system, borrowing and seeking aid abroad to do so, which pushed the system into a financial crisis in the 1980s. Many physicians left the country, and demand for health services overwhelmed supply, so that health services were increasingly rationed by a longer waiting time. For Cumper the appropriate response would have been to privatize part of the system, or to recover some of its costs from people who could afford to pay, which would have avoided the need to close facilities and lay off staff.[17]

In yet a third interpretation, Damien King argues that Jamaica's reforms toward economic liberalization were halfhearted until the 1990s, which left the island behind Caribbean and Latin American neighbors that reformed earlier and more enthusiastically.[18] While successive governments professed to implement IMF policies, in fact they responded to the real effects of economic stagnation on the population and to popular demands for more effective policies to relieve poverty.

From all of these points of view, commentators have warned about stress on the health care system, hinting or arguing directly that deterioration in the quantity of health services provided by the public sector would lead to higher levels of infant mortality and lower life expectancy. Thus structural adjustment led scholars and analysts in Jamaica and in Latin America to pay closer attention to health statistics and to scrutinize official data because they feared that health conditions would begin to deteriorate.[19]

[17] George E. Cumper, "Should We Plan for Contraction in Health Services? The Jamaican Experience," *Health Policy and Planning*, 8 (1993): 113–21.

[18] King, "The Evolution of Structural Adjustment and Stabilisation Policy." See also Evelyne Huber and John D. Stephens, "Changing Development Models in Small Economies: The Case of Jamaica from the 1950s to the 1990s," *Studies in Comparative International Development*, 27 (1992): 57–92.

[19] In addition to the sources already cited, see Felix Abdala, Rosa N. Geldstein, and Sonia M. Mychaszula, "Economic Restructuring and Mortality Changes in Argentina: Is There any Connection?," in Giovanni Andrea Cornia and Renato Paniccià, eds., *The Mortality Crisis in Transitional Economies* (Oxford, 2000), pp. 328–50; and M. C. Gulliford, "Health and Health Care in the English-speaking Caribbean: A British Public Health Physician's View of the Caribbean," *Journal of Public Health Medicine*, 16 (1994): 263–69.

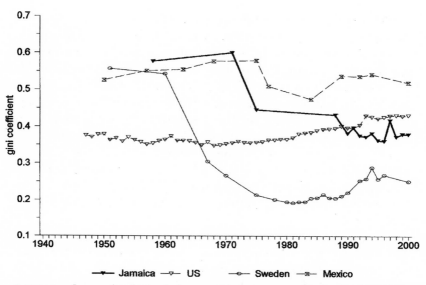

FIGURE 6.3. Income distribution in four countries, 1945–2000. *Sources:* For JAMAICA: E. Ahiram, "Income Distribution in Jamaica, 1958," *Social and Economic Studies,* 13 (1964), 313–69; Derick A.C. Boyd, *Economic Management, Income Distribution, and Poverty in Jamaica* (New York, 1988), p. 100; Jamaica, Planning Institute of Jamaica, *Jamaica Survey of Living Conditions* (Kingston, various years). MEXICO: Samuel Morley, *The Income Distribution Problem in Latin America and the Caribbean* (Santiago, 2001), p. 168; and UNDP, World Income Inequality Database, at www.undp.org/poverty/initiatives/wider/wiid.htm. UNITED STATES: U.S. Census Bureau, Historical Income Tables-Families, Table F-4, Gini Ratios for Families, by Race and Hispanic Origin of Householder: 1947 to 2001, at www.census.gov/hhes/income/histinc/f04.html. SWEDEN: Anthony B. Atkinson, Lee Rainwater, and Timothy M. Smeeding, *Income Distribution in OECD Countries: Evidence from the Luxembourg Income Study* (Paris, 1995), p. 74; and UNDP, World Income Inequality Database, at www.undp.org/poverty/initiatives/wider/wiid.htm. The coefficients for 2000 for Sweden and Mexico have been taken from UNDP, *Human Development Report 2001* (New York, 2001), pp. 182–84.

THE DISTRIBUTION OF INCOME AND CONSUMPTION

Jamaica entered the 1970s with income distribution skewed toward the elite, in a position quite common in Latin America but less so in other world regions. It ended the period with the most equitable distribution of consumption among larger countries in Latin America. Figure 6.3 shows trends in the distribution of income and consumption over time in Jamaica, Mexico, the United States, and Sweden.[20]

---

[20] On the distribution in Latin America, see Samuel A. Morley, *The Income Distribution Problem in Latin America and the Caribbean* (Santiago, 2001), p. 21 and passim. In

IMF policies undermined the government's moral authority because they obliged it to disfavor wage earners.[21] In the early stages of the economic slowdown in the 1970s, observers usually found that the distribution of income and consumption was becoming more skew. In the longer run, however, it emerged that Jamaica was moving toward considerably greater equality in at least the distribution of consumption. As Figure 6.3 shows, the Gini coefficient dropped below 0.45 by 1989, when the Survey of Living Conditions began to produce data, and by 1998–2000 to a position between 0.37 and 0.38.[22] At that level Jamaica resembled Australia and the United Kingdom and had a distribution slightly more equitable than the United States.[23] Thus during a period of economic reforms, "inequality declined while poverty rose."[24]

Economists and economic historians have often discussed the effects that a particular distribution of income and consumption may have on economic growth,[25] but less often how changes in the distribution across time may affect growth and social development. The principal gains from a distribution skewed toward an elite, as Jamaica's was in 1958 and also in 1972, would in theory come on the supply side in the form of higher savings and more capital available for investment. But Jamaica's skewed distribution had not provided enough savings for investment, so that successive prime ministers struggled with the problem of attracting outside capital to Jamaica to develop mining, tourism, and manufacturing. The chief gains from a more even distribution would come on the demand side in the form of higher levels

Figure 6.3 coefficients for the United States are for family income; for Jamaica for household income; for Mexico they are for family income for 1950–1975 and for household income per capita for 1977–1994; and for Sweden for household income.

[21] Norman Girvan, Richard Bernal, and Wesley Hughes, "The IMF and the Third World: The Case of Jamaica, 1974–80," *Development Dialogue*, 2 (1980): 113–55.

[22] Planning Institute of Jamaica, *Survey of Living Conditions 2000* (Kingston, 2001), p. 27. Those estimates differ from the figures provided by the World Income Inequality Database. It seems likely that a measurement of the distribution of wealth would find it considerably more skew. Likewise a comprehensive gauge of income, especially including income from all sources including those not reported to tax authorities, would probably find its distribution more skew.

[23] United Nations Development Programme, *Human Development Report 2001* (New York, 2001), pp. 183–85.

[24] Damien King and Sudhanshu Handa, "Changes in the Distribution of Income and the New Economic Model in Jamaica," *Social and Economic Studies*, 50 (2001): 159.

[25] See Peter H. Lindert and Jeffrey G. Williamson, "Growth, Equity, and History," *Explorations in Economic History*, 22 (1985): 341–77, for an introduction to the issues and the literature.

of personal spending on housing, consumer goods, education, health care, and other goods and services. Since such a large proportion of the populace was poor, redistribution would also reduce poverty and add to the size of the middle class. In the event that was the path followed.

Students of poverty in Jamaica, like their counterparts elsewhere, have been unable to set a threshold of poverty or to keep its definition constant over time. M. G. Smith's 1975 survey of 1,093 households depicts some of the leading characteristics. Poverty was (and has remained) more often rural than urban, the ghettoes of Kingston notwithstanding, and more often a condition of the young.[26] In their housing the poor often have not had electricity, piped water, toilets, baths, or kitchens. Average attendance at school has been lower among poor children, and their parents less often have known about government and private agencies providing assistance.[27] Derek Gordon's estimates for 1992–93, which use diet as a threshold, suggest that at that point about 38 percent of the population was poor.[28]

HOW DID PEOPLE COMPENSATE IN THIS ERA OF HARD TIMES?

The hard times of 1973 and thereafter are plainly evident in official statistics, whether reported by Jamaican authorities or the corrected estimates provided by the World Bank, the IMF, and other international agencies. But in Jamaica people do not necessarily live just in the world described by those statistics, and certainly not to the same degree as their counterparts in the Unite States or Western Europe. Two developments after 1973 offered people ways to compensate for the hard times. One of those arose from the combination of a more equitable distribution of income and consumption with higher levels of government spending on public services, and the other from activity

---

[26] Mariana Williams et al., Assessing Equity in Jamaica, unpublished report, 2000, prepared for the Canadian International Development Agency. See also Dennis Brown, Aldrie Henry-Lee, and Heather Ricketts, Poverty and Its Correlates: The Social Characteristics of Those below the Poverty Line, unpublished paper, 1996, prepared for the Planning Institute of Jamaica; and, for details on poverty in sugar-growing areas in the 1990s, Michelle Harrison, *King Sugar: Jamaica, the Caribbean and the World Sugar Economy* (New York, 2001).

[27] M. G. Smith, *Poverty in Jamaica* (Kingston, 1989), pp. 70–75, 109, and 140.

[28] Derek Gordon, Estimates of Poverty in Jamaica: For the Years 1992 and 1993, unpublished paper, 1995 (available at SALISES).

outside the formal sector of the economy and, to a lesser degree, remittances from Jamaicans living in the United States, Canada, and Britain. In the 1970s Jamaica developed a dual economy, with the formal sector providing comparatively well paid jobs for skilled workers and the parallel but not closely related informal economy providing a way to supplement income for people who could not make ends meet or for the jobless to earn a living. Higglering and many forms of legal and nearly legal entrepreneurship as well as illegal activities played a growing role in the economic opportunities of lower-income groups. People were pushed into petty trading and other coping strategies, including theft, prostitution, the ganja trade, and other illicit activities also by the restriction of price controls and food subsidies in the mid-1970s and by the long period of inflation. Ironically the informal and illicit segments of the economy featured aggressive capitalism.[29] Regulations and laws that pertained to licit and formal enterprises did not apply there.

The number of people engaged in petty trade increased in the 1970s and thereafter and became more structured. In the 1980s higglers still supplied urban residents with fresh produce, as they had long done, but less often with produce that the higglers had grown and more often with goods purchased in the countryside for resale. Men temporarily out of work took up unlicensed taxi driving if they had access to a car, so that a license plate indicating an authorized taxi might be driven by an unauthorized driver, and many people provided taxi services with no licensing. Women and some men set up stands here and there selling food and drink, tobacco products, electrical goods, and other items as higglering diversified. Most higglers dealt in locally produced goods, but some obtained used clothing from the United States and elsewhere for resale, even traveling by air to Miami to buy used clothing in bulk. Estimates of the scale of informal economic activity in all its forms are necessarily rough. Those available suggest that the informal sector may have totaled some 8 percent of the official gross domestic product in 1962. It reached perhaps 15 percent in 1975, 23 percent in 1985, and 39 percent in 1989.[30] On that scale it is apparent that the official estimates of domestic product, even those that attempt to include certain activities

[29] This point is made by Paul L. Buchanan, *Community Development in the 'Ranking' Economy* ([Kingston], [1986?]), pp. 59–61. "Ranking" refers to gunmen in the urban ghettoes.
[30] Michael Witter and Claremont Kirton, "The Informal Economy in Jamaica: Some Empirical Exercises," ISER Working Paper No. 36, 1990 (available at SALISES); and

in the informal sector, may seriously understate actual earnings. Understatement increased in the 1980s and 1990s. It is therefore possible that stagnation in the formal economy coexisted with an expanding informal economy that delivered more prosperity to Jamaicans, rather than the stagnation of GDPpc indicated in Figure 6.1.

Remittances, too, often escape detection. Ransford Palmer provides estimates for remittances from the United States alone in the period 1962–72, which capture a fraction of the total.[31] In earlier times Jamaicans emigrated chiefly for unskilled and low-wage jobs, which, nevertheless, paid more than what could be earned at home. By the 1960s, however, emigration had two modes, one composed of people who found work as domestic servants, laborers, and the like, and the other of people working in professional and technical jobs. The new class of emigrants could afford to send more money back home. By the 1990s the net amount of private transfers to Jamaica from the United States totaled at least the 9.1 percent of GDP reported by the Bank of Jamaica.[32] As another sign of the importance of people living abroad and their resources, Jamaicans changed part of their burial practices. Whereas formerly people were usually buried two days after their deaths, emigration led to the practice of waiting for 10 days or more to allow relatives living abroad time to get home.[33] For 1971–72, Palmer's estimates represent a mere 0.17 percent of the gross domestic product. Even though the actual total must have been much higher,

Claremont P. Kirton, Informal Economic Activities in Selected Caribbean Countries, unpublished paper, March 1991 (available at SALISES).

[31] Ransford W. Palmer, "A Decade of West Indian Migration to the United States, 1962–72: An Economic Analysis," *Social and Economic Studies*, 23 (1974): 571–84.

[32] Elizabeth Thomas-Hope, "Return Migration to Jamaica and Its Development Potential," *International Migration*, 37 (1999): 183–207. According to official statistics remittances rose from about U.S.$ 130 million in 1990 to nearly U.S.$ 600 million in the late 1990s. Actual remittances were probably higher. Elsie Le Franc and Andrew Downes, "Measuring Human Development in Countries with Invisible Economies: Challenges Posed by the Informal and Remittance Sectors in Jamaica," *Social and Economic Studies*, 50 (2001): 181 and 183–84; and Sudhanshu Handa and Damien King, "Structural Adjustment Policies, Income Distribution and Poverty: A Review of the Jamaican Experience," *World Development*, 25 (1997): 915–30. Le Franc and Downes argue that those remittances accounted for the reduction in poverty, since the informal economy, while still large, failed to grow during the 1990s and may have shrunk slightly. They also argue that both official and SLC data tend to overstate improvements in levels of consumption, and thus to understate poverty. See also Aldrie Henry-Lee, "The Dynamics of Poverty in Jamaica, 1989 to 1999," *Social and Economic Studies*, 50 (2001): 199–228, for another explanation of poverty reduction.

[33] Barry Chevannes, *Rastafari: Roots and Ideology* (Syracuse, NY, 1994), p. 25.

remittances would appear to represent a smaller supplement to income than transactions in the informal economy.

Le Franc's interviews with higglers in the Kingston Metropolitan Area in the mid-1980s led her to conclude that most petty traders used their profits for consumption. Asked about their reasons for higglering, many argued that this was a way "to ensure the education of their children."[34] Few people remained petty traders for very many years but used this form of entrepreneurship to provide an income during periods of joblessness in the formal economy.

Women, who have consistently earned less than men even when they have the same level of education and experience,[35] continued to dominate higglering. A. Lynn Bolles studied how Jamaican working women coped in the late 1970s, in the immediate aftermath of policy changes demanded by the IMF. The IMF program weakened food subsidies and controls, and behind this confusion merchants seized the opportunity to mark prices up, causing most of the 1978 price spike (Figure 6.2). Bolles found, as other scholars had earlier, that a high proportion of women carried the main financial responsibility for their households. Even though women in stable unions usually identified their domestic partners as the head of the household, "they also clearly identified themselves as the important decision maker in the home." Women deployed a set of coping strategies that enabled them to sustain their households through difficult times, such as periods without a male partner or without support from their partner, unemployment, or sudden increases in the price of food and other necessities. In addition to petty trading, they shared goods, services, cash, and credit across households.[36]

[34] Elsie Le Franc, "Petty Trading and Labour Mobility: Higglers in the Kingston Metropolitan Area," in Keith Hart, ed., *Women and the Sexual Division of Labour in the Caribbean* (Kingston, 1989), pp. 99–132, quote from p. 115. On coping strategies see also Aldrie Henry-Lee, Barry Chevannes, Mary Clarke, and Sybil Ricketts, *An Assessment of the Standard of Living and Coping Strategies of Workers in Selected Occupations Who Earn a Minimum Wage* (Kingston, 2001).

[35] Derek Gordon, "Women, Work and Social Mobility in Post-war Jamaica," in Keith Hart, ed., *Women and the Sexual Division of Labour in the Caribbean* (Kingston, 1989), pp. 67–80, comparing results for 1943 and 1984.

[36] A. Lynn Bolles, *Sister Jamaica: A Study of Women, Work and Households in Kingston* (Lanham, MD, 1996), pp. 61–95, quote from p. 71. Elisa Janine Sobo, *One Blood: The Jamaican Body* (Albany, NY, 1993), esp. pp. 29–50, discusses Jamaican perceptions of physiology, especially matters of physical comfort and social health, on the basis of field work she did in 1988–89. On food subsidies and the later food stamp program see Margaret E. Grosh, "Five Criteria for Choosing among Poverty

Thus, at the very least, people compensated for hard times. Greater evenness in the distribution of consumption meant that lower-income groups fared better compared to higher income groups and relative to conditions in the 1950s and 1960s. Rapid expansion in the informal sector along with its creative use by the jobless and the poor also favored poorer groups. These two developments help explain why both the proportion of the population living below the poverty line and malnutrition, assessed by height and weight for age among children, diminished during a period of stable or declining per capita income in the formal sector.[37] The share of the population living in poverty has been estimated annually since 1989 in the Survey of Living Conditions from data about household consumption, which probably capture informal sector activity and remittances. This proportion dropped from 30.9 percent of Jamaicans in 1989 to 16.9 percent in 1999.[38] Although most petty traders would be considered poor by the scale of their activities and earnings, petty trading allowed households, usually female-headed, to keep children in school, even into secondary schools, when that would have been otherwise impossible. This activity cushioned the effects of high levels of unemployment in the formal economy and low levels of wage labor force participation for women. Official statistics about unemployment, overstated in the first place by inclusion in the denominator of people not looking for work, are overstated also by failing to include petty traders in the numerator. That people have the option of petty trading, and that female household heads so often turn to it, may also help explain why gender is no longer an independent predictor of poverty.[39]

In sum, ordinary Jamaicans adapted to hard times. Official statistics understate mortality, especially infant mortality. But official statistics

Programs," in Nora Lustig, ed., *Coping with Austerity: Poverty and Inequality in Latin America* (Washington, 1995), pp. 146–86, for a comparison of Jamaican experience with other countries in the region.

[37] World Bank, *World Development Indicators 2002*, CD-ROM (Washington, 2003). But see also Wilma Bailey, "The Socioeconomic Context of Undernutrition in Jamaica," pp. 171–87 in Connie Weil and Joseph L. Scarpaci, eds., *Health and Health Care in Latin America During the Lost Decade: Insights for the 1990s* (Iowa City, 1992), for evidence of a spike in child undernutrition during the 1980s.

[38] See the analysis of data from the survey for 1990–1994 by Elizabeth Susan Emanuel, The Impact of Socio-economic Factors on Health Status in Jamaica, unpublished Master's thesis, UWI, Mona, 1997.

[39] Elsie Le Franc and Aldrie Henry-Lee, Poverty and Gender in the Caribbean, typescript, 1999, prepared for the Caribbean Development Bank, p. 24 (available at SALISES).

also overstate unemployment and understate the scale of economic activity, omitting, as they do, most earnings within the informal sector. Jamaica did not fare as badly in its economic transition from the good times of the 1950s and 1960s to the hard times after 1972, as did many countries formerly within the Soviet Union, because Jamaicans adapted quickly and imaginatively to the new circumstances and because the government adopted a rhetoric that appealed to the IMF but maintained or expanded its activities in health and education and its role as a leading employer.

PRIMARY HEALTH CARE

Driven more by cost than by a deliberate policy favoring primary health care, Jamaica in the 1960s began to move away from a hospital-based system and toward investing more in training medical providers, especially doctors, nurses, and health aides, building primary care facilities, providing a wider range of health care services to mothers and children, and initiating a community-level program of health education directed at pregnant women and new mothers.[40] By the mid-1970s, under Manley and the PNP, the government openly and deliberately placed less emphasis on hospitals, medical specialists, and even physicians, and more emphasis on health care workers with briefer training but in immediate touch with the people who, in the sense of the term used in poor countries, could provide "primary care."[41] In 1977 the core of Jamaica's health care system remained hospital care: 30 hospitals with something over 6,700 employees provided 7,547 beds, of which, on average, 82 percent were in use. The same year there were also 382 health centers, rural maternity centers, and clinics employing 2,072 people in all. The hospital sector more or less maintained its size, while a primary care sector grew. The number of physicians attending patients at publicly funded facilities remained much the same, for the time being, but more and more patients presented to community health aides, midwives, public health and regular staff nurses at the health centers, and nurse practitioners. By the first half of the 1980s, nurse practitioners, a profession created in the late 1970s, were attending nearly as many

[40] Estimates for numbers of nurses, assistant nurses, and other health care workers are given in Statistical Institute of Jamaica, *Statistical Yearbook of Jamaica* (Kingston, various years), e.g., for 1981 (Kingston, 1983), p. 473.

[41] Also Jamaica temporarily collaborated with Cuba. See Douglas Manley, *Cuban Doctors Aid Jamaica's Health Service* (n.p., 1977).

patients at health centers in the Kingston area as were physicians. Also in the 1970s, more houses were provided with treated water.[42]

In the long-standing hospital-based program, each parish had at least one hospital with facilities concentrated in population centers. But in the 1970s Jamaicans still lived mostly outside urban centers, often in widely dispersed villages. The new program's community health aides and nurse practitioners were meant to carry health care to the people and to engage the local community in recognizing their health needs. The Bureau of Health Education, in operation since 1926, was called on to promote the community health program and the formation of local health committees while continuing to inform the public and school children about health issues.[43] For a time, from the mid-1970s into the early 1980s, Jamaica had a thriving system of primary health care, vigorous efforts to improve maternal and child health services, and enthusiastic support from the parts of the population being served.

In the international arena, primary health care is associated with the World Health Organization's Alma Ata meeting in 1978, where delegates pledged to bring good health to everyone by the year 2000 by making basic health care available everywhere. The Jamaican delegation attended the 1978 meeting as a body of experts able to advise about primary health care from experience because of their country's long history of engagement in primary care and because of these more recent steps toward expanding the program.[44] The Jamaican plan was to see that every person should live within 10 miles walking distance of a clinic, toward which the Ministry of Health planned to build and staff 430 new health centers, which itself required much higher investments from international aid agencies. Most of those centers (365) were built, and most people obtained a clinic within 10 miles of their

---

[42] J. P. Figueroa, Annual Report: Public Health Department: Kingston and St. Andrew Corporation, unpublished, 1983 and following years (available at the Ministry of Health); and Planning Institute of Jamaica, Economic and Social Survey: Jamaica, 1977 (Kingston, n.d.), pp. 314–17 and 328.

[43] See Planning Institute of Jamaica, Economic and Social Survey: Jamaica, 1977 (Kingston, n.d.), pp. 317–23.

[44] Affette McCaw-Binns and C. O. Moody, "The Development of Primary Health Care in Jamaica," West Indian Medical Journal, 50, suppl. 4 (2001): 6–10; A. M. McCaw-Binns, C. O. Moody, and K. L. Standard, "Forty Years: An Introduction to the Development of a Caribbean Public Health," West Indian Medical Journal, 47, suppl. 4 (1998): 8–12; and Ronnie Linda Leavitt, Disability and Rehabilitation in Rural Jamaica: An Ethnographic Study (Rutherford, 1992), pp. 77–79.

residences. Five levels of clinics were to be built and staffed. Type I health centers, each to serve up to 4,000 people, were to have a midwife and two community health aides, a position created in 1967.[45] Trained in the classroom for eight weeks and then for an additional period in service, their chief task was to furnish maternal and child health care; to educate the public about health, nutrition, and family planning; and to immunize. Each aide would serve about 600 people, making home visits and targeting households with young children. By 1978 there were 1,326 community health aides at work. Their training manual covered many topics, none of them in much detail, leaving the trainees with a sense of the health problems they would face but little specific information about what to do or what to recommend to the people who approached them seeking help.[46]

Type II centers, serving up to 12,000 people, had in addition a public health nurse, a public health inspector, and a staff nurse, and were to be visited regularly by a pharmacist and a doctor or a nurse practitioner. Type III centers were to hold daily clinic hours with a resident doctor. Type IV centers, located in hospitals, could provide laboratory and diagnostic services, and type V centers served the major cities with comprehensive services. Since most of these diagnostic and treatment facilities were already available, primary health care in Jamaica was meant chiefly to provide more accessible treatment and to make preventive health care available to pregnant women, mothers, and young children, along with family planning services.[47]

---

[45] Kenneth L. Standard and Olive Ennever, "The Community Health Aide in the Commonwealth Caribbean with Special Reference to Jamaica," in Kenneth Standard and José R. Teruel, eds., *Four Decades of Advances in Health in the Commonwealth Caribbean* (Washington, 1979), pp. 102–12; and Thomas Joseph Marchione, Health and Nutrition in Self-Reliant National Development: An Evaluation of the Jamaican Community Health Aide Programme, unpublished Ph.D. dissertation, University of Connecticut, 1977, pp. 101–27.

[46] *Manual for Community Health Workers*, rev. ed. (Mona, 1983).

[47] On primary health care see also Dinesh O. Sinha, Ann O. Diloreto, and Isabel Rojas-Aleta, Primary Health Care in Jamaica, unpublished paper, 1981 (available at SALISES); John W. Peabody, Omar Rahman, Kristin Fox, and Paul Gertler, "Quality of Care in Public and Private Primary Health Care Facilities: Structural Comparisons in Jamaica," *Bulletin of the Pan American Health Organization*, 28 (1994): 122–41; and Brian Abel-Smith in World Health Organization, *Recurrent Costs in the Health Sector: Problems and Policy Options in Three Countries: Costa Rica, Jamaica, Mali* (Washington, 1989), p. 96.

For a critique of Jamaica's health care system in the 1980s, see George E. Cumper, *The Evaluation of National Health Systems* (Oxford, 1991). Peabody et al., "Quality of Care," assess the merits of public vs. private facilities.

These innovations came to Jamaica at a difficult moment. The government was compensating for the effects of economic decline by borrowing while also sharply expanding its level of activity. For a few years in the latter 1970s, loans and more aid from the outside permitted the construction and staffing of health centers, expanded hospital casualty services, and paid for more hospital beds, more doctors, and many more community health workers.[48] In 1984, for example, eight health centers were opened, four funded by the World Bank, three by UNICEF, and one by the Netherlands.[49] But especially from 1984 the health sector was constricted; recurrent costs were more difficult to meet and maintenance of facilities and equipment deteriorated.[50] By 1998 some primary care facilities had been closed and the number of health centers in operation had dropped to 318.[51] Still, 90 percent of the population lived within five miles of a clinic. During the 1980s and 1990s more nurses and doctors emigrated, and the government laid off many of the community health workers it had so recently engaged. Foreign aid continued to supply money for new initiatives, including programs to combat HIV transmission. Jamaica participated in the World Health Organization's Expanded Program on Immunization, vaccinating against the principal childhood infections and in the 1980s reaching most children.[52] But the problem of meeting recurrent costs remained.

The introduction in the 1980s of fees for the use of health facilities – by 2000 such fees contributed nearly 10 percent of the health budget – helped ease pressure. So did the growth of private sector health services. In 1980 most health spending, about 70 percent, came from the treasury. By the mid-1990s private health services had expanded to

[48] G. E. Cumper, "Jamaica: A Case Study in Health Development," *Social Science & Medicine*, 17 (1983): 1983–93.

[49] Jamaica, Ministry of Health, *Annual Report of the Chief Medical Officer 1984* (Kingston, 1986), p. 14.

[50] George E. Cumper, "Should We Plan for Contraction in Health Services? The Jamaican Experience," *Health Policy and Planning*, 8 (1993): 113–121; and World Health Organization, *Recurrent Costs in the Health Sector: Problems and Policy Options in Three Countries: Costa Rica, Jamaica, and Mali* (Washington, 1989).

[51] Statistical Institute of Jamaica, *Statistical Yearbook of Jamaica 1999* (Kingston, 2000), pp. 104–5.

[52] For information about health programs and facilities as of 2000, see Planning Institute of Jamaica, *Economic and Social Survey: Jamaica 2000* (Kingston, 2001), pp. 23.1–23.19; and on vaccination levels see Center for International Health Information, *Jamaica: Health Situation and Statistics Report, 1994* (Arlington, VA, 1994), pp. 4–5.

about 65 percent of all health spending.[53] But most Jamaicans could not afford private care. Only about a tenth of the population bought health insurance. Furthermore, the private sector delivered health services at appreciably higher cost and with favoritism. Patients complained that doctors, allowed to use public hospitals to treat private patients, gave some patients a favored position.[54]

Even though more people were using private facilities more often, attendance at publicly funded health centers averaged 1.8 million visits per year in the period 1996–2000.[55] The overall effect of a health program emphasizing primary care was not only to reduce the cost to the public sector associated with each attendance but also to provide care to people who had not previously been served or who had been underserved. At the entry level the theory was that a health worker with no more than brief training could provide valuable services. Questions were quickly raised about whether such providers might lead people to expect greater competence than community health workers possessed and whether the standard of care would be as high as promised.

It is difficult, in the nature of things, to assess the contribution of primary health care or community health workers to survival. Perhaps the quality of health services would diminish as nurses and nursing assistants attended a larger proportion of patients, and physicians a smaller portion. But of course the comparison would, in many cases, be between people previously unattended, or attended only in the later stages of an ailment, with people now attended albeit by someone with little training. In Jamaica the community health aides were meant mostly to detect problems and to advise about nutrition and childcare, thereby to fill roles that had not previously been performed. One evaluation, carried out by Thomas Marchione in 1973–75 in St. James

[53] PAHO, *Health in the Americas, 2002 Edition*, 2 vols. (Washington, 2002), Vol. I, p. 161, reports an even split in 2000: 2.7 percent of GDP in public sector spending on health, or U.S.$89 per capita, and 2.7 percent of GDP in private sector spending, or U.S.$89.60 per capita.

[54] J. P. Figueroa, "Health Trends in Jamaica: Significant Progress and a Vision for the 21st Century," *West Indian Medical Journal*, 50, suppl. 4 (2001): 15–22; Planning Institute of Jamaica, *Economic and Social Survey: Jamaica, 2000* (Kingston, 2001), pp. 23.1 to 23.19; and, on favoritism, Jill Armstrong, *Jamaica Health Sector Review: Present Status and Future Options* (Washington, 1994), p. 5, in a study commissioned by the World Bank.

[55] Jamaica, Ministry of Health, *Annual Report 2000* (Kingston, 2001), p. 23. Attendances at health centers peaked in 1984 at 2.4 million. See Armstrong, *Jamaica Health Sector Review*, p. 65.

parish, which includes Montego Bay, suggested that the community health aides knew the material they had been taught and that they visited an average of five households a day. But most effects were slight or indeterminate. Thus nutrition improved during the study period, but Marchione did not find that gains were greater in households visited by community health aides than in those that were not.[56]

More critical demands were put on other elements of Jamaica's health care system, but those, too, have proved to be difficult to analyze in ways that speak to changes in survival.[57] In a description of its response to structural adjustment policies, called the Social Well-being Programme, the government argued that the physical facilities of the health system had deteriorated during the 1980s and, without elaboration or evidence, that the "quality of health care administered" had also declined.[58]

In Jamaica, as nearly everywhere else, practical judgments about quality were left to be made by patients who typically entered the system at a level where they were attended by less extensively trained providers, and then graduated to practitioners with higher levels of training according to the attendants' judgments about a patient's needs and to the patient's own determination to demand further care. In a system where people in general seek medical advice for everyday health problems, survivorship is at risk in fewer patient-provider contacts than it is in a system where people lack inexpensive access to care and tend to wait to seek advice until they are convinced they have a serious problem.

In any case, the demographic measures most often used to assess population-level health – life expectancy, infant mortality, and maternal mortality – do not indicate deterioration in the quality of health

---

[56] Marchione, Health and Nutrition, pp. 220–84, summarized on pp. 284–88. See also Peter A. Berman, Davidson R. Gwatkin, and Susan E. Burger, "Community-based Health Workers: Head Start or False Start towards Health for All?" *Social Science & Medicine*, 25 (1987): 443–59, who reviewed programs in 1987.

[57] Victor Lavy, Michael Palumbo, and Steven N. Stern, *Health Care in Jamaica: Quality, Outcomes, and Labor Supply* (Washington, 1995), attempt to grade health care facilities as of 1989 by quality in order to assess whether the quality of health care could be associated with labor force participation. They find evidence of an association between some characteristics of health care facilities and health, especially in distinctions between private and public facilities but none with labor force participation. In 1989 private facilities served a small fraction of the population with superior equipment and more highly trained personnel.

[58] Jamaica, *The Social Well-Being Programme: A Programme for Social Development* (Kingston, 1988), p. 37.

services.[59] A 1995 report from the Ministry of Health identified malnutrition among children less than five years old and too many low
birth weight infants as unresolved issues, in addition to rising HIV infection.[60] Other observers added violence to the list, referring to the
rising homicide rate.[61] A team from Boston University visiting in 1994–
95, like earlier observers, warned of an impending crisis and urged
Jamaican health authorities to ration expensive treatments and the care
of chronic ailments among older people in order to maintain the ability to serve poorer groups.[62] But even the sternest critics of Jamaica's
health system, especially those who most sharply questioned reporting
of deaths, acknowledged that Jamaicans continued to the end of the
century to enjoy good health despite the country's ongoing economic
difficulties.

Perhaps the most unexpected development was the continuing decline in mortality at higher ages. Jamaica had built and modified its
health care system chiefly around the idea of providing widely available health services to people whose leading problems were infectious
diseases. That system could, and did, adjust in the 1960s and 1970s
by adding services for maternal and child health. In the meantime,
by the 1980s, Jamaica's disease profile had changed to include more
people dying at higher ages from chronic diseases. Those people, too,
could obtain care in the health clinics and hospitals, but little had
been done to provide early screening for diabetes, heart disease, and
cancer; to add diagnostic equipment; or to train health providers in
geriatric medicine. Jill Armstrong's 1994 report for the World Bank
warned of yet another impending crisis. This one would develop as

---

[59] Cumper, "Should We Plan for Contraction in Health Services?"; and Affette McCaw-
Binns et al., "Access to Care and Maternal Mortality in Jamaican Hospitals: 1993–
1995," *International Journal of Epidemiology*, 30 (2001): 796–801, comparing ratios
across the period 1981–1995.

[60] Jamaica, Ministry of Health, Report on the Major Problems in the Health Sector:
The Reforms Adopted and/or Could be Adopted, unpublished report, 1995, p. 5
(available at SALISES).

[61] E. R.-M. Le Franc, Health Situation Analysis: Jamaica, unpublished report to PAHO,
May 1996 (available at SALISES). See also Caroline Moser and Jeremy Holland,
Urban Poverty and Violence in Jamaica (Washington, 1997), who report from field
work.

[62] William J. Bicknell, Jamaican Health Sector Assessment: Policy Implications and
Recommendations, 1994; and Vaira Harik, Michael Trisolini, and William Bicknell,
The Jamaican Health Sector: A Chartbook, 1995, both being unpublished reports
produced for the Jamaican Ministry of Health. I obtained copies from the Center for
International Health, School of Public Health, Boston University.

the burden of chronic diseases grew, so that Jamaica would, with its limited resources, sooner or later face an inescapable choice. Would publicly funded health services be able to keep up the investment in primary health care while also meeting a rising demand for chronic care services? Armstrong supposed that economic growth would begin in the mid-1990s leading to higher government revenues and a greater ability for people to buy health services privately.[63]

Moreover Jamaica seemed, because of the characteristics of its population and widespread sexual behaviors, to be open to high rates of infection with HIV and to high AIDS mortality. Edward Green reported that the prevalence of HIV infection declined in the early 1990s, and he attributed this trend to a successful U.S.-funded but Jamaican-run program featuring surveillance of infections and modified behaviors in the population, including fewer sexual partners, wider condom use, and later onset of sexual activity. AIDS education in the schools complemented community-level AIDS awareness programs.[64] But a more recent survey shows that the number of AIDS cases reported and the incidence of HIV infection rose in the period 1995–2002.[65]

The crises that Armstrong anticipated and that HIV infection portended had not yet appeared by mid-2004. By 2000, people who could afford private care for chronic ailments obtained it, often in the United States, but most of the population could not. In the meantime shortages in the public sector drove more people into the private sector for their medications. Even so, despite the maintenance of a health system oriented chiefly toward acute and communicable diseases and the health problems of younger people and despite growing difficulties in acquiring medications, especially for poorer people, survival at higher ages continued to rise. And, faced with the threat posed by HIV infections, Jamaican health authorities followed a program similar to Uganda's, educating the public in leading risk factors, reintroducing health education into the schools and reviving a program of community-level health education aimed at adults. They may have slowed the spread of HIV/AIDS, but they did not manage to

---

[63] Armstrong, *Jamaica Health Sector Review*. Armstrong recommended that Jamaica change from having a full service publicly funded health system to one that concentrated on a smaller range of services.

[64] Edward C. Green, *Rethinking AIDS Prevention: Learning from the Successes in Developing Countries* (Westport, CT, 2003), pp. 253–61.

[65] Bilali Camara et al., *Status and Trends: Analysis of the Caribbean HIV/AIDS Epidemic, 1982–2002* (Port of Spain, 2004), pp. 109–15.

halt it. By 2000, AIDS was the leading cause of death among people aged 25–44.

CONCLUSION

Jamaica's hard times had not, as late as 2004, undermined progress in health indicators. Life expectancy rose; infant mortality declined; mortality at ages 65–84 fell; and levels of literacy and schooling improved, especially in secondary and university enrollments. Jamaican and outside observers expected health indices to show the same signs of strain apparent in the economic system, but they did not.

By the mid-1980s Jamaica had the health system of a richer country in its hospitals and medical school and the health system of a poor country with community health aides and health clinics. It also had one of the best-developed public health systems among poor countries in its training facilities for public health workers, public health nurses, sanitary inspectors, vaccination programs, and other facilities; but it still fell far short of rich countries in the provision of safe water to homes and the construction of waterborne sewage disposal systems. Examining descriptions of this system's institutional framework,[66] it is not difficult to imagine that such a system could control disease risks. What is important to notice, however, is that disease control showing up in rising life expectancy and declining infant mortality developed along with, usually ahead of, these institutional supports.

Since 1972 Jamaica has continued to rely heavily on health institutions funded by the public sector. The abiding strength of its health system in the 1970s and 1980s rested on democratic access to health care, counseling about infant and maternal health, and immunizations. The element of self-reliance, which had been so strong in the 1920–50 period, weakened as the government and the health system relied more on foreign aid and remittances from Jamaicans living abroad and less on domestic resources. Older people gained better access to health care providers in the 1970s, but they also had to put up with the rationing of health services, beginning their search for care with nursing assistants and moving on to care given by doctors and hospitals only by a combination of need and persistence. Older people have gained no more than selective access to such procedures as kidney dialysis, heart

---

[66] Each year, *Economic and Social Survey* summarizes the budget and Ministry of Health programs.

surgery, and magnetic resonance imaging, unless they can afford to buy these services outside Jamaica.

From the mid-1980s the publicly funded system began to lose some of its importance, and private health care to gain position. Even amid stagnation in the official economic indicators, poverty waned and the Jamaican middle class grew in the period 1985–2000. More people could afford private health care. By 2000 Jamaica had a dual health system, part of it publicly funded, which served chiefly lower income groups, and part of it private, which served the people who could afford it.

Now is the time to try to answer the questions posed at the beginning of this chapter. Did Jamaicans after about 1985 merely defer an inescapable health crisis, drawing down the health infrastructure, or was the crisis not as close as observers feared? Did the economy really stagnate so decisively across the period 1972–2000, or was there surreptitious growth in the informal sector that actually improved the standard of living of poorer groups? Certainly Jamaica drew down its health infrastructure, as doctors left the country and as facilities and equipment forewent maintenance and upgrading. But the system that remained, complemented by a growing private sector, was strong enough to provide adequate health care. In the 1980s observers worried that infant mortality might rise, but it did not. In the 1990s they worried that public spending for the treatment of chronic diseases in older age groups was deficient and that mortality at those ages might rise, but it did not. It may be, as of 2004, that the Jamaican health system stands on the brink of crisis. But it seems likelier that the system had more resilience than was suspected, that the combination of a shrinking public and a growing private sector has served the country adequately, and that infant mortality may continue to decline while life expectancy continues to rise. If that is true, the main explanation for it must lie in the skill with which people, especially the poor, have adapted to hard times, the growing informal sector, and the redistribution of consumption toward the poor.

7

CONCLUSION

Jamaica is and has been a low-income country where many people are poor. These disadvantages notwithstanding, Jamaica has attained a life expectancy nearly as high as that of the rich countries. By the end of the 1990s Jamaica had a cause-of-death profile like that of the rich countries with heart attacks, stroke, and cancer causing most deaths and most deaths occurring in old age.[1]

Jamaica and Jamaicans made rapid progress at reducing mortality in nearly all age groups from the 1920s onward. None of the three periods into which this study has divided the search for explanations – 1920–50, 1950–72, and 1972–2000 – would appear to hold special promise for a greater capacity to manage risks to survival. Many people were poor in each period; they and their successive governments had little to spend on medicine or public health. Antibiotics and immunizations gave an advantage in the years from 1949 or 1950 onward, but most of the diseases open to management or prevention by antibiotics and the new immunizations had already been brought under control. Foreign aid, in particular the sizable investments made in public health since about 1970 by agencies interested in promoting primary health care and in controlling the spread of HIV/AIDS, lent an advantage to the most recent period. But it was in the years 1920–50 that Jamaica made the most rapid progress in disease control, when the people were

---

[1] Compare causes of death in Jamaica and the United States from Statistical Institute of Jamaica, *Demographic Statistics 2000* (Kingston, 2001), pp. 61–62; and United States National Center for Health Statistics, "Deaths: Final Data for 1999," *National Vital Statistics Reports*, Vol. 49, No. 8, pp. 27–30, at www.cdc.gov/nchs/releases/01facts/99mortality.htm. On causes of death in Jamaica in the 1990s see also Jill Armstrong, *Jamaica Health Sector Review: Present Status and Future Options* (Washington, 1994).

the least well endowed in public or private resources to have done that.

The medical establishment that existed in 1920 was, compared to most regions of the world, well developed, in that there were hospitals and doctors trained in Europe, and the hospitals and doctors were dispersed around the country. But neither the inauguration nor the expansion of that system had been enough to begin a reduction in mortality. Mortality began to decline when certain public health activities were added to the medical program, activities emphasizing the education of people in how they could protect themselves from leading diseases. The foundational element in the Jamaican experience has three components: the prior development of education, especially the elementary schools; interventions from the outside, especially the importation of ideas about how to control the country's major killer diseases, captured in pithy advice in the writings of the educator McFarlane and the colonial civil servant Lucie-Smith, and in the public health program that Benjamin Washburn organized on behalf of the Rockefeller Foundation; and the things people learned to do for themselves in the first period of gains in survival. The schools and the schooling of Jamaicans, in which most people attended for three or four years but not longer and learned by rote memorization, enabled them to master new information about how to manage disease hazards, while ideas drawn from the filth and germ theory jumpstarted the process of managing those hazards.

British colonial authorities and planters regarded Afro-Jamaicans as a willful and disobedient people. It is tempting to dismiss that characterization as mere British racism. The evidence reviewed here, which depicts Jamaicans as a capable and self-reliant people, considers the same traits but portrays them in a favorable way. Two emphatic signs of these traits consisted, in the 1920s and 1930s, of popular mastery and application of lessons about health and disease prevention, which up to about 1950 led the decline in mortality from diarrheal diseases, malaria, and tuberculosis, and, since the 1970s, of the development of the legal and quasi-legal activities in the informal economy to earn livelihoods. The particularly Jamaican features of mortality control, the factors that lead in explaining the Jamaica paradox, emerged in the 1920s and 1930s from the alliance between self-reliant action by the people with effective leadership from public health authorities, including outsiders, in selecting useful and effective steps that people could take for themselves.

The personal qualities of Benjamin Washburn also mattered. Unlike some other Rockefeller agents, who could not bear to touch people of color or who let feelings of superiority to their patients hinder them, Washburn made Jamaicans his partners and played a key part in creating an Afro-Jamaican public health establishment. Unlike some other agents, who could not give up science for medicine, Washburn was willing to write and talk again and again about the same basic public health lessons. Washburn even catered to the willful, or self-reliant, nature of Jamaicans, inviting them to express their opinions, writing in Jamaican English, and, for the schools, composing plays and stories that made health lessons some of the most interesting things children were exposed to in school.

Only later, in the comparatively brief heyday of primary health care, from about 1970 to about 1990, can it be said that medical care reached the Jamaican people universally and democratically enough to make a major difference by itself. Thus Jamaican experience underscores the potential of an alliance between public health authorities and the people in which the authorities find ways to present ideas and suggestions about behavior in ways that appeal to the people, and the people are open to learning and implementing those ideas and suggestions.

There are still, early in the twenty-first century, many elements in the Jamaican situation that work against high life expectancy and good health. The population is still only 56 percent urban; thus nearly half of Jamaicans contend with the lower survival prospects, poorer access to hospitals and technocratic medicine, and more limited economic opportunities of rural areas. In 2000 Jamaica had 0.53 physicians per 1000 people, compared to 5.9 in the United States and 5.3 in Cuba, and 41 percent of the rural population lacked access to improved water, compared to 19 percent of the urban population. Most people in cities could use improved sanitary facilities, but 35 percent of the rural population did not have such things. Many people lived in poverty. Even though Jamaicans devoted 5.7 percent of GDP to health care in the 1990s, this proportion meant only U.S.$202 per person, against U.S.$3,950 spent per person in the United States. Toward the end of the 1990s unemployment totaled 16 percent, and 23 percent for women. A quarter of the potential urban labor force worked at least part time in the informal sector.[2]

---

[2] World Bank, *World Development Indicators: 2001* (Washington, 2001), passim; Pan American Health Organization, "Jamaica: Basic Country Health Profiles,

Will it last? Will Jamaica and Jamaicans be able to continue adding years of life expectancy and reducing infant mortality if the economic problems of the period since 1972 persist? Has the country drawn down its health capital – the number and quality of the people providing health services, the understanding that people have of health threats and how to avoid them, the educational system that furnishes people with the literacy necessary to become informed about health risks and health care options and, still to some degree, directly about health risks – to a dangerously low point? Is Jamaica in danger of entering the kind of reversal of fortune in life expectancy that occurred in Russia and some other states formerly part of the Soviet Union?

Not yet. It may be that the marginalization of males that worries Errol Miller and Barry Chevannes will be serious enough, or of the right kind, to threaten Jamaican males with the reversal in survivorship that confronted males in Russia in the 1980s and 1990s. That is one of the things that demographers should assess when they scrutinize Jamaican mortality data, along with the important issues of infant and maternal mortality. The Jamaican model of social development, which joins capitalism made seemingly inescapable by the need to export minerals and crops to high levels of government spending on health and education, remains at risk. But it has not yet shown evidence of deteriorating health indicators.

Jamaica's attainment of good health without high income shows some similarities to the experience of other countries where life expectancy is high but per capita income low. As in Costa Rica, Kerala, and Sri Lanka, females have operated with more autonomy in Jamaica than in many poor countries with low life expectancy; they have attended schools; and, in some ways, they have asserted themselves. But female autonomy in Jamaica is and has been, on closer examination, quite different from the case Caldwell made about female autonomy in Costa Rica, Kerala, and Sri Lanka. Jamaicans admire the strong independent woman who, exploiting her social capital, finds a way to raise, provide for, and educate her children despite the irregular presence in the household of a man sharing the costs and responsibilities of

Summaries 1999," at www.paho.org/English/SHA/prfljam.htm; and Sanjay Kathuria et al., *The Road to Sustained Growth in Jamaica* (Washington, 2004). See also the online version of the United States Central Intelligence Agency's World Factbook at www.odci.gov/cia/publications/factbook/geos/jm.html; and Transparency International, Corruption Perceptions Index 2002, at www.transparency.org/pressreleases_archive/2002/2002.08.28.cpi.en.html.

parenting. But strength and independence in working-class women in Jamaica has not been a statement about female autonomy so much as an adaptation to desperate conditions and subordinate status. It would not be accurate to claim that women have joined the Jamaican political or business leadership in large numbers. Girls get more schooling than boys and working-class women find ways to make ends meet, but there remains a point in the scheme of things at which men take charge.

In Jamaica, too, schooling developed early, and people began to describe themselves as literate and came to prize education. A closer examination of schooling in Jamaica shows that, until the 1950s or 1960s, few people completed more than four years; the schools were poorly served in buildings, equipment, and educational material; and many teachers struggled with their own inadequate training. In Jamaica it is not so much a case of students learning to read and becoming literate masters of their own destiny as it is of students being drilled in certain information, which, in the 1920s and 1930s especially, included basic lessons about disease avoidance. And there the expectation that children taught their parents things they had learned and been indoctrinated in at school coexists with the idea that parents with some schooling, or with more years of schooling, learned things that enabled them to protect their children better.

In Latin American and the Caribbean, Jamaica has become an outlier. For many countries in the region, larger investments in human resources coincided with, and perhaps sponsored, higher rates of economic growth in the period 1965–90, as Jere Behrman has argued. This appears to have been true for Jamaica somewhat earlier, during 1950–72, but not from 1972 to 2000.[3] In those years human resources were not a sufficient endowment for economic growth. Many Jamaicans, to whom local resources had provided secondary and higher education and professional training, found livelihoods and lived abroad, in contrast to earlier periods when most emigrants were unskilled workers. Emigration of the elite has responded to the difficulty of satisfying expectations and ambitions at home. But it has also deprived the nation of many of its most talented members and has undermined prospects for applying human resources to foster economic growth.

Certainly Jamaica shares with Costa Rica, Kerala, and Sri Lanka a history of lively and open public discussion of political and social

---

[3] Jere R. Behrman, *Human Resources in Latin America and the Caribbean* (Washington, 1996), pp. 23, 49, and passim.

issues, and popular engagement in the political process. But in Jamaica corruption in the political system and the rise of unlawful economic activity, especially in the narcotics trade, have undermined much of the effect of political openness. By the end of the twentieth century Jamaicans tended to be cynical not just about their political system but also about any prospects for an improvement in it.

The way that Jamaica most obviously differs from Caldwell's explanation for high life expectancy in Costa Rica, Kerala, and Sri Lanka lies, however, in the realm of social justice. To a significant degree, if covertly, and below the notice of the IMF and the World Bank, Jamaica moved in the 1970s, 1980s, and 1990s to a position in which consumption was more equitably distributed while the government spent aggressively on health and education and employed a much larger proportion of the population than had ever been true before. But Jamaica moved to that position after having long resisted it. Government spending on health and education had been rising since the 1920s from a low beginning level. Income distribution long remained uneven, to the point that into the 1970s Jamaica resembled Latin American countries more closely than it did the rest of the world.

The Jamaican way of elevating life expectancy rested on two pillars, individuals' capacity to fend for themselves and the government provision of schools, public health resources, and health care. In the early decades of the health transition, the 1920s and 1930s, individuals fending for themselves played the stronger part, but the leadership of public health authorities was important. In the 1950s and 1960s the balance shifted toward institutional health care and the public provision of health and medical resources. Not until the 1970s could it be said that public sector facilities in health and education had developed to a point of matching or surpassing what individuals did for themselves. A weak version of social justice figured as an ideal in a way that can be seen in articles about poverty in Kington published in the *Daily Gleaner* in the period 1896–1920, in the popular attitudes toward income distribution uncovered in the survey Wendell Bell did in the early 1960s, and in Michael Manley's experiment in social democracy. But a more equitable distribution of consumption developed only very late, in the 1980s and 1990s.

Six tactical areas – public health, medicine, economic development, nutrition, individual and household behavior, and literacy and education – encompass the policies and programs that different countries have followed in making persistent gains in life expectancy. Each country has had a distinctive history in the combination of programs and policies that it deployed, and Jamaica is no exception. There, economic development played only a small role in life expectancy gains; incomes rose slowly and belatedly even in the period of rising prosperity, from 1950 to 1972. Before and during the era of survival gains, up to the 1970s, nutrition remained sufficient in quantity but often poor in quality. The provision of neither doctors nor modern medicines and vaccines altered the course of mortality.

In Jamaica public health mattered more than medicine, and within public health what mattered most was the mass dissemination of useful information selected by a few public health authorities. Primary school teachers, trained to be health educators, and sanitary inspections, who visited households and identified problems, played an ancillary role. Householders built latrines. Individual and household behavior changed, not just in the construction and maintenance of latrines but also in the ways that people learned to recognize and protect themselves against specific diseases and disease vectors. Schooling counted more than literacy because indoctrination played a more important role in the way people mastered lessons about disease prevention than did the informed reading of printed material. Jamaicans developed a cooperative and collaborative attitude toward learning health lessons, and public health authorities found ways to work with people rather than trying to impose advice upon them. Thus in Jamaica, gains in life expectancy up to the 1970s were led by improvements in public health, individual behavior, and schooling.

Collectively this approach let Jamaicans improve survival chances within the limits of their meager resources. There was no possibility of following a rich-country path toward lower mortality. None of the pertinent actors, neither British colonial authorities nor parochial boards nor householders, could afford that route. Up to the 1970s each of the programs and policies that led survival gains is distinctive for its modest costs. In Jamaica health capital was built more from human effort than from new investments. The gains were nevertheless rapid and secure. In fact Jamaica made faster progress in reducing mortality in the period before such biomedical interventions as antibiotics and the new vaccines than had any of the high-income countries in the analogous periods of their own health transitions. Thus Jamaica's health transition was not a weak or second-best substitute in the programs and policies followed, but the robust demonstration of an alternative path.

Especially since the 1970s Jamaicans have often described their national position as one of hopelessness. They may not know enough about the remarkable features of achieving a life expectancy that matches, or nearly matches, the life expectancy of rich countries to be as pleased with that achievement as they might be.

Poor countries can look to the Jamaican system as something that can be created without first becoming rich, and rich countries can look to it as a model of "efficiency," which is the word George Cumper used to describe a system that attends the people at low cost but in ways that suffice to protect people from most risks to their survival.[4] The Jamaican case makes fewer demands, should any other country elect to try to replicate it, than do the cases of Costa Rica, Kerala, or Sri Lanka, for it does not require a reformation of basic values and attitudes. In Jamaica the schools taught about hygiene and health from the 1920s into the 1940s. In a short burst of intensive indoctrination, practice, and learning, Jamaicans mastered filth and germ theory and a set of useful lessons about how to protect themselves from the most dangerous diseases in their environment. It was apparently enough that one generation learned these things and incorporated them into the health lessons taught at home.

For people who think about and work on the problem of finding ways to elevate life expectancy where it is low, this book's chief lessons deal with the benefits of schooling, even if by indoctrination; providing people with pertinent information about the health risks they face; encouraging people to speak their minds; and finding ways for public health authorities to collaborate with the people.

---

[4] George E. Cumper, "Should We Plan for Contraction in Health Services? The Jamaican Experience," *Health Policy and Planning*, 8 (1993): 113–21.

APPENDIX I

_____

ESTIMATES OF LIFE EXPECTANCY,
1881–1964

Table A.1 gives annual estimates of life expectancy for Jamaica for the period 1881–1964. These values are correctly labeled as estimates. The number of people at risk in each age group has been drawn from the annual report of births and, for ages 1 and above, from straight-line interpolation for intervening years of numbers in age groups as reported in the censuses of 1881, 1891, 1911, 1921, 1943, 1960, and 1970.[1] The 1881 census did not report ages for 1.4 percent of the people tallied, and no attempt has been made to distribute these people by age. Later censuses were more complete in reporting age. Some deaths were recorded without ages, but those are few enough in number to be disregarded.[2]

Official statistics show that Jamaicans experienced heavy mortality at ages 1 and 2, making it desirable to treat these ages separately. (Combining the population at risk and deaths at ages 1–4 would produce higher life expectancy estimates.) Thus life tables have been estimated from these ages: infancy, 1, 2, 3, 4, 5–9, 10–14, 15–19, 20–24, and then for 10-year groups up to closure with 85 years and older. Under some circumstances it would be desirable to estimate the population at risk at lower ages, through 4, from reported births and deaths in previous years. But Jamaicans displayed a continuing preference for overstating

[1] For 1881–89, deaths are reported for a registration year ending September 30; for 1890–1915, one ending on March 31; and for 1916–60, one ending on December 31. (Thus the estimates for 1889 and 1890 overlap.) Estimates for population at risk keep the census date, in early April, as the midpoint except for 1890–1915, during which a further adjustment was made so that the death registration year matches the period for which the midpoint population has been estimated.

[2] For the method of life table construction see Chin Long Chiang, *The Life Table and Its Applications* (Malabar, FL, 1984).

Year	Females	Males	Both	Year	Females	Males	Both
1881	35.8	32.7	34.2	1923	39.1	36.8	38.0
1882	41.8	38.4	40.1	1924	39.4	37.7	38.6
1883	39.0	37.2	38.1	1925	39.9	37.8	38.9
1884	37.9	36.6	37.2	1926	41.9	39.5	40.7
1885	39.0	36.7	37.8	1927	40.7	38.0	39.4
1886	37.9	35.9	36.9	1928	42.5	40.6	41.6
1887	36.5	34.4	35.5	1929	44.1	41.8	43.0
1888	39.2	37.9	38.6	1930	46.4	44.1	45.3
1889	39.1	36.1	37.6	1931	43.9	41.1	42.7
1890	34.8	33.7	34.3	1932	45.5	42.8	44.2
1891	38.3	36.3	37.3	1933	43.1	40.2	41.6
1892	40.2	38.2	39.2	1934	46.2	42.7	44.4
1893	40.1	37.1	38.6	1935	45.9	42.4	44.0
1894	40.2	37.7	39.0	1936	45.6	43.2	44.4
1895	38.5	36.9	37.4	1937	48.7	45.6	47.2
1896	38.6	36.6	37.6	1938	46.9	44.9	45.9
1897	38.3	35.6	37.0	1939	49.9	47.1	48.5
1898	40.3	37.8	39.1	1940	48.7	46.5	47.6
1899	38.6	36.5	37.6	1941	51.0	47.4	49.4
1900	38.9	36.7	37.8	1942	51.5	48.2	49.8
1901	39.3	37.0	38.1	1943	52.0	48.7	50.3
1902	41.6	39.2	40.4	1944	50.6	47.7	49.1
1903	35.6	33.7	34.6	1945	51.1	47.1	49.1
1904	34.7	32.6	33.6	1946	52.7	50.1	51.4
1905	38.5	36.7	37.6	1947	52.0	48.9	50.4
1906	33.8	31.0	32.4	1948	53.0	50.4	51.7
1907	30.6	28.4	29.5	1949	55.7	52.0	53.9
1908	38.0	35.7	36.8	1950	56.4	52.8	54.6
1909	38.1	36.5	37.3	1951	55.8	52.9	54.4
1910	37.9	35.4	36.7	1952	57.1	53.6	55.4
1911	39.0	36.8	37.9	1953	59.0	56.2	57.7
1912	35.5	33.4	34.4	1954	59.1	55.3	57.2
1913	38.9	36.2	37.5	1955	60.6	57.3	58.9
1914	39.0	37.5	38.2	1956	62.2	58.6	60.4
1915	38.1	35.9	37.0	1957	63.4	59.6	61.5
1916	37.3	34.0	35.6	1958	62.6	59.4	61.1
1917	33.3	30.1	31.7	1959	61.3	57.8	59.6
1918	27.8	25.0	26.4	1960	64.5	60.2	62.4
1919	38.2	34.9	36.6	1961	64.9	60.7	62.7
1920	36.9	33.9	35.4	1962	64.9	61.2	63
1921	31.6	29.8	30.7	1963	64.2	60.5	62.3
1922	37.9	36.0	37.0	1964	66.6	62.8	64.7

Sources: Kalman Tekse, *Population and Vital Statistics: Jamaica, 1832–1964: A Historical Perspective* (Kingston, 1974), pp. 30–36, 168–72, and 256–67; Jamaica, *Annual Report of the Registrar General for 1945* (Kingston, 1946), pp. 27 and 32; and *Recent Population Movements in Jamaica* (Paris, 1974), p. 179.

the ages of young children, so that the censuses enumerate fewer children aged 1 year than they do for those aged 2, and fewer 2 than 3.[3] My assumption is that the same preferences governed parents in reporting the ages of children who had died.

Greater confidence in the quality of registration of births and deaths, especially in the early years, might strengthen the argument for trying to estimate the population at risk at ages less than 5 from births and from deaths at earlier ages. But information about the scale of underregistration across time is lacking, whereas the census counts are reported to be reliable. Interpolation gives satisfactory estimates, if only because errors that occur at one age less than 5 will (more or less) be corrected in the other ages if the sum of populations and deaths is accurate. This will not always be true, especially for years immediately following a surplus or deficit of births or for 1919, the year after the influenza epidemic.[4] However, sensitivity tests indicate that even in those years estimates of life expectancy across all age groups differ by less than 0.5 years, and usually less than 0.2 years, compared to the estimate that would be given from adjusting the population at risk to account for recent events.

After having adjusted census results, George W. Roberts and Jack Harewood reestimated population levels for Jamaica and other Caribbean countries between the 1943 and 1960 censuses.[5] Although they do not discuss methods or inferences in detail, it is apparent that they found two defects in the Jamaican census data. First, they concluded that births were understated, and adjusted the population at ages 0–1 and 1–2 (but not any higher ages) upward (for 1943 by nearly

[3] This preference is apparent in the census estimates. See also the April 1927 report of hookworm unit number 1 in RAC, RF, RG 5, Series 3, 437, Box 181, folder 2250. The medical director for this unit was called on April 24 to attend a seriously ill patient who had been treated for hookworm, one Daniel Record Williams said to be two years old. But the doctor reported that he was actually not quite one. (Williams was treated for broncho-pneumonia, but he died. Initially there was some concern that he had developed chenopodium poisoning from the hookworm treatment.)

[4] Influenza epidemics occurred in 1890–91 and the last months of 1918. Adopting Killingray's higher estimate of deaths from influenza would of course reduce life expectancy, but Killingray does not supply estimates of ages at death. David Killingray, "The Influenza Pandemic of 1918–1919 in the British Caribbean," *Social History of Medicine*, 7 (1994): 71 and 81.

[5] Census Research Programme, University of the West Indies, *Estimates of Intercensal Population by Age and Sex and Revised Vital Rates for British Caribbean Countries, 1946–1960* (n.p., 1964), pp. 14–15. See also George E. Cumper, *Preliminary Analysis of Population Growth and Social Characteristics in Jamaica, 1943–60* ([Mona], 1963).

TABLE A.2. *Official estimates of life expectancy at birth*

Period	Females	Males
1879–82	39.8	37.02
1889–92	38.3	36.74
1910–12	41.41	39.04
1920–22	38.2	35.89
1945–47	54.58	51.25
1950–52	58.89	55.73
1959–61	66.63	62.65

Source: Kalman Tekse, *Population and Vital Statistics: Jamaica, 1832–1964: A Historical Perspective* (Kingston, 1974), pp. 236–37.

21 percent at age 0–1 and 16 percent at 1–2). Second, they noticed a tendency to report too few people at ages 10–14 and too many at ages 15–19. Both shortcomings may characterize earlier censuses, and they may also show up in reports of deaths at ages 10–19. Although there was a temptation to use their estimates for the population at risk for the years between 1943 and 1960, it was resisted because there are no equivalent adjustments available for the ages of people dying. Using their estimates alone would therefore produce misleadingly low mortality, and high life expectancy, for those years.

In all likelihood, births and infant deaths have been underreported in Jamaica throughout the period of civil registration.[6] There is no particular reason to suppose that errors on one side cancel out those on the other. Until further research has been done on this issue, however, there are no bases on which to suggest corrections to the official statistics for births and deaths, and no corrections have been attempted here for the period up to 1960. From 1960 a second set of life expectancy estimates incorporates corrections made by the authorities who produce the *World Development Indicators* and who have reestimated Jamaican infant mortality to try to take underregistration into account.[7]

---

[6] A glance at the registered number of deaths by age, reproduced by Tekse, suggests that registration improved in the first years, from 1879 to 1881, which is usually the case.

[7] There are other sources, too, offering estimates of life expectancy in Jamaica for some years since 1960, but many of them, such as the CIA's World Factbook, rely on registered births and infant deaths. See also United Nations, *Demographic Yearbook:*

The 1881–1964 estimates provided here do not match the life tables constructed by colonial authorities (Table A.2), who used different age groups and evidently also a different way of calculating Lx and Tx values.

Historical Supplement, CD-ROM (Washington, 2000); United States Census Bureau, International Data Base, at blue.census.gov/cgi-bin/ipc/ibdsprd; and Planning Institute of Jamaica, *Jamaica Human Development Report 2000* (Kingston, 2000), p. 135.

OFFICIAL SOURCES FOR QUANTITATIVE INFORMATION TO 1964

Most of the data analyzed and reported here come from official sources. Typically in the colonial period, these data are available in two sets of annual publications, one being the *Annual General Report of Jamaica, together with the Departmental Reports* (AGR), and the department reports themselves, which were also published separately. (Nearly all items have variations in their titles over the years.) From 1946 the Colonial Office published the *Annual Report on Jamaica*, which gives a much-abridged version of what had appeared in the AGRs, but annual departmental reports continued for some years to be published in full.[1] Census reports were published separately and as part of the AGR.

The first series of official reports used here is *The Governor's Report on the Blue Book and Departmental Reports*, called simply the Blue Book. Private publishers drew heavily on official publications to make the *Handbook of Jamaica*, published occasionally, giving histories of the island, summaries of government activity, lists of people holding official or professional positions, revenues and expenditures, schools and enrollments, significant news of the period, and much more.

The following are the most extensively used departmental reports:

1. The registrar general recorded births, deaths, and marriages; certified deaths by cause; and compiled other population estimates for Jamaica and for the 14 parishes, and reported those annually from 1879 to 1964.

---

[1] This series had been issued from 1938 as the *Annual Report on the Social and Economic Progress of the People of Jamaica.*

2. The Education Department, later the Ministry of Education, compiled information about the schools, enrollments, attendance, teachers and their training; selected inspectors and published their reports; and supervised education.

3. The Island Medical Department, later the Ministry of Health, organized and reported about specific activities, such as vaccinations and hospital or clinic construction; published annual reports from the district medical officers and later from parish health departments; and described specific health campaigns, such as the hookworm campaign.

In addition, many units within the government issued annual or occasional reports. These include the principal hospitals, the Board of Health, and the main teacher-training colleges. Reported quantities sometimes differ or are unclear about the reference period, and in such cases I elected to rely on and use the department reports.

BIBLIOGRAPHY

ABBREVIATIONS

AGR   Jamaica, *The Annual General Report of Jamaica, together with the Departmental Reports*
BEW   Benjamin E. Washburn
EPICA   Ecumenical Program on Central America and the Caribbean
PAHO   Pan American Health Organization
RAC   Rockefeller Archive Center
RF   Rockefeller Foundation papers
RG   Record Group
SALISES   Sir Arthur Lewis Institute of Social and Economic Studies, UWI, Mona
UWI   University of the West Indies

MANUSCRIPTS

Jamaica Archives, Spanish Town
Water and Sewerage Board reports, Box 7.
Rockefeller Archive Center, Sleepy Hollow, New York, Rockefeller Foundation Archives
   RG 1, Series 100, Box 5
   RG 1.1, Series 437, Boxes 1–11
   RG 5, International Health Board/Division
     Series 1, 437, Boxes 263–264, 302
     Series 1.2, Boxes 12, 33, 50, 67, 83, 100, 121, 142, 169, 199, 230, 263–264, and 302
     Series 2, 437, Box 43
     Series 3, 437, Boxes 179–187
   RG 12, 437, Washburn diaries for 1934–1939
   RG 13 Oral History, Interviews with Benjamin E. Washburn, Sept. 15–17, 1970, by Mary Boccaccio
   Photograph Collection, Boxes 115–116
   Special Collections, Benjamin E. Washburn Papers, Boxes 1–9

INTERVIEWS

Peter Figueroa
Aldrie Henry-Lee
Affette McCaw-Binns
Michael Witter

PRINTED MATERIAL

Abdala, Felix, Rosa N. Geldstein, and Sonia M. Mychaszula. "Economic Restructuring and Mortality Changes in Argentina: Is There any Connection?" In Giovanni Andrea Cornia and Renato Paniccià, eds., *The Mortality Crisis in Transitional Economies* (Oxford, 2000), pp. 328–50.

Abdula, Norma, ed. *Trinidad and Tobago 1985: A Demographic Analysis.* n.p., n.d.

Agricultural Policy Committee of Jamaica. *Nutrition in Jamaica.* Kingston, 1945.

Ahiram, E. "Income Distribution in Jamaica, 1958," *Social and Economic Studies*, 13 (1964): 313–69.

Alexander, Jack. "The Culture of Race in Middle-Class Kingston, Jamaica." *American Ethnologist*, 4 (1977): 413–35.

Alter, George. "Infant and Child Mortality in the United States and Canada." In Alain Bideau, Bertrand Desjardins, and Hector Perez-Brignoli, eds., *Infant and Child Mortality in the Past* (Oxford, 1997), pp. 91–108.

Andersen, Otto. "The Decline in Danish Mortality before 1850 and Its Economic and Social Background." In Tommy Bengtsson, Gunnar Fridlizius, and Rolf Ohlsson, eds., *Pre-Industrial Population Change: The Mortality Decline and Short-Term Population Movements* (Stockholm, 1984), pp. 115–26.

Anderson, Beverley Joy. The Decline of Friendly Societies of Jamaica: A Traditional Voluntary Association in a Developing Society. Unpublished Ph.D. dissertation, Boston College, 1985.

André, Robert, and José Pereira-Roque. *La démographie de la Belgique au XIXe siècle.* Brussels, 1974.

Andreev, Kirill F. *Evolution of the Danish Population from 1835 to 2000.* Odense, 2002.

Annual Departmental Reports Relating to the Gold Coast and British Togoland (microfilm). Wakefield, 1979–1980.

Armstrong, Jill. *Jamaica Health Sector Review: Present Status and Future Options.* Washington, 1994.

Asbury, Charles E. "Public School System of Jamaica," *United States Bureau of Education Bulletin*, 49 (1919): 30–37.

Ashcroft, M. T. "Immunization against Typhoid Fever," *West Indian Medical Journal*, 12 (1963): 82–89.

Ashworth, Ann, and J. C. Waterlow. *Nutrition in Jamaica, 1969–70.* Kingston, 1970.

Atkinson, Anthony B., Lee Rainwater, and Timothy M. Smeeding. *Income Distribution in OECD Countries: Evidence from the Luxembourg Income Study.* Paris, 1995.

Austin, Diane J. *Urban Life in Kingston, Jamaica: The Culture and Class Ideology of Two Neighborhoods.* New York, 1984.

Austin-Broos, Diane J. *Jamaica Genesis: Religion and the Politics of Moral Orders.* Chicago, 1997.

Bacon, Edgar Mayhew. *The New Jamaica, Describing the Island.* New York, 1890.

Bailey, Wilma. "The Socioeconomic Context of Undernutrition in Jamaica." In Connie Weil and Joseph L. Scarpaci, eds., *Health and Health Care in Latin America During the Lost Decade: Insights for the 1990s* (Iowa City, 1992), pp. 171–87.

Balfour, Andrew, and Henry Harold Scott. *Health Problems of the Empire Past, Present and Future.* London, 1924.

Bayer, Marcel. *Jamaica: A Guide to the People, Politics and Culture.* New York, 1993.

Beckford, George L. *Persistent Poverty: Underdevelopment in Plantation Economies of the Third World.* London, 1973.

Beckford, George, and Michael Witter. *Small Garden...Bitter Weed: The Political Economy of Struggle and Change in Jamaica.* Morant Bay, Jamaica, 1982.

Beckles, Hilary, and Verene Shepherd, eds. *Caribbean Freedom: Society and Economy from Emancipation to the Present.* Kingston, 1993.

Beckwith, Martha Warren. *Black Roadways: A Study of Jamaican Folk Life.* Chapel Hill, 1929.

Behrman, Jere R. *Human Resources in Latin America and the Caribbean.* Washington, 1996.

Bell, Wendell. "Equality and Attitudes of Elites in Jamaica," *Social and Economic Studies,* 11 (1962): 409–32.

Benham, Frederic. "The National Income of Jamaica, 1942," *Development and Welfare in the West Indies,* Bulletin No. 5. Bridgetown, 1942.

Berman, Peter A., Davidson R. Gwatkin, and Susan E. Burger. "Community-based Health Workers: Head Start or False Start towards Health for All?" *Social Science & Medicine,* 25 (1987): 443–59.

Bethel, Jeanette. "Some National Income Aggregates for Jamaica: At Constant Prices," *Social and Economic Studies,* 10 (1961): 128–56.

Bhat, P. N. Mari. "Mortality and Fertility in India, 1881–1961: A Reassessment." In Tim Dyson, ed., *India's Historical Demography: Studies in Famine, Disease and Society* (London, 1989), pp. 73–118.

Bicknell, William J. Jamaican Health Sector Assessment: Policy Implications and Recommendations. Unpublished report, Center for International Health Information, Boston University, 1994.

Blake, Judith. *Family Structure in Jamaica: The Social Context of Reproduction.* New York, 1961.

Blayo, Yves. "La mortalité en France de 1740 à 1829," *Population,* Special Number, 30 (Nov. 1975): 123–42.

Blum, Alain. *Naître, vivre et mourir en URSS, 1917–1991*. Paris, 1994.

Bolland, O. Nigel. *The Politics of Labour in the British Caribbean: The Social Origins of Authoritarianism and Democracy in the Labour Movement.* Kingston, 2001.

Bolles, A. Lynn. *Sister Jamaica: A Study of Women, Work and Households in Kingston.* Lanham, MD, 1996.

Booker, Cedella Marley, and Anthony C. Winkler. *Bob Marley, My Son.* Lanham, MD, 1996.

Boot, Adrian. *Jamaica: Babylon on a Thin Wire.* London, 1976.

Bourbeau, Robert, and Jacques Légaré. *Evolution de la mortalité au Canada et au Québec, 1831–1931: Essai de mesure par génération.* Montreal, 1982.

Boyce, Robert W. *Health Progress and Administration in the West Indies.* London, 1910.

Boyd, Derick A. C. *Economic Management, Income Distribution, and Poverty in Jamaica.* New York, 1988.

Boyd, Mark F., and F. W. Aris. "A Malaria Survey of the Island of Jamaica," *American Journal of Tropical Medicine*, 9 (1929): 309–99.

Brand, Jeanne L. *Doctors and the State: The British Medical Profession and Government Action in Public Health, 1870–1912.* Baltimore, 1965.

Briercliffe, Rupert. *Development and Welfare in the West Indies 1941–42, Public Health, Jamaica.* n.p., 1941.

Brodber, Erna. The Second Generation of Freemen in Jamaica, 1907–1944. Unpublished Ph.D. dissertation, University of the West Indies, Mona, 1984.

Brodber, Erna "Socio-cultural Change in Jamaica." In Rex Nettleford, ed., *Jamaica in Independence: Essays on the Early Years* (Kingston, 1989), pp. 55–74.

Brothwell, Don R. "Yaws." In Kenneth F. Kiple, ed., *The Cambridge World History of Human Disease* (Cambridge, 1993), pp. 1096–1100.

Brown, Dennis, Aldrie Henry-Lee, and Heather Ricketts. Poverty and Its Correlates: The Social Characteristics of Those below the Poverty Line. Unpublished paper, 1996, prepared for the Planning Institute of Jamaica.

Bryan, Patrick. "The Black Middle Class in Nineteenth Century Jamaica." In Hilary Beckles and Verene Shepherd, eds., *Caribbean Freedom: Society and Economy from Emancipation to the Present* (Kingston, 1993), pp. 284–95.

Bryan, Patrick. *The Jamaican People 1880–1902: Race, Class and Social Control.* London, 1991.

Bryan, Patrick. *Philanthropy and Social Welfare in Jamaica: An Historical Survey.* Kingston, 1990.

Bryder, Linda. *Below the Magic Mountain: A Social History of Tuberculosis in Twentieth-Century Britain.* Oxford, 1988.

Buchanan, Paul L. *Community Development in the 'Ranking' Economy.* [Kingston], [1986].

Burnard, Trevor. "'The Countrie Continues Sicklie': White Mortality in Jamaica, 1655–1780," *Social History of Medicine*, 12 (1999): 45–72.

Caldwell, John. C. "Education as a Factor in Mortality Decline: An Examination of Nigerian Data," *Population Studies*, 33 (1979): 395–413.

Caldwell, John. C. "Population." In Wray Vamplew, ed., *Australians: Historical Statistics* (Cambridge, 1987), pp. 23–41.

Caldwell, John. C. "Routes to Low Mortality in Poor Countries," *Population and Development Review*, 12 (1986): 171–220.

Camara, Bilali, et al. *Status and Trends: Analysis of the Caribbean HIV/AIDS Epidemic, 1982–2002*. Port of Spain, 2004.

Campbell, Carl C. *Colony and Nation: A Short History of Education in Trinidad and Tobago, 1834–1986*. Kingston, 1992.

Campbell, E. A. Glen. *Public Health Administration in Jamaica with Some Modern Ideas for Improvement*. Kingston, 1925.

Carley, Mary Manning. *Education in Jamaica*. London, 1942.

Carley, Mary Manning. *Medical Services in Jamaica*. Kingston, 1943.

Carnegie, James. *Some Aspects of Jamaica's Politics: 1918–1938*. n.p., 1973.

Census Research Programme, University of the West Indies. *Estimates of Intercensal Population by Age and Sex and Revised Vital Rates for British Caribbean Countries, 1946–1960*. n.p., 1964.

Center for International Health Information, Boston University. *Jamaica: Health Situation and Statistics Report, 1994*. Arlington, VA, 1994.

Chandler, Asa C. *Hookworm Disease: Its Distribution, Biology, Epidemiology, Pathology, Diagnosis, Treatment and Control*. New York, 1929.

Chandler, Asa C., and Clark P. Read. *Introduction to Parasitology, with Special Reference to the Parasites of Man*. 10th ed. New York, 1961.

Chevannes, Barry. *Learning to Be a Man: Culture, Socialization and Gender Identity in Five Caribbean Communities*. Kingston, 2001.

Chevannes, Barry. *Rastafari: Roots and Ideology*. Syracuse, NY, 1994.

Chiang, Chin Long. *The Life Table and Its Applications*. Malabar, Florida, 1984.

Chomsky, Aviva. *West Indian Workers and the United Fruit Company in Costa Rica, 1870–1940*. Baton Rouge, 1996.

Clarke, Colin G. *Kingston, Jamaica: Urban Development and Social Change, 1692–1962*. Berkeley, 1975.

Clarke, Edith. *My Mother Who Fathered Me: A Study of the Family in Three Selected Communities in Jamaica*. London, 1966.

Cleland, John G., and Jerome K. van Ginneken. "Maternal Education and Child Survival in Developing Countries: The Search for Pathways of Influence." In John C. Caldwell and Gigi Santow, eds., *Selected Readings in the Cultural, Social, and Behavioural Determinants of Health* (Canberra, 1991), pp. 79–100.

Clyde, David F. *History of the Medical Services of Tanganyika*. Dar es Salaam, 1962.

Coleman, Walter Moore. *The People's Health: A Textbook of Sanitation and Hygiene for the Use of Schools*. New York, 1914.

Conniff, Michael L. *Black Labor on a White Canal: Panama, 1904–1981*. Pittsburgh, 1985.

Conway, Dennis. "The Importance of Migration for Caribbean Development," *Global Development Studies*, 2 (1999 – 2000): 73–105.

Cory, R. A. S. "Changing Trends in the Treatment of Pulmonary Tuberculosis in Jamaica," *West Indian Medical Journal*, 4 (1955): 5–8.

Craton, Michael. "Jamaican Slave Mortality: Fresh Light from Worthy Park, Longville and the Tharp Estates," *Journal of Caribbean History*, 3 (1971): 1–27.

Craton, Michael. *Searching for the Invisible Man: Slaves and Plantation Life in Jamaica*. Cambridge, Mass., 1978.

Cromwell, Jerry. "The Size Distribution of Income: An International Comparison," *Review of Income and Wealth*, Series 23, No. 3 (1977): 291–308.

Cumper, George E. "Incomes of Upper 2.5 per cent and 8.5 per cent of Income Tax Payers in Relation to National Income, Jamaica, 1951–65," *Social and Economic Studies*, 20 (1971): 362–68.

Cumper, George E. "Jamaica: A Case Study in Health Development," *Social Science & Medicine*, 17 (1983): 1983–93.

Cumper, George E. *Preliminary Analysis of Population Growth and Social Characteristics in Jamaica, 1943–60*. [Mona], 1963.

Cumper, George E. "Should We Plan for Contraction in Health Services? The Jamaican Experience," *Health Policy and Planning*, 8 (1993): 113–121.

Cumper, George E. *The Social Structure of Jamaica*. Kingston, 1949.

Cumper, George E., ed. *The Economy of the West Indies*. Kingston, 1960.

Cumper, George E. *The Evaluation of National Health Systems*. Oxford, 1991.

Cumper, George E. "Two Studies in Jamaican Productivity," *Social and Economic Studies*, 1 (1953): 3–83.

Cundall, Frank. *Jamaica in 1928*. London, 1928.

Curtin, Philip D. *Death by Migration: Europe's Encounter with the Tropical World in the Nineteenth Century*. Cambridge, 1989.

Dancer, Thomas. *The Medical Assistant; or Jamaica Practice of Physic: Designed Chiefly for the Use of Families and Plantations*. Kingston, 1801.

Daniels, Anders. "Economic Reforms in Jamaica," *Journal of Inter-American Studies and World Affairs*, 38 (1996): 97–108.

Davis, Kingsley. "The Amazing Decline of Mortality in Underdeveloped Areas," *American Economic Review*, 46 (1956): 305–18.

Deane, Phyllis. *The Measurement of Colonial National Incomes: An Experiment*. Cambridge, 1948.

De Lisser, Herbert. *Jane's Career: A Story of Jamaica*. New York, 1971, reprint of 1914 ed.

Desai, P. et al. "Infant Mortality Rate in Three Parishes of Western Jamaica, 1980," *West Indian Medical Journal*, 32 (1983): 83–87.

Development and Welfare in the West Indies. London, various years.

Devos, Isabelle. Allemaal Beestjes: Mortaliteit en morbiditeit in Vlaanderen, 18de-20ste eeuw. Unpublished Ph.D. dissertation, Universiteit Gent, 2003.

Díaz-Briquets, Sergio. "Determinants of Mortality Transition in Developing Countries before and after the Second World War: Some Evidence from Cuba," *Population Studies*, 35 (1981): 399–411.

Díaz-Briquets, Sergio. "Mortality in Cuba." In Ira Rosenwaike, ed., *Mortality of Hispanic Populations: Mexicans, Puerto Ricans, and Cubans in the United States and in the Home Countries* (New York, 1991), pp. 55–77.

Dominguez, Virginia R. *From Neighbor to Stranger: The Dilemma of Caribbean Peoples in the United States.* New Haven, 1975.

Douglas, Ronald Lloyd. *General Science with Health and Hygiene for West Indian Schools.* Kingston, n.d.

Douglass, Lisa. *The Power of Sentiment: Love, Hierarchy, and the Jamaican Family Elite.* Boulder, 1992.

D'Oyley, Vincent Roy. *Jamaica: Development of Teacher Training through the Agency of the Lady Mico Charity from 1835 to 1914.* Toronto, 1964.

D'Oyley, Vincent Roy, and Reginald Murray, eds. *Development and Disillusion in Third World Education with Emphasis in Jamaica.* Toronto, 1979.

Ebanks, G. Edward. *Infant and Child Mortality and Fertility: Trinidad and Tobago, Guyana, and Jamaica*, World Fertility Survey No. 75. Voorburg, June 1985.

Edie, Carlene J. *Democracy by Default: Dependency and Clientelism in Jamaica.* Boulder, 1991.

Eisner, Gisela. *Jamaica 1830–1930: A Study in Economic Growth.* Manchester, 1961.

Elkins, W. F. *Street Preachers, Faith Healers and Herb Doctors in Jamaica, 1890–1925.* New York, 1977.

Emanuel, Elizabeth Susan. The Impact of Socio-economic Factors on Health Status in Jamaica. Unpublished Master's thesis, University of the West Indies, Mona, 1997.

EPICA Task Force. *Jamaica, Caribbean Challenge: A People's Primer.* Washington, 1979.

Ettling, John. "Hookworm Disease." In Kenneth F. Kiple, ed., *The Cambridge World History of Human Disease* (Cambridge, 1993), pp. 784–88.

Ewbank, Douglas C. "History of Black Mortality and Health before 1940," *Milbank Quarterly*, 65, Suppl. 1 (1987): 100–28.

Farley, John. *To Cast Out Disease: A History of the International Health Division of the Rockefeller Foundation (1913–1951).* Oxford, 2004.

Feinstein, C. H. *National Income, Expenditure and Output of the United Kingdom 1855–1965.* Cambridge, 1972.

Figueroa, J. P. Annual Report: Public Health Department: Kingston and St. Andrew Corporation. Unpublished, 1983 and following years (available at the Ministry of Health).

Figueroa, J. P. "Health Trends in Jamaica: Significant Progress and a Vision for the 21st Century," *West Indian Medical Journal*, 50, Suppl. 4 (2001): 15–22.

Figueroa, J. P., et al. "A Profile of Health Research in Jamaica 1991–1995," West Indian Medical Journal, 47 (1998): 89–93.

Figueroa, John J. "Education for Jamaica's Needs," *Caribbean Quarterly*, 15 (1969): 5–33.

Fincham, J. E., M. B. Markus, and V. J. Adams. "Could Control of Soil-transmitted Helminthic Infection Influence the HIV/AIDS Pandemic?" *Acta Tropica*, 86 (2003): 315–33.

Flahiff, E. W. *The Epidemiology of Tuberculosis in Large Towns, Small Towns and Rural Areas of Jamaica.* Kingston, 1938.

Foner, Nancy. *Status and Power in Rural Jamaica: A Study of Educational and Political Change.* New York, 1973.

Forrest, A. S. and John Henderson. *Jamaica.* London, 1906.

Fox, Kristin. Infant Mortality Rates in Jamaica, 1993. Unpublished paper, 1994 (available at SALISES).

Francis, Sybil. "The Evolution of Community Development in Jamaica (1937–1962)," *Caribbean Quarterly*, 15 (1969): 40–59.

Furnia, Arthur H. *Syncrisis: The Dynamics of Health: An Analytic Series on the Interactions of Health and Socioeconomic Development XX. Jamaica.* n.p., 1976.

Gallagher, Nancy Elizabeth. *Egypt's Other Wars: Epidemics and the Politics of Public Health.* Syracuse, NY, 1990.

Garcia Quiñones, Rolando. *La transition de la mortalidad en Cuba: Un estudio sociodemográfico.* Havana, 1996.

Gardarsdóttir, Ólöf. *Saving the Child: Regional, Cultural and Social Aspects of the Infant Mortality Decline in Iceland, 1770–1920.* Umeå, 2002.

Gayle, Carol Evadne. An Assessment of the Extent of Registration of Stillbirths and Neonatal Deaths in Jamaica. Unpublished Master's thesis, University of the West Indies, Mona, 1989.

Gayle, Carol Evadne. The Political Economy of Health Care in Jamaica: An Historical Analysis, 1962–1983. Typescript, 1985.

Girvan, Norman, ed. *Working Together for Development: D.T.M. Girvan on Cooperatives and Community Development, 1939–1968.* Kingston, 1993.

Girvan, Norman, Richard Bernal, and Wesley Hughes. "The IMF and the Third World: The Case of Jamaica, 1974–80," *Development Dialogue*, 2 (1980): 113–55.

Gjonça, Arjan. *Communism, Health and Lifestyle: The Paradox of Mortality Transition in Albania, 1950–1990.* Westport, CT, 2001.

Gjonça, Arjan, Chris Wilson, and Jane Falkingham. "Paradoxes of Health Transition in Europe's Poorest Country: Albania 1950–90," *Population and Development Review*, 23 (1997): 585–609.

Glasser, Jay H. "Implications of Declining Mortality for the Organization of Health Care: The Case of Jamaica." In Harald Hansluwka et al., eds., *New Developments in the Analysis of Mortality and Causes of Death* (Bangkok, 1986), pp. 509–26.

Golding, John S. R. *Ascent to Mona: A Short History of Jamaican Medical Care.* Kingston, 1994.

Gordon, Derek. Estimates of Poverty in Jamaica: For the Years 1992 and 1993. Unpublished paper, 1995 (available at SALISES).

Gordon, Derek. "Women, Work and Social Mobility in Post-war Jamaica." In Keith Hart, ed., *Women and the Sexual Division of Labour in the Caribbean* (Kingston, 1989), pp. 67–80.

Gordon, Shirley C. *A Century of West Indian Education: A Source Book.* London, 1963.

Gordon, Shirley C. *Reports and Repercussions in West Indian Education, 1835–1933.* London, 1968.

Goulbourne, Harry. *Teachers, Education and Politics in Jamaica, 1892–1972.* London, 1988.

Grant, L. S., and S. E. Anderson, "The Problem of Medical Care in the Caribbean," *West Indian Medical Journal,* 4 (1955): 105–108.

Grant, S. Jacqueline, and Toby Shillito. "Island in a Turbulent World." In Deepa Narayan and Patti Petesch, eds. *Voices of the Poor from Many Lands* (New York, 2002), pp. 429–60.

Great Britain. Colonial Office. *Annual Report on the Social and Economic Progress of the People of Jamaica.* London, various years.

Great Britain. Development and Welfare Organization in the West Indies. *Development and Welfare in the West Indies.* London, various years.

Green, Edward C. *Rethinking AIDS Prevention: Learning from the Successes in Developing Countries.* Westport, CT, 2003.

Grosh, Margaret E. "Five Criteria for Choosing among Poverty Programs." In Nora Lustig, ed., *Coping with Austerity: Poverty and Inequality in Latin America* (Washington, 1995), pp. 146–86.

Grosh, Margaret E. *The Household Survey as a Tool for Policy Change: Lessons from the Jamaican Survey of Living Conditions.* Washington, 1991.

Gulliford, M. C. "Health and Health Care in the English-Speaking Caribbean: A British Public Health Physician's View of the Caribbean," *Journal of Public Health Medicine,* 16 (1994): 263–69.

Gunatilleke, Godfrey, ed. *Intersectoral Linkages and Health Development: Case Studies in India (Kerala State), Jamaica, Norway, Sri Lanka, and Thailand.* Geneva, 1984.

Gutiérrez, Hector. "La mortalité par cause à Cuba avant et après la Révolution," *Population,* 39 (1984): 383–88.

Haines, Michael R. "Estimated Life Tables for the United States, 1850–1910," *Historical Methods,* 4 (1998): 149–69.

Hall, Douglas. *Free Jamaica 1838–1865: An Economic History.* New Haven, 1959.

Halstead, Scott B., Julia A. Walsh, and Kenneth S. Warren, eds. *Good Health at Low Cost.* New York, 1985.

Hancock, Graham. *Lords of Poverty: The Power, Prestige, and Corruption of the International Aid Business.* New York, 1989.

Handa, Sudhanshu. "The Impact of Education, Income, and Mortality on Fertility in Jamaica," *World Development,* 28 (2000): 173–86.

Handa, Sudhanshu, and Damien King. "Structural Adjustment Policies, Income Distribution and Poverty: A Review of the Jamaican Experience," *World Development,* 25 (1997): 915–30.

Handbook of Jamaica. London and Kingston, various years.

Harewood, Jack. *The Population of Trinidad and Tobago.* Paris, 1975.

Harik, Vaira, Michael Trisolini, and William Bicknell. The Jamaican Health Sector: A Chartbook. Unpublished report, 1995.

Harrison, Gordon. *Mosquitoes, Malaria and Man: A History of the Hostilities since 1880.* New York, 1978.

Harrison, Michelle. *King Sugar: Jamaica, the Caribbean and the World Sugar Economy.* New York, 2001.

Hart, Richard. "The Labour Rebellions of the 1930s." In Hilary Beckles and Verene Shepherd, eds., *Caribbean Freedom: Society and Economy from Emancipation to the Present* (Kingston, 1993), pp. 370–75.

Heller, Peter. "The Strategy of Health-Sector Planning." In Myron E. Wegman, Tsung-yi Lin, and Elizabeth F. Purcell, eds., *Public Health in the People's Republic of China: Report of a Conference* (New York, [1973]), pp. 62–107.

Henriques, Fernando. *Family and Colour in Jamaica.* 2nd ed. London, 1968.

Henry-Lee, Aldrie. "The Dynamics of Poverty in Jamaica, 1989 to 1999," *Social and Economic Studies,* 50 (2001): 199–228.

Henry-Lee, Aldrie, et al. *An Assessment of the Standard of Living and Coping Strategies of Workers in Selected Occupations Who Earn a Minimum Wage.* Kingston, 2000.

Henry-Wilson, Maxine. "The Status of the Jamaican Woman, 1962 to the Present." In Rex Nettleford, ed., *Jamaica in Independence: Essays on the Early Years* (Kingston, 1989), pp. 229–53.

Higman, B.W. "Domestic Service in Jamaica, since 1750." In B. W. Higman, ed., *Trade, Government and Society in Caribbean History 1700–1920* (Mona, 1983), pp. 117–38.

Higman, B.W. *Slave Population and Economy in Jamaica, 1807–1834.* Cambridge, 1976.

Hill, Allan G., and Lincoln C. Chen, *Oman's Leap to Good Health: A Summary of Rapid Health Transition in the Sultanate of Oman.* Muscat, 1996.

Historisk statistik för Sverige. 3 vols. Stockholm, 1969.

Hobcraft, John. "Women's Education, Child Welfare and Child Survival: A Review of the Evidence," *Health Transition Review* 3 (1993): 159–75.

Holland, Celia V. and Malcolm W. Kennedy, eds. *The Geohelminths: Ascaris, Trichuris, and Hookworm.* Boston, 2001.

Holt, Thomas C. *The Problem of Freedom: Race, Labor, and Politics in Jamaica and Britain, 1832–1938.* Baltimore, 1992.

Home Care of the Sick. Kingston, 1943.

Howes, H. W. *Fundamental, Adult, Literacy and Community Education in the West Indies.* n.p., 1955.

Huber, Evelyne, and John D. Stephens. "Changing Development Models in Small Economies: The Case of Jamaica from the 1950s to the 1990s," *Studies in Comparative International Development,* 27 (1992): 57–92.

Human Mortality Database at www.mortality.org.

Humphreys, Margaret. *Malaria: Poverty, Race, and Public Health in the United States.* Baltimore, 2001.

Hutchinson, Sharmaine Elaine. Health, Nutrition and Social Determinants of School Achievement in Rural Jamaican Primary School Children. Unpublished Master's thesis, University of the West Indies, Mona, 1996.

International Bank for Reconstruction and Development. *The Economic De-velopment of Jamaica*. Baltimore, 1952.

International Conference on Health Problems in Tropical America (1924 Kingston Jamaica). Boston, 1924.

International Monetary Fund. *International Financial Statistics Yearbook*. Washington, various years.

Jamaica. *The Annual General Report of Jamaica, together with the Departmental Reports*. Kingston, various years.

Jamaica. *Annual Report of the Ministry of Education*. Kingston, various years.

Jamaica. *Annual Report of the Registrar General's Department*. Kingston, various years.

Jamaica. *Annual Report on Jamaica*. London and Kingston, various years from 1948, succeeding the *Annual General Report of Jamaica, together with the Departmental Reports*.

Jamaica. Colonial Reports. *Annual Report on the Social and Economic Progress of the People of Jamaica*. London, various years.

Jamaica. Colonial Reports. *Report for [the Year]*. London, various years.

Jamaica. Department of Statistics. *Census of Jamaica, 7th April 1960*. 2 vols. Kingston, n.d.

Jamaica. Department of Statistics. *Expenditure Patterns of Working Class Households*. Kingston, 1967.

Jamaica. Department of Statistics. *Statistical Abstract*. Kingston, various years.

Jamaica. Division of Censuses and Surveys. Department of Statistics. *Population Census 1970*. Kingston, 1970–1979.

Jamaica. Education Department. *Annual Report of the Education Department*. Kingston, various years.

Jamaica. *The Governor's Report on the Blue Book and Departmental Reports*. Kingston, various years.

Jamaica. Ministry of Education. *Annual Report of the Ministry of Education*. Kingston, various years.

Jamaica. Ministry of Education and Social Welfare. *A Review of the Developments in Education and Social Welfare in Jamaica During the Period 1944–1954*. Kingston, 1954.

Jamaica. Ministry of Health. *Annual Report of the Chief Medical Officer*. Kingston, various years.

Jamaica. Ministry of Health. Health Status Report 1991. Typescript, April 1993 (available at the Ministry of Health).

Jamaica. Ministry of Health. *Report of the Medical Services of Jamaica and Its Dependencies for 1955*. Kingston, n.d.

Jamaica. Ministry of Health. Report on the Major Problems in the Health Sector: The Reforms Adopted and/or Could Be Adopted. Unpublished essay, Sept. 1995 (available at SALISES).

Jamaica. Planning Institute of Jamaica. *Economic and Social Survey*. Kingston, various years.

Jamaica. Planning Institute of Jamaica. *Human Development Report 2000*. Kingston, 2000.

Jamaica. Planning Institute of Jamaica. *Jamaica Survey of Living Conditions*. Kingston, various years.

Jamaica. Schools Commission. *Annual Report of the Jamaica Schools Commission, 1938*. Kingston, n.d.

Jamaica. *The Social Well-Being Programme: A Programme for Social Development*. Kingston, 1988.

Jamaica. Statistical Institute of Jamaica. *Demographic Statistics*. Kingston, various years.

Jamaica. Statistical Institute of Jamaica. *Population Census, 1982*. 12 vols.; Kingston, 1982–1991.

Jamaica. Statistical Institute of Jamaica. *Statistical Yearbook*. Kingston, various years.

Jamaica Public Health [bulletin published by the Bureau of Health Education]. Kingston, 1926–1971.

Jefferson, Owen. *The Post-war Economic Development of Jamaica*. Kingston, 1972.

Johansen, Hans Chr. *Danish Population History 1600–1939*. Odense, 2002.

Johansen, Hans Chr. *The Decline in Danish Tuberculosis Mortality before World War II*, Danish Center for Demographic Research, Research Report 10 1999. Odense, 1999.

Jones, Edwin, and Gladstone E. Mills. "The Institutional Framework of Government." In Rex Nettleford, ed., *Jamaica in Independence: Essays on the Early Years* (Kingston, 1989), pp. 105–30.

Kathuria, Sanjay, et al. *The Road to Sustained Growth in Jamaica*. Washington, 2004.

Killingray, David. "The Influenza Pandemic of 1918–1919 in the British Caribbean," *Social History of Medicine*, 7 (1994): 59–87.

King, Damien. "The Evolution of Structural Adjustment and Stabilisation Policy in Jamaica," *Social and Economic Studies*, 50 (2001): 1–53.

King, Damien, and Sudhanshu Handa. "Changes in the Distribution of Income in the New Economic Model in Jamaica," *Social and Economic Studies*, 50 (2001): 127–68.

Kirkpatrick, W. *A Short History of the First One Hundred Years of the Public Water Supply in the Kingston and Liguanea Area, 1849–1949*. Kingston, 1949.

Kirton, Claremont P. *Informal Economic Activities in Selected Caribbean Countries*. Unpublished paper, March 1991 (available at SALISES).

Kosa, John, Aaron Antonovsky, and Irving Kenneth Zola, eds. *Poverty and Health: A Sociological Analysis*. Cambridge, MA, 1969.

Kuczynski, R. R. *Demographic Survey of the British Colonial Empire*. 3 vols. London, 1948–1953.

Kuper, Adam. *Changing Jamaica*. London, 1976.

LaGuerre, John. *The Social and Political Thought of the Colonial Intelligentsia*. Mona, 1982.

Lavy, Victor, Michael Palumbo, and Steven N. Stern. *Health Care in Jamaica: Quality, Outcomes, and Labor Supply*. Washington, 1995.

Leavitt, Ronnie Linda. *Disability and Rehabilitation in Rural Jamaica: An Ethnographic Study*. Rutherford, 1992.

Le Franc, Elsie, ed. *Consequences of Structural Adjustment: A Review of the Jamaican Experience*. Kingston, 1994.

Le Franc, Elsie. Health Situation Analysis: Jamaica. Unpublished report to PAHO, May 1996 (available at SALISES).

Le Franc, Elsie. "Petty Trading and Labour Mobility: Higglers in the Kingston Metropolitan Area." In Keith Hart, ed., *Women and the Sexual Division of Labour in the Caribbean* (Kingston, 1989), pp. 99–132.

Le Franc, Elsie. "The Bauxite Labor Force in Jamaica: A High Wage Sector in a Dual Economy," *Social and Economic Studies*, 36 (1987): 217–68.

Le Franc, Elsie. "The Co-operative Movement in Jamaica: An Exercise in Social Control," *Social and Economic Studies*, 28 (1979): 21–43.

Le Franc, Elsie, and Andrew Downes. "Measuring Human Development in Countries with Invisible Economies: Challenges Posed by the Informal and Remittance Sectors in Jamaica," *Social and Economic Studies*, 50 (2001): 169–98.

Le Franc, Elsie, and Aldrie Henry-Lee. Poverty and Gender in the Caribbean. Typescript, 1999, prepared for the Caribbean Development Bank.

LePrince, J. A. "Can We Get Better Anopheles-Control and More Malaria-Control at Less Cost?" In *Proceedings of the International Conference on Health Problems in Tropical America held at Kingston, Jamaica, B.W.I., July 22 to August 1, 1924* (Boston, 1924), pp. 157–64.

Lescene, G. T. "Brief Historical Retrospect of the Medical Profession in Jamaica," *West Indian Medical Journal*, 4 (1955): 217–42.

Lewis, Arthur. "The 1930s Social Revolution." In Hilary Beckles and Verene Shepherd, eds., *Caribbean Freedom: Society and Economy from Emancipation to the Present* (Kingston, 1993), pp. 376–92.

Lewis, Rupert. *Marcus Garvey: Anti-colonial Champion*. Trenton, NJ, 1988.

Lindert, Peter H., and Jeffrey G. Williamson. "Growth, Equity, and History," *Explorations in Economic History*, 22 (1985): 341–77.

Livingstone, W. P. *Black Jamaica: A Study in Evolution*. London, 1899.

Lloyd, Edna Hogwood. Education, Health and Labor in Jamaica since 1900. Unpublished Master's thesis, University of Illinois, 1941.

Lobdell, Richard A. *Economic Structure and Demographic Performance in Jamaica, 1891–1935*. New York, 1987.

Looney, Robert E. *The Jamaican Economy in the 1980s: Economic Decline and Structural Adjustment*. Boulder, 1987.

Lopez, A. D., et al. *World Mortality in 2000: Life Tables for 191 Countries*. Geneva, 2002.

Lorimer, Frank. *The Population of the Soviet Union: History and Prospects*. Geneva, 1946.

Lucie-Smith, J. D., ed. *A Text Book for Teachers of Hygiene, Malaria, Hookworm*. Kingston, 1921.

Luft, Harold S. *Poverty and Health: Economic Causes and Consequences of Health Problems*. Cambridge, MA, 1978.

Macmillan, W. M. *Warning from the West Indies: A Tract for Africa and the Empire.* London, 1936.

Maddison, Angus. *The World Economy: A Millennial Perspective.* Paris, 2001.

Magoon, E. H. *Drainage for Health in the Caribbean Area.* n.p., 1945.

Mandle, Jay R. "The Decline of Mortality in British Guiana, 1911–1960," *Demography,* 7 (1970): 301–15.

Mandle, Jay R. *The Plantation Economy: Population and Economic Change in Guyana 1838–1960.* Philadelphia, 1973.

Manley, Douglas. *Cuban Doctors Aid Jamaica's Health Service.* n.p., 1977.

Manley, Michael. *Up the Down Escalator: Development and the International Economy: A Jamaican Case Study.* Washington, 1987.

Manual for Community Health Workers. Rev. ed. Mona, 1983 (1st ed. 1972).

Marchione, Thomas Joseph. Health and Nutrition in Self-Reliant National Development: An Evaluation of the Jamaican Community Health Aide Programme. Unpublished Ph.D. dissertation, University of Connecticut, 1977.

Marier, Roger. *Social Welfare Work in Jamaica: A Study of the Jamaica Social Welfare Commission.* Paris, 1953.

Martin, Tony. "Marcus Garvey, the Caribbean, and the Struggle for Black Jamaican Nationhood." In Hilary Beckles and Verene Shepherd, eds., *Caribbean Freedom: Society and Economy from Emancipation to the Present* (Kingston, 1993), pp. 359–69.

Mata, Leonardo, and Luis Rosero. *National Health and Social Development in Costa Rica: A Case Study of Intersectoral Action.* Washington, 1988.

May, Jacques M., and Donna L. McLellan. *The Ecology of Malnutrition in the Caribbean.* New York, 1973.

McCaw-Binns, Affete. "Jamaica, 1991–1995." In Marjorie A. Koblinsky, ed., *Reducing Maternal Mortality: Learning from Bolivia, China, Egypt, Honduras, Indonesia, Jamaica, and Zimbabwe* (Washington, 2003), pp. 123–30.

McCaw-Binns, Affette M., and C. O. Moody. "The Development of Primary Health Care in Jamaica," *West Indian Medical Journal,* 50, Suppl. 4 (2001): 6–10.

McCaw-Binns, Affette M., C. O. Moody, and K. L. Standard. "Forty Years: An Introduction to the Development of a Caribbean Public Health," *West Indian Medical Journal,* 47, Suppl. 4 (1998): 8–12.

McCaw-Binns, Affette M., Valerie Nam, and Deanna Ashley. An Evaluation of Issues Associated with Registration of Deaths in Jamaica: 1996 and 1998. Unpublished draft, Spring 2002.

McCaw-Binns, Affette M., et al. "Access to Care and Maternal Mortality in Jamaican Hospitals: 1993–1995," *International Journal of Epidemiology,* 30 (2001): 796–801.

McCaw-Binns, Affette M., et al. "Registration of Births, Stillbirths and Infant Deaths in Jamaica," *International Journal of Epidemiology,* 25 (1996): 807–13.

McFarlane, A. Bruce. *Hints on Hygiene for Elementary Schools with Special Reference to the Tropics.* Kingston, 1912.

McKenzie, Herman I., et al. "Child Mortality in Jamaica," *Milbank Memorial Fund Quarterly*, 45 (1967): 303–20.

McKenzie, S. I. Alleyne, and K. L. Standard. "Reported Illness and Its Treatment in a Jamaican Community," *Social and Economic Studies*, 16 (1967): 262–79.

McLewin, Philip J. *Power and Economic Change: The Response to Emancipation in Jamaica and British Guinea 1840–1865*. New York, 1987.

McLure, Charles E., Jr. "The Incidence of Jamaican Taxes, 1971–72," *Social and Economic Studies*, 29 (1980): 101–33.

Meksi, Ermelinda, and Gianpiero Dalla Zuanna, "La mortalité générale en Albanie (1950–1990)," *Population*, 49 (1994): 607–35.

Meslé, France, and Jacques Vallin. "Reconstitution de tables annuelles de mortalité pour la France au XIXe siècle," *Population*, 44 (1989): 1121–58.

Miller, Errol. "Church, State and Secondary Education in Jamaica 1912–1943." In Ruby Hope King, ed., *Education in the Caribbean: Historical Perspectives* (Kingston, 1987), pp. 109–44.

Miller, Errol. "Educational Development in Independent Jamaica." In Rex Nettleford, ed., *Jamaica in Independence: Essays on the Early Years* (Kingston, 1989), pp. 205–28.

Miller, Errol. *Marginalization of the Black Male: Insights from the Development of the Teaching Profession*. 2nd ed. Mona, 1994.

Mintz, Sidney Wilfred. *Caribbean Transformations*. Chicago, 1974.

Moody, Christine. The History of Public Health in Jamaica. Unpublished paper, 1998.

Moore, Brian L., and Michele A. Johnson, eds. *The Land We Live In: Jamaica in 1890*. Mona, 2000.

Moore, Brian L., and Michele A. Johnson, eds. *Squalid Kingston, 1890–1920: How the Poor Lived, Moved and Had Their Being*. Mona, 2000.

Morley, Samuel A. *The Income Distribution Problem in Latin America and the Caribbean*. Santiago, 2001.

Morris, Morris David. *Measuring the Condition of the World's Poor: The Physical Quality of Life Index*. New York, 1979.

Moseley, Benjamin. *A Treatise on Tropical Diseases, and on the Climate of the West Indies*. London, 1787.

Moser, C. A. *The Measurement of Levels of Living with Special Reference to Jamaica*. London, 1957.

Moser, Caroline, and Jeremy Holland. *Urban Poverty and Violence in Jamaica*. Washington, 1997.

Moulton, Forest Ray. *A Symposium on Human Malaria, with Special Reference to North America and the Caribbean Region*. Washington, 1941.

Munro, Dana Gardner. *Intervention and Dollar Diplomacy in the Caribbean, 1900–1921*. Princeton, 1964.

Munroe, Trevor. *Jamaican Politics: A Marxist Perspective in Transition*. Kingston, 1990.

Munroe, Trevor. *Renewing Democracy into the Millennium: The Jamaican Experience in Perspective*. Kingston, 1999.

Munroe, Trevor. *Social Classes and National Liberation in Jamaica*. n.p., 1983.

Munroe, Trevor. *The Politics of Constitutional Decolonization: Jamaica, 1944–62*. Mona, 1972.

Murray, Cynthia. *Maternal and Infant Care*. Kingston, 1941.

Nettleford, Rex M. *Caribbean Cultural Identity: The Case of Jamaica: An Essay in Cultural Dynamics*. Kingston, 2003.

Nettleford, Rex M. *Identity, Race and Protest in Jamaica*. New York, 1972.

Nettleford, Rex M. ed. *Jamaica in Independence: Essays on the Early Years*. Kingston, 1989.

Neville-Rolfe. *Report on Social Hygiene May, 1936*. Kingston, 1936.

Newton, Velma. *The Silver Men: West Indian Labour Migration to Panama, 1850–1914*. Kingston, 1984.

Olivier, Sydney Haldane. *Jamaica: The Blessed Island*. New York, 1936.

Opie, Eugene L., Persis Putnam, and E. Joyce Saward. "The Fate of Negro Persons of a Tropical Country, Jamaica, B.W.I., after Contact with Tuberculosis." In *Studies on Tuberculosis* (Baltimore, 1941), pp. 55–95.

PAHO. *Health Conditions in the Caribbean*. Washington, 1997.

PAHO. *Health in the Americas, 2002 Edition*. Washington, 2002.

PAHO. *Health Statistics from the Americas*. Washington, various years.

Pawlowski, Z. S., G. A. Schad, and G. J. Stott. *Hookworm Infection and Anaemia: Approaches to Prevention and Control*. Geneva, 1991.

Peabody, John W., Omar Rahman, Kristin Fox, and Paul Gertler. "Quality of Care in Public and Private Primary Health Care Facilities: Structural Comparisons in Jamaica," *Bulletin of the Pan American Health Organization*, 28 (1994): 122–41.

Peach, Ceri. *West Indian Migration to Britain: A Social Geography*. London, 1968.

Pemberton, Rita. "A Different Intervention: The International Health Commission/Board, Health, Sanitation in the British Caribbean, 1914–1930." *Caribbean Quarterly*, 49 (2003): 87–103.

Perez, Eduardo A., and Betsy Reddaway. *Designing a Sanitary Program for the Urban Poor: Case Study from Montego Bay, Jamaica*, U.S. Agency for International Development, EHP Activity Report No. 34. Arlington, VA, 1997.

Petras, Elizabeth McLean. *Jamaican Labor Migration: White Capital and Black Labor, 1850–1930*. Boulder, 1988.

Phelps, O. W. "Rise of the Labour Movement in Jamaica," *Social and Economic Studies*, 9 (1960): 417–68.

Platt, B. S. *Nutrition in the British West Indies*. London, 1946.

Post, Ken. *Arise Ye Starvelings: The Jamaican Labour Rebellion of 1938 and its Aftermath*. The Hague, 1978.

Post, Ken. *Strike the Iron: A Colony at War: Jamaica 1939–1945*. Atlantic Highlands, NJ, 1981.

Preston, Samuel H., and Michael R. Haines. *Fatal Years: Child Mortality in Late Nineteenth-Century America*. Princeton, 1991.

Price, Lilian. *A Healthy Home in Healthy Surroundings*. Kingston, 1943.

Puffer, Ruth Rice, and Carlos V. Serrano. *Patterns of Mortality in Childhood.* Washington, 1973.

Putnam, Persis, et al. *Studies on Tuberculosis.* Baltimore, 1941.

Ramer, Samuel. "Who Was the Russian Feldsher?" *Bulletin of the History of Medicine,* 50 (1976): 213–25.

Recent Population Movements in Jamaica. Paris, 1974.

Richardson, Bonham C. *Panama Money in Barbados, 1900–1920.* Knoxville, 1985.

Ricketts, Heather. Equity Issues as Highlighted by the Jamaican Survey of Living Conditions (JSLC) and Other Data Sources. Unpublished paper, July 2000 (available at SALISES).

Riley, James C. *Rising Life Expectancy: A Global History.* Cambridge, 2001.

Roberts, George W. "A Life Table for a West Indian Slave Population," *Population Studies,* 5 (1951–52): 238–43.

Roberts, George W. *The Population of Jamaica.* Cambridge, 1957. Reprinted 1979 with a new introduction by the author.

Roberts, George W., and Dorian L. Powell. "Mortality." In *Recent Population Movements in Jamaica* (Paris, 1974), pp. 94–123.

Rojas-Aleta, Isabel, and James A. Murray. Primary Health Care in Jamaica: Framework for Strengthening of the Parish Level. Unpublished paper sponsored by PAHO, WHO, and the Ministry of Health, 1984 (available at SALISES).

Sargent, Carolyn, and Michael Harris. "Bad Boys and Good Girls: The Implications of Gender Ideology for Child Health in Jamaica." In Nancy Scheper-Hughes and Carolyn Sargent, eds., *Small Wars: The Cultural Politics of Childhood* (Berkeley, 1998), pp. 202–27.

Saward, E. Joyce, Persis Putnam, and Eugene L. Opie. "The Spread of Tuberculosis in Negro Families of Jamaica, B.W.I." In *Studies on Tuberculosis* (Baltimore, 1941), pp. 1–53.

Shapiro, Joel, and Harry Diakoff. *Antibiotics in Historical Perspective.* David L. Cowen and Alvin B. Segelman, eds. n.p., 1981.

Shepherd, Verene. The Education of East Indian Children in Jamaica, 1879–1949. Unpublished seminar paper, University of the West Indies, Mona, 1983.

Sherlock, Philip, and Hazel Bennett. *Story of the Jamaican People.* Kingston, 1998.

Sigerist, Henry E. *Medicine and Health in the Soviet Union.* New York, 1947.

Simey, T. S. *Welfare and Planning in the West Indies.* Oxford, 1946.

Sinclair, Sonja A., and Barbara M. Boland. "Characteristics of the Population." In *Recent Population Movements in Jamaica* (Paris, 1974), pp. 11–23.

Sinha, Dinesh P. *Children of the Caribbean, 1945–1984: Progress in Child Survival, Its Determinants and Implications.* Kingston, 1988.

Sinha, Dinesh P., Ann O. Diloreto, and Isabel Rojas-Aleta. Primary Health Care in Jamaica. Unpublished paper, 1981 (available at SALISES).

The Situation and Recent Trends of Mortality in the World, Population Bulletin of the United Nations, No. 6, 1962 (New York, 1963).

Slaughter-Defoe, D. T., W. A. Addae, and C. Bell. "Toward the Future School-ing of Girls: Global Status, Issues, and Prospects," *Human Development*, 45 (2002): 34–53.

Smith, F. B. *The Retreat of Tuberculosis, 1850–1950*. London, 1988.

Smith, M.G. *Poverty in Jamaica*. Kingston, 1989.

Smith, Raymond T. *Kinship and Class in the West Indies: A Genealogical Study of Jamaica and Guyana*. New York, 1988.

Smith, M. G., Roy Augier, and Rex Nettleford. *The Ras Tafari Movement in Kingston, Jamaica*. Mona, 1960.

Smith, Shirley J. Industrial Growth, Economic Opportunities, and Migration within and from Jamaica, 1943 to 1970. Unpublished Ph.D. dissertation, University of Pennsylvania, 1975.

Sobo, Elisa Janine. *One Blood: The Jamaican Body*. Albany, NY, 1993.

St. Pierre, Maurice. "The 1938 Jamaica Disturbances: A Portrait of Mass Re-action against Colonialism," *Social and Economic Studies*, 27 (1978): 171–96.

Standard, Kenneth L., and Olive Ennever. "The Community Health Aide in the Commonwealth Caribbean with Special Reference to Jamaica." In *Four Decades of Advances in Health in the Commonwealth Caribbean* (Washington, 1979), 102–12.

Stephens, Evelyne Huber, and John D. Stephens. *Jamaica's Democratic Socia-list Experience*. Washington, 1985.

Stiglitz, George. *Globalization and Its Discontents*. New York, 2000.

Stockdale, Frank. *Development and Welfare in the West Indies, 1940–1942*. London, 1943.

Stockdale, Frank. *Development and Welfare in the West Indies, 1943–44*. London, 1945.

Stolberg, Claus F., ed. *Jamaica 1938: The Living Conditions of the Urban and Rural Poor: Two Social Surveys*. Kingston, 1990.

Stone, Carl. *Class, State, and Democracy in Jamaica*. New York, 1986.

Stone, Carl. *Power in the Caribbean Basin: A Comparative Study of Political Economy*. Philadelphia, 1986.

Stycos, J. Mayone, and Judith Blake. "The Jamaican Family Life Project: Some Objectives and Methods," *Social and Economic Studies*, 3 (1954): 342–49.

Sundbärg, Gustav. *Bevölkerungsstatistik Schwedens 1750–1900*. Stockholm, 1970 reprint.

Susser, Mervyn. "Health as a Human Right: An Epidemiologist's Perspective on the Public Health," *American Journal of Public Health*, 83 (1993): 418–26.

Tanzi, Vito, and Ludger Schuknecht. *Public Spending in the 20th Century: A Global Perspective*. Cambridge, 2000.

Taylor, Frank Fonda. "From Hellshire to Healthshire: The Genesis of the Tourist Industry in Jamaica." In B. W. Higman, ed. *Trade, Government and Society in Caribbean History 1700–1920* (Mona, 1983), pp. 139–54.

Taylor, Frank Fonda. "The Tourist Industry in Jamaica, 1919–1939," *Social and Economic Studies*, 22 (1973): 205–28.

Taylor, Frank Fonda. *To Hell with Paradise: A History of the Jamaican Tourist Industry*. Pittsburgh, 1993.

Taylor, LeRoy. *Government's Expenditure on the Health Services, Jamaica, 1977–1986*. Kingston, 1991.

Tekse, Kalman. *Population and Vital Statistics: Jamaica, 1832–1964: A Historical Perspective*. Kingston, 1974.

Thomas, Herbert T. *The Story of a West Indian Policeman or Forty-Seven Years in the Jamaica Constabulary*. Kingston, 1927.

Thomas-Hope, Elizabeth. "Return Migration to Jamaica and Its Development Potential," *International Migration*, 37 (1999): 183–207.

Thorne, Alfred P. "Revisions, and Suggestions for Deflating the Gross Product Estimates for Jamaican-type Economies," *Social and Economic Studies*, 9 (1960): 41–56.

Thorne, Alfred P. "Size, Structure and Growth of the Economy of Jamaica," *Social and Economic Studies*, 4 Supplement (1955): 1–112.

Todd, John L. "Tropical Medicine, 1898–1924." In *Proceedings of the International Conference on Health Problems in Tropical America* (Boston, 1924), pp. 17–27.

Transparency International. 2002 Corruption Perceptions Index, at www.transparency.org/pressreleases_archive/2002/2002.08.28.cpi.en.html.

United Fruit Company. Medical Department. *Annual Report*. Boston, various years.

United Nations. *Demographic Yearbook, Historical Supplement 1948–1997*. New York, 2000 (CD-ROM and print versions).

United Nations Development Program. *Human Development Report*. New York, various years.

United Nations Development Program. World Income Inequality Database, at www.undp.org/poverty/initiatives/wider/widd.htm.

United Nations Population Division. *Selected World Demographic Indicators by Countries, 1950–2000*, Working Papers No. 55. n.p., 1975.

UNESCO. *Jamaica: National Literacy Programme: Project Findings and Recommendations*. Paris, 1976.

United States. *Historical Statistics of the United States: Colonial Times to 1970*. 2 vols. Washington, 1975.

United States Census Bureau. *Country Demographic Profiles: Jamaica*. Washington, 1977.

United States Census Bureau. Historical Income Tables – Families, Table F-4, Gini Ratios for Families, by Race and Hispanic Origin of Householder: 1947 to 2001, at www.census.gov/hhes/income/histinc/fo4.html.

United States Census Bureau. International Data Base, at blue.census.gov/cgi-bin/ipc/ibdsprd.

United States Census Bureau. *Poverty in the United States: 2000*. Washington, 2001.

United States Central Intelligence Agency. *World Factbook*, at www.cia.gov/cia/publications/factbook.

United States Department of Health, Education, and Welfare. *Vital Statistics of the United States 1950.* 3 vols. Washington, 1954.

United States National Center for Health Statistics. *National Vital Statistics Reports*, Vol. 49, No. 8, *Deaths: Final Data for 1999*, at www.cdc.gov/nchs/releases/01facts/99mortality.htm.

Veys, D. *Cohort Survival in Belgium in the Past 150 Years: Data and Life Table Results, Shortly Commented.* Leuven, 1983.

Washburn, Benjamin Earle. *A Country Doctor in the South Mountains.* Asheville, NC, 1955.

Washburn, Benjamin Earle. *As I Recall.* New York, 1960.

Washburn, Benjamin Earle. *The Health Game.* London, 1930.

Washburn, Benjamin Earle. *Jamaica Health Stories and Plays.* Kingston, 1929.

Washburn, Benjamin Earle. "Report of the Co-operative Public Health Work in Jamaica during 1926." Extract from the *Jamaica Gazette*, Suppl., Vol. 70, No. 3, May 12, 1927.

Wedderburn, C.C. "The Development of Public Health in Jamaica." In *Four Decades of Advances in Health in the Commonwealth Caribbean.* (Washington, 1979), pp. 18–25.

Wedenoja, William. "Mothering and the Practice of 'Balm' in Jamaica." In Carol Shepherd McClain, ed. *Women as Healers: Cross-Cultural Perspectives* (New Brunswick, 1989), pp. 76–97.

Wells, C. W., and H.H. Smith. *The Epidemiology of Tuberculosis in Kingston, Jamaica, B.W.I.* Kingston, 1938.

West India Royal Commission 1938–39. *Statement of Action Taken on the Recommendations.* London, 1945.

West Indies Population Census. *Census of Jamaica, Apr. 7, 1960.* 2 vols. Kingston, n.d.

Whitbourne, Dahlia. "History of the School Medical Services, Kingston, Jamaica (1934–1959)," *West Indian Medical Journal*, 14 (1965): 167–79.

Whyte, Millicent. *A Short History of Education in Jamaica.* London, 1977.

Wilgus, A. Curtis, ed. *The Caribbean: Its Health Problems.* Gainesville, 1965.

Wilkins, Nadine Joy. "Doctors and Ex-Slaves in Jamaica, 1834–1850," *Jamaican Historical Review*, 17 (1991): 19–30.

Williams, Mariana et al. Assessing Equity in Jamaica. Unpublished report, 2000, prepared for the Canadian International Development Agency.

Williams, Eric. *Education in the British West Indies.* Port of Spain, 1950.

Winkler, Anthony C. *Going Home to Teach.* Kingston, 1995.

Winkler, Anthony C. *The Painted Canoe.* Chicago, 1989.

Witter, Michael, and Patricia Anderson. The Distribution of the Social Cost of Jamaica's Structural Adjustment 1977–1989. Unpublished paper, 1991 (available at SALISES).

Witter, Michael, and Claremont Kirton. The Informal Economy in Jamaica: Some Empirical Exercises. ISER Working Paper No. 36, 1990 (available at SALISES).

Wood, E. F. L. *Report by the Honourable E. F. L. Wood, M.P., on his Visit to the West Indies and British Guinea.* London, 1922.

World Bank. *World Development Indicators 2002*, CD-ROM. Washington, 2003.

World Health Organization. *Recurrent Costs in the Health Sector: Problems and Policy Options in Three Countries: Costa Rica, Jamaica, and Mali.* Washington, 1989.

Wrigley, E. A., and R. S. Schofield. *The Population History of England, 1541– 1871: A Reconstruction.* Cambridge, 1989.

INDEX

Howard, H. H., Rockefeller agent, 83, 103
hygiene, knowledge about, 105–21; *see also* health education, public health

immigration to Jamaica, 14–5, 23
income and wealth, distribution of, 4, 15–16, 66–7, 142–3, 146–9, 158, 160, 169, 171–3, 177, 193
income level, and life expectancy, 1–6, 9–13, 20, 21–23, 38
    compared across globe, 11–2
    see also gross domestic product
indentured laborers, 15, 49
independence, 18, 121–9, 140, 155
India, 23, 25, 34–5
Indians, in Jamaica, 15; *see also* indentured laborers
Industrialization by Invitation, 139–40
infant deaths, registration of, 28
infant health transition, 29; *see also* infant mortality
infant mortality, 28–9, 36–8, 41, 69, 73–4, 81, 148, 163, 177
inflation, 165–6, 174
influenza in 1918, 59–60, 199
informal economy, 161, 174–5, 187, 189–90; *see also* higglering, criminal activities
informal practitioners, 51; *see also* myalism, obeah
insects, as disease vectors, 14, 58
    see also houseflies, mosquitoes
International Health Board, 83–4, 89–90, 130; *see also* Rockefeller Foundation
International Monetary Fund, 164–5, 168–70, 172–3, 176, 193
investments from North America, 122
Island Medical Department, 51, 116, 203; *see also* Island Medical Service, Medical Department
Island Medical Service, 50

Jacobs, H. P., colonial official, 129
Jamaica Board of Education, 52
Jamaica Hookworm Commission, 83, 120
Jamaica Labour Party, 18, 123, 155
Jamaican model of social development, *see* political economy
Jamaica paradox, 189; *see also* "good health at low cost", income level

Jamaica Public Health, 98, 112–5, 117
Jamaica Social Welfare Commission, 115–6, 120, 123, 126
Jamaica Tuberculosis Commission, 98
Jamaica Union of Teachers, 71
Jamaica Welfare, 115–6, 120, 123, 125–6, 144
Jamaica Yaws Commission, 92
Jamaicans
    attitude toward inequality, 148
    attitude toward the poor, 62
    compensation during hard times, 173–8, 187
    defecation habits, 84, 103–5
    demands for public health improvements, 85–6, 90, 132–3
    emigrate for jobs, 16, 34–6, 61, 139, 160, 175, 192
    expectations about themselves, 19–20
    health habits modified, 104–5, 119–21, 129–33
    height and weight comparisons, 78, 138, 177
    invited to express opinions, 87
    knowledge about disease, 129–31; *see also* health education, health propaganda
    origins of, 14–5
    self perception, 146
    sense of being trapped, 166, 195
    and social barriers, 146
    vision of the future, 122, 129
    water sources, 102; *see also* water piping
    women, strength and independence, 149–50
Jefferson, Owen, scholar, 7, 139–40
Jews, in Jamaica, 15

Kerala, 2–5, 11–2, 23, 191–5
King, Damien, scholar, 170
Kingston, 29, 39, 58–9, 80–1, 107, 122, 124, 147, 149, 173
    causes of death in, 45
    described, 63
    housing in, 63
    immigration to, 16
    mortality decline in, 38–47, 102
    nutrition in, 77–8